109175

WOMEN CLERGY

WOMEN CLERGY

BREAKING

THROUGH

GENDER

BARRIERS

Edward C. Lehman, Jr.

Transaction Books

New Brunswick (U.S.A.) and Oxford (U.K.)

Library of Congress Catalog Number: 84-5644
ISBN: 0-88738-071-9 [cloth]
Printed in the United States of America

Library of Congress Cataloging in Publication Data

Lehman, Edward C.
  Women clergy.

  Includes bibliographies and index.
  1. Women clergy—United States. I. Title.
BV676.L43   1985   262'.14   84-5644
ISBN 0-88738-071-9

Table of Contents

CHAPTER 3

Where Do the Clergy Stand?

CHAPTER 4

Explaining Differences in Receptivity

CHAPTER 8

Explaining Contact's Effect Upon Receptivity . 193

CHAPTER 9

Getting into the System:
What Makes a Difference? 227

CHAPTER 10

Preface

Church members have experienced many changes in their organizations during the twentieth century. There have been mergers of major denominations, times of boom and decline in membership, periods of cooperation and times of conflict. One major change in church life which has occurred during the last third of the century is the entrance of large numbers of women into theological seminaries and eventually into the ranks of ordained clergy. This book deals with those events—the impact of the feminist movement on the churches and their reactions to that encounter. It reports the results of a study of the ways in which church members responded to women serving their congregations as ordained clergy.

The research is basically sociological in its approach. Its goal was to describe how church members felt about the issue. It portrays their perceptions of women ministers, including some of their stereotypes. It shows the areas of clear preference for male church leadership as well as points of ambivalence. It depicts their tendencies to discriminate against women clergy.

With this picture in mind, the study also tried to detect *why* people felt the way they did, focusing on social backgrounds, differences in religious commitment, the types of churches involved and the ways in which members try to protect their organizations from the disruptions of congregational conflict. Each of these kinds of influences affect people's reactions to having a woman as their minister.

Of particular interest is the way church members' attitudes change once they personally experience a woman working in the role of their pastor. With this kind of direct contact seem to come major alterations in what they think clergywomen are like and how they feel about working with women as ministers. The evidence suggests that antipathies associated with changing sex roles can be modified by some of the same techniques as those used to reduce hostilities among racial and ethnic groups.

The research project is national in scope. It focused on one major Protestant denomination, the United Presbyterian Church, U.S.A., a large "middle-of-the-road" body which resembles many other religious groups in the United States. The Vocation Agency of that denomination provided the impetus for the work and defrayed the costs of data collection and analysis.

Research is not an individualistic enterprise, especially as it is conducted today by investigators working within the context of highly structured professions and in conjunction with modern bureaucratic organizations. Many people contribute. Authors must pay their debts to those who help them along the way. This author is primarily indebted to Ann Dubois and Penelope Morgan Colman, both of whom were working with the Vocation Agency of the UPC when the study began. In fact it was these women's insight and initiative which gave birth to the entire undertaking. And it was in the context of a fruitful exchange with them that the objectives and design of the study took shape. To Ann and Penny, "Thanks!" Thanks for letting an old Baptist take a hard look at you Presbyterians! And thanks for your incisive criticism and other feedback along the way!

The research would not have succeeded without the excellent cooperation of the clergywomen and their church members. The women ministers who participated in the study endured many protracted telephone calls which probed deeply into their professional lives. I appreciate their trust and their forebearance. The members of their congregations likewise were willing to open up to a total stranger and to discuss candidly what was going on in their communities. Many of them will never know it, of course, but they have my heartfelt thanks too.

The thoroughly social nature of modern research is also apparent in the support provided by branches of the organizations associated with the work. The Research Division of the Support Agency of the United Presbyterian Church conducted the data collection for two sections of the study—the Presbyterian Panel, which served as the national sample of laity and clergy, and the survey of clergywomen focusing on their placement experiences during job searches. We appreciate their support. We especially thank Gay Tennis for her consultation and other work on the Panel.

The State University College at Brockport, New York, also played an important role in the undertaking. I am grateful to my colleagues in the Department of Sociology for letting me structure my work there so as to allow time for conducting the research. I am probably more indebted to them than I know, also, for the forgotten insights they provided (but which I now claim) during the course of dozens of conversations in the office and over lunch. I must also thank the Academic Computing Center at Brockport for their assistance with the data analysis.

One thing that can make or break an otherwise good research project is a secretary, that infinitely discreet person who covers up most of the author's mistakes. Two such wonderful creatures were involved in this study—Brenda Perry of the Vocation Agency, UPC, whose skill in dealing with mountains of correspondence was indispensable; and Gloria Condoluci of the Department of Sociology at SUC Brockport, at whose hands every page of manuscript was typed. Well done, both of you!

Two persons provided important services as research assistants. These were Mark Lehman and Faith Rogers, both students at the State University College at Brockport. Their content analysis of church members' comments provided important "meat" for the "bare bones" of the survey statistics.

As usual several people were involved in the drudgery of reviewing early versions of the manuscript and making important recommendations for modifications. These vital contributions were made by Ann Dubois, Penny Colman, Jackson Carroll, Barbara Hargrove, and Adaire Lummis. A few persons provided feedback on specific chapters of the book, and these include Dean Hoge, Jean Spade, Doris Jones and Phyllis Henry. Publication of research results also involves a series of reviewers who remain anonymous. They also have my gratitude, even though in their protected status they must continue to be nameless.

Finally, and yet profoundly, my gratitude goes to Johnnie Lehman, whose patience, understanding and encouragement make most things I try to do worthwhile.

Edward C. Lehman, Jr.
Brockport, New York

June, 1983

CHAPTER 1

The Advent of Clergywomen

"Breakthrough!" The word almost always generates excitement. It distracts us from daily routines and draws attention to the source of the claim. It lifts our expectations. Sometimes it engenders suspicion that the claim is exaggerated. Most of the time it makes us just a little envious.

The term provokes such responses, because any claim to a breakthrough is an assertion that one has accomplished things which some people considered unattainable—the "impossible dream." It signifies instances of human achievement where seemingly insurmountable obstacles have been overcome and transcended. Few events really qualify.

Most recent events we would consider breakthroughs are basically physical in nature. Included among them would be things like test pilot Chuck Yeager breaking through the sound barrier, Roger Bannister breaking through the four-minute mile, Jonas Salk developing the vaccine against polio, and Marie Curie isolating radium. These were all significant events in humanity's efforts to manipulate the world.

In this book we shall be dealing with another kind of breakthrough. Instead of focusing on people adapting to the physical world around them, we shall concentrate on the problem of relating to other people—trying to get by in society. Getting by can be a serious problem. Other people don't always act in the way we want them to act. They get in our way, not physically but by constructing customs, rules, values, attitudes and prejudices that work against us. Anyone who has seriously tried to buck these things knows that they are very real barriers, even though they are by nature intangible and hard to put your finger on.

From time to time, people produce flashes of insight and create social innovations that remove some of these barriers. Some such developments are a part of recent American history— the institution of universal suffrage, the desegregation of public facilities, the 1964 Civil Rights Act, and so forth. Other such changes are still struggling for acceptance, such as the Equal Rights Amendment and nuclear disarmament. As these instances of social change occur, even though they meet with strenuous resistance from those whose vested interests are threatened at the time, they take on the status of "breakthroughs." Given only a few years of retrospection, even those who previously opposed them come to view them as socially desirable. Eventually no serious observer would advocate a return to the situation which existed prior to the institutionalization of the change.

This book examines what may be a breakthrough "in progress." It describes what is happening as women seek acceptance in fields of endeavor previously dominated by men, in this case the ordained clergy. As has happened as women become practitioners in other fields—medicine, law, space flight, politics—as women seek ordination as ministers, they encounter resistance from others in the organization. Denominational leaders, other clergy, and lay church members all include individuals who are not prepared to accept women as clergy.

Some of this resistance stems from age-old assumptions about what is "naturally" male and female about us as human beings. Patterns of thought and action which men and women learn from their culture appear to have an inevitability about them that some people regard as inviolable. They so think that "of course" men and women differ in their temperament, moods, intellectual abilities, etc., that the movement of persons of one sex into a field considered the appropriate province of the other sex appears to be a contravention of nature.

Nevertheless, bolstered by a growing body of literature which suggests that many of these sex differences are only obliquely linked to basic biological differences between men and women, increasing numbers of women are moving into fields previously dominated by men. This is the case with the clergy. Women are entering theological seminaries and training to become ministers, priests and rabbis. As they complete their theological education, they are seeking placement as pastors, chaplains, teachers of religion, and in other forms of ministry. They are trying to break through the gender barrier that identifies the ministry as a male-only occupation.

Our analysis looks at the encounter between the woman minister and the ultimate "consumers" of her ministry, the lay church members. It is probably in the context of this interface that the barrier will (or will not) eventually come down. Acceptance of women in ministry on the part of church members may constitute another social "breakthrough." As of now, what do church members think of the prospect of having a woman as pastor? What kinds of feelings do clergywomen arouse in laypersons? How do church members respond to the challenge? Why do they react as they do? As women encounter barriers from church members, what can they do to overcome them? These are the questions we'll address in the pages to follow.

The Feminist Movement as Background

The movement of women into the ranks of ordained clergy is but one of a large number of social movements taking place in twentieth-century America. These social movements call attention to problems in virtually every area of life—politics, the economy, the family, education, religion, etc. Everything is open to question. In political movements people have demythologised national and local leaders. Economic movements have placed capitalism itself on trial. Marriage is no longer viewed as either natural or inevitable by many devoted couples. Religious leaders no longer enjoy a knee-jerk response to their pronouncements and directives. It is an age in which Americans are questioning conventional wisdom—an exciting and frustrating time.

Some of these movements seem to have existed for a long time, e.g., pressures for civil rights, free speech, Fundamentalism and the Social Gospel. We have been dealing with these concepts in one form or another for decades. Others appear to be new—concerns about nuclear energy, environmentalism, gay rights, "grey power" and the "right to life." At least they have assumed dimensions that, for whatever reasons, have not been apparent before. Whether new or old, they all clamor for our attention simultaneously, and they have the potential to revolutionize our daily lives.

The Current Feminist Movement

In this book we will focus on but one of these movements, one which is clearly manifesting its potential for revolutionizing life in the United States. This is the Women's Liberation Movement. Some observers trace this movement's origins back to Susan B. Anthony, Elizabeth Cady Stanton and others in the Women's Suffrage Movement early in this century. To others the real momentum appeared with Margaret Sanger and the birth control movement about a generation later. Yet most observers see the current phase—the "Women's Liberation Movement" per se—as having begun with the appearance of Betty Friedan's Book, *The Feminine Mystique* (1963), a work which most publishers considered "too hot to handle" in 1963 but whose profits they wish they had reaped.

In the early '60's a number of conditions seemed to converge to unleash a nation-wide social movement of women (and men) to redress inequities in sex roles in this society (Freeman, 1975). The inequities themselves certainly seem to have been one such condition—inequities in law, education, politics, occupations, credit, family roles and even religious life. It seems as though the effects of many of these inequities were largely unrecognized at first; nevertheless, little "consciousness raising" was required to put them clearly in mind a bit later on.

A second condition was the unfocused dissatisfaction of many middle-class women. In a period of relative prosperity, they had most of the basic material goods they needed—they were "taken care of" by their provider-husbands/fathers. But something was missing. They were bored. Their lives seemed to lack intrinsic meaning. What they didn't realize at the time was that their very dependency itself was oppressive, but—again—many of them didn't define the situation that way. If anything was wrong, it had to be themselves. Their problem, they thought, was in being "ungrateful" or not being "content." After all, "What else could they want?" They soon found out.

The third condition, and the one which appears to have provided the catalyst for changing these perceptions and for mobilization to systematically attack sex-role subordination itself, was the development of some networks of communication. These sets of relationships initially took the form of a series of national and state "Commissions on the Status of Women" established by President John F. Kennedy. The national commission provided a structure primarily for documenting sex-role problems, and the state commissions became arenas within which implications of the problems could be articulated. In these contexts, and within a series of more spontaneous, informal women's groups that appeared to emerge as "spin-offs" from the peace movement, women found themselves able to compare notes and develop sets of shared redefinitions of the situation. Before entering these groups, women tended to view themselves as privileged but ungrateful, and therefore regretful. Having experienced the exchange and support that existed in most of the groups, women came to define themselves instead as oppressed and hoodwinked, and therefore resentful.

In addition to serving as media for communication and transformation of consciousness, the commissions provided the initial bases from which women could begin to organize themselves to change the situation on a societal level. The best known of these formal organizations, of course, is the National Organization for Women. But many others were created too, such as the National Women's Political Caucus and the Women's Equity Action League. Working within these structures, women mounted effective campaigns for political, legal, economic and educational reforms. The literature which coincided with these organizations, such as *MS* magazine, became another medium for communication and consciousness raising. More local groups formed. The movement took off.

Today, after more than two decades of work, the women's liberation movement has wrought significant transformations of

life in American society. These range from highly formal decisions, such as appointing a woman to the United States Supreme
Court, to very informal routines such as who takes the initiative in
making love. Getting one's own credit rating, being admitted into
a professional school, having access to child-care facilities, being
taken seriously as a candidate for public office, having legal control over one's body, etc.—these aspects (and many others) of
women's life situations have been dramatically improved largely
through the impact of the women's liberation movement. The
changes have been broad and exhilarating. They have also been
frustrating and disquieting for both women and men, for the
movement has been revising roles for everyone in the society,
and no one is quite sure what the final version should look like.
But, frustrating or not, the movement has developed its own
momentum, and most of the transformations are likely to be more
permanent than transitory.

Women's Occupations

The world of work is one arena in which women's roles have
been changing in ways that are relatively easy to document
(Stromberg and Harkess, 1978). Today more women are formally
active in the labor force than ever before. For many years now a
majority of American women have held jobs other than that of
homemaker. At the end of the 1970's, 60 percent of all women
between the ages of 16 and 64 were employed outside the home
(Department of Labor, 1980). The percentage of all married
women with such employment was 50. The figure was 59 percent
for women with school-age children, and it was 43 percent for
women with children in the pre-school years. Some of this movement of women into gainful employment is directly attributable to
pressures for change brought about by the women's liberation
movement, especially their concerted drives for increases in the
number and quality of day-care facilities. Without these arrangements most women with pre-school and school-age children
would find it difficult to justify their departure from the mother
role during "working hours," although many more such facilities
are needed.

The particular *kind* of occupational activity women are engaged
in is another indicator of changes in women's opportunities in the
labor market. Table 1.1 shows the number of men and women in
some selected occupations at roughly the beginning and end of

the 1970's. The patterns in the table illustrate the kinds of shifts that have been occurring in the world of work partly as a result of the current feminist movement. The sex composition of a few fields remains relatively unchanged. The number of women in the traditionally female occupations of secretary and elementary school teacher, for example, increased slightly in terms of absolute numbers. However, the percentage of female workers in those occupations presents a different picture, i.e., the *proportion* of women in those fields was basically unchanged. They are still considered "women's fields." Stenographers, however, another traditionally female field, *decreased* in absolute numbers. There were fewer stenographers at the end of the period than at the outset. This reduction is probably due to the increased use of electronic word processing in offices across the country. Nevertheless, notice again that the *proportion* of women who were stenographers remained stable. Stenography is still considered primarily a woman's field.

While these traditionally female occupations have not lost their feminine labels, there is evidence that many traditional male occupations are opening up to women. The advent of Title VII of the 1964 Civil Rights Act, along with the introduction of guidelines for implementing both "equal opportunity" and "affirmative action," has clearly required accountability of the federal government as an employer. The number of "letter carriers" who are female, for example, increased by 66 percent from early to late 1970's. Furthermore, the proportion of persons in that occupation who were women increased by 75 percent. While it is still perceived as a field in which males predominate, its sex-composition is changing. (Bureau of the Census, 1979).

Discrimination legislation has also affected sex-composition of the professions. During the 1970's, the legal profession appears to have changed more than any other. The number of women working as lawyers and judges increased by 286 percent. The proportion of these legal professionals who are women increased by 147 percent. The practice of law is diminishing as a "men's club." Over the same period, medicine, pharmacy and higher education opened up to women at about the same rates. The number of women in these professions increased by just under 50 percent. In terms of proportions of females in these occupations, however, pharmacy appears to have been the most receptive to females. The rate of change in medicine is more gradual, with that for college teachers somewhere in between. At whatever rate of change,

TABLE 1.1   CHANGES IN THE SEX COMPOSITION OF SELECTED OCCUPATIONS: 1972 TO 1978*

Occupation:	Females in 1972: number**	percent	Females in 1978: number	percent	Percent change in number	Rate of change in proportion
mail carrier	18,000	6.7	30,000	11.7	66	75
secretary	2,922,000	99.1	3,561,000	99.2	22	0****
stenographer	113,000	90.4	85,000	90.4	-25	0****
elementary school teacher	1,065,000	85.1	1,095,000	84.0	3	0****
lawyer & judge	12,000	3.8	50,000	9.4	286	147
physician	33,000	10.1	48,000	11.3	47	12
pharmacist	16,000	12.7	23,000	16.9	44	33
college teacher	129,000	28.0	190,000	33.8	47	21
religious worker	37,000	11.0	48,000	14.8	30	35
TOTAL***	31,047,000	38.0	94,373,000	42.1	25	11

*Source: Bureau of the Census, Statistical Abstracts: 1979, pp. 416–418.
**Numbers rounded to the nearest thousand in the source.
***Total figures include all types of occupations, i.e., more than those selected for inclusion in the table.
****Rate of change less than 1%.

these professions are becoming less exclusively the domain of males, reflecting in part the impact of the women's liberation movement (Bureau of the Census, 1979).

One reason professions such as these have admitted at least some additional women is the advent of Title VII of the Civil Rights Act, legislation for which feminist organizations lobbied strenuously. Law schools, medical schools, colleges of pharmacy and graduate programs in the liberal arts depend heavily on federal grants to support programs of research and graduate training. Any schools receiving such aid who are found guilty of sex discrimination stand in danger of losing their grant status. With this jeopardy, many of them have adjusted their admissions procedures to allow the entry of more women and have placed fewer other barriers in the way of women seeking to complete programs of study once admitted. Most of these colleges and universities have also appointed affirmative action officers to oversee such policies. Most large industrial and commercial firms employing women in traditionally male fields such as management and technical areas have also installed "watch dogs" in their personnel divisions in order to avoid the loss of federal and state contracts. By being institutionalized in law, the pressures against sex discrimination practices in education and employment have effected institutional changes. They are enforceable.

The last category in Table 1.1 consists of "religious workers." The number of women in religious vocations increased by 30 percent. And the rate of change in this proportion was about 35 percent. Women are moving into religious occupations more rapidly than men. The rate of change in the proportion of religious workers who are female roughly approximates the degree of change associated with pharmacy. However, in the case of religious occupations, Title VII does not apply due to the First Amendment to the Constitution—the separation of church and state doctrine. There is no law which says religious organizations must employ women. Yet there appears to be significant change in that occupational classification.

The category "religious workers" is heterogeneous in terms of the sex-typing of occupations. Applied to Roman Catholics, for example, it includes bishops, priests, and nuns. Among main-line Protestants, it embraces pastors, directors of religious education, youth workers and choir directors. Its diversity *masks* an important change that is taking place in the leadership of religious institutions in this country. The 30 to 35 percent increase of women in the "religious worker" classification (Bureau of the Census, 1979) includes both old and new patterns. Not all of these women are moving into church-related work where women have been found traditionally—youth workers, music directors, organists, educational directors, and foreign missionaries. True, these fields still attract large numbers of women today. However, what these census figures do not reveal is the fact that *large numbers of women are moving into religious vocations previously thought to be the exclusive province of men. Many of them are entering the pastoral ministry.*

The Women-In-Ministry Movement

The current feminist movement has been making inroads into the leadership of religious institutions in the United States (see Daly, 1975). One of the clearest indicators of this trend is the pattern of recent increases in female enrollments in theological seminaries (Taylor, 1982). Total enrollments grew from 29,815 students in 1969 to 49,611 in 1980, an increase of 66 percent. Breaking down those gross figures by sex reveals that this growth involves significant movement of women into theological education. Table 1.2 portrays the rates of increase of selected seminary enrollments during the 1970's. While total enrollments went up by about 66 percent, the increases were but 31 percent for males while they

TABLE 1.2   RATES OF INCREASE IN SELECTED
SEMINARY ENROLLMENTS: 1972–1980*

Program	Rate of increase
total enrollment	66%
male enrollments	31%
female enrollments	223%
enrollment in professional tracks:	
males	36%
females	248%
female enrollments in "ordination"	
degree programs	241%

*Source: Marvin J. Taylor, ed. *Fact Book on Theological Education: 1980–81.* American Association of Theological Schools, Vandalia, Ohio, pp. 1–10.

were 223 percent for females. Most of these increases were in educational programs leading to professional involvements in church leadership—a 36 percent increase for men but a 248 percent upsurge for women. The rate of increase of female enrollments in degree programs leading specifically to *ordination* was 241 percent. Information obtained in personal conversations with seminary staff suggests that at the time they enter seminary most of these women in "ordination tracks" are seriously interested in becoming pastors of local churches.

Female Students Making An Impact

The most dramatic increases in seminary enrollments of females took place during the 1970's. Once these women were members of the student bodies, they were instrumental in promoting other changes in seminary education. One important change was structural. Taking cues from the women's movement in the larger society (Freeman, 1975), female seminary students organized support groups on their local campuses. These groups appear to have performed the same functions within the seminary as did their counterparts in secular circles. First, they became "rap groups" in which students could vent their frustrations about sexist components of seminary life—unenlightened faculty and students, inappropriate curricular materials, biased administrative policies, offensive traditional language, etc. By airing feelings of disappointment and resentment about such obstacles in a supportive milieu, women seminarians were able to "hand in and hang loose" and cope successfully.

A previous study (Lehman, 1981 b) of trends such as these in another denomination—the American Baptists—reveals an even more interesting pattern, i.e., that in some instances the women are actually replacing men in the ordination degree programs due to a decline in the number and quality of male applicants for admission to these tracks. Table 1.3 contains enrollment figures from American Baptist seminaries for the academic years 1970–71 and 1979–80. The male enrollments in the "master of divinity" (M.DIV.) track, the traditional path to the pastorate and typically a seminary's "bread-and-butter" program, increased by only 7 percent during the period, while female enrollments in M.DIV. programs increased by 570 percent.

Furthermore, this shift is most readily noticeable in the Northern states among predominantly white seminaries where the primary thrust of the denomination's theological education has been located. In the seminaries catering mostly to white students, there was an overall 9 percent *decline* of males in the M.DIV. programs and an increase of 657 percent among the females. The figures in Table 1.3 pertain to one denomination, i.e., the American Baptists. Nevertheless, personal conversations and anecdotal reports suggest that the pattern is not unique to them but may be found in other denominations as well.

TABLE 1.3   ENROLLMENTS OF MEN AND WOMEN IN AMERICAN BAPTIST SEMINARY M.DIV. PROGRAMS: 1970–71 and 1979–80*

Total of all seminaries		
	M.Div. Enrollments	
Year	men	women
1970–71	709	47
1979–80	762	315
% increase	07	570

Predominantly black seminaries		
	M.Div. Enrollments	
Year	men	women
1970–71	205	12
1979–80	302	50
% increase	47	317

Predominantly white seminaries		
	M.Div. Enrollments	
Year	men	women
1970–71	504	35
1979–80	460	265
% increase	−09	657

*Source: Edward C. Lehman, Jr., "Organizational Resistance to Women in Ministry" *Sociological Analysis*, 42:2 (1981), p. 114.

Denominational figures published by the American Association of Theological Schools (Taylor, 1982) indicate that in most religious bodies by 1980 the number of women enrolled in professional programs in general and in the M.DIV. programs (and B.D. programs which parallel them) in particular had increased substantially. Those figures are contained in Table 1.4. The body whose seminaries showed the largest numerical gains in female enrollments in professional programs was the non-denomination schools. Of the denominational seminaries, the greatest numerical gains in professional enrollments were in the Southern Baptist institutions. The Roman Catholic schools showed a large number of women in professional tracks too.

Focusing on the relative picture, however, i.e., the percentages of women enrolled, shows a different pattern. The denomination whose seminaries showed the greatest *proportion* of women enrolled in professional tracks is the United Church in Canada (even though they had the smallest actual number). The Roman Catholic Church in Canada had the second-highest percentage of women in this category. In the United States, the body with the highest proportion of female professional enrollments was the United Church of Christ.

The patterns shift even more dramatically when we focus on the M.DIV. programs specifically—the track leading to the pastorate. The denomination whose seminaries had the highest number of females enrolled in M.DIV. programs was the United Methodist Church, reflecting their established policy of ordaining women to the pastoral ministry, as well as their relatively centralized placement system, an attractive factor to women seeking placement after seminary. In terms of proportions of M.DIV. students who are women, the denomination whose schools had the highest rate was the United Church of Christ, both in the United States and in Canada. Note that Southern Baptists, whose seminaries had the highest number of women in professional tracks, had one of the lowest percentages of M.DIV. students who were women. Only the Roman Catholic Church had a smaller proportion of female M.DIV. students than Southern Baptists. These low rates are consistent with widely-held impressions that both official policy and unofficial attitudes toward the concept of clergywomen in these denominations tends strongly toward conservatism.

Beyond these extremes, however, the general pattern in the table indicates that in the seminaries of most denominations the force of movement of women into professional and M.DIV. programs is significant. Nearly one-third of the students in professional programs in 1980 were women. Nearly one-fourth of those specifically in the M.DIV. programs were women.

Partly due to the context of collectively dealing with each other's problems of coping, while considering ways of approaching various manifestations of sexism, some of the local support groups became strategy groups. The supportive role of the groups remained, but an insurgent role came to coexist. This is an important

TABLE 1.4 ENROLLMENTS IN SELECTED SEMINARY PROGRAMS BY SEX, PROGRAM AND DENOMINATION: 1980*

	Professional Programs			B.D./M.DIV. Programs		
	male	female	(percent female)	male	female	(percent female)
Canada Roman Catholic	382	237	(38)	233	33	(12)
Canada United Church	211	166	(44)	141	101	(42)
American Baptist	807	240	(23)	424	137	(24)
Southern Baptist	7110	1606	(18)	4220	403	(09)
Christian Church	599	206	(26)	337	117	(26)
Lutheran: LCA	800	257	(24)	544	173	(24)
United Methodist	2816	1129	(29)	1765	736	(29)
Presbyterian: U.S.	564	194	(26)	165	43	(21)
United Presbyterian	2161	523	(19)	809	376	(32)
Episcopal	669	304	(31)	509	192	(27)
Roman Catholic: US	4194	1188	(22)	3005	208	(06)
United Church of Christ	834	423	(34)	340	275	(45)
Non-Denominational	5991	1827	(23)	3426	678	(17)
TOTALS	27,138	8,300	(31)	15,918	3,472	(22)

*Source: Marvin J. Taylor, ed., Fact Book on Theological Education: 1980–81. American Association of Theological Schools, Vandalia, Ohio, pp. 72, 74.

transformation. It marked the end of an exclusively defensive posture toward sexism in the seminary, and it signified the beginning of a more aggressive stance. Functionally the groups changed from purely adaptive structures to become mechanisms for reform as well.

As a result of the support groups becoming more overtly transformative in their agendas, a number of other changes appeared on seminary campuses. Some were programmatic. Female seminarians objected to sexism they perceived in the seminary curriculum and they asked for curricular change. Most schools responded with two modifications: (1) the introduction of new courses dealing with feminist issues in religious life, and (2) modification of existing courses to make them less offensive to women and more inclusive of women's concerns.

Other changes involved seminary personnel. One obvious fact of life on seminary campuses for many years has been the male domination of the faculty (see Taylor, 1982). In 1971 there were but 73 full-time female seminary faculty constituting 3.2 percent of the whole, and 104 part-time women faculty comprising 6.9 percent of all part-timers. Women in seminary called for increases in female faculty. By 1980 the number of full-time female seminary faculty had increased to 195, and the proportion had risen to 7.9 percent. The number of part-time women had increased to 386 or 16.3 percent of the whole. Early in the 1980's the male dominance is still clearly present, but most schools have begun to incorporate women among the faculty (Taylor, 1982). (One problem in answering the initial calls for female seminary faculty was the paucity of women with the appropriate academic credentials, a situation which is gradually changing.)

Another complaint of the female seminarians focused on the schools' administration. Where were the female administrators? In 1971 there were but 103 women among the professional seminary administrative personnel. These women amounted to 12.2 percent of the total. The students' pressure seemingly brought results. In 1980 there were 193 women among the seminary administrators, or 18.8 percent of the total (Taylor, 1982).

It is interesting to note that recruiting more women as administrators was accomplished with greater success than was installing women as full-time faculty. If one were to give the incumbent seminary faculty the benefit of the doubt, this pattern was plausibly due to highly specialized credentials being required for most faculty posts in theological schools and the simple fact that there were very few women with such training. A broader range of backgrounds would qualify one for an administrative position. However, anecdotal evidence suggests that many schools were slow to recruit female faculty on the basis of intransigence on the part of some individuals who were in the seminary administration and faculty at that time. Reality is most likely at neither extreme but somewhere in between.

Another important way in which groups of female seminary students appear to have resembled women's groups associated with the broader liberation movement was in the development of networks of communication among groups. Women from seminary campuses in various geographical regions met periodically, sometimes formally and at other times informally, to share notes about their quality of life and strategies for change. They developed linkages across many geographical and denominational boundaries. This "networking" activity had several consequences. First, it further developed the sense of "sisterhood" and of being joined in a common struggle. These contacts broadened the arena within which they saw themselves as pressing for changes in seminary life and in the church. Eventually the object of strategy was conceptualized as the whole denomination and the society around it. Seminary women were no longer thinking in terms of changing curricula. They were dealing with ways of changing people's understanding of the entire community of faith. It had to be an exhilarating perception.

Women's groups in seminaries also brought pressure to bear on the hierarchical structures of the denominations associated with their schools. (Some such contacts were necessary to achieve the curricular and personnel changes in the seminaries outlined above.) Through a variety of strategies—in denominational offices, at regional and national conventions, via denominational media, through seminary administrators—they obtained recognition of the legitimacy of their complaints. They successfully linked the desire for eliminating sexist elements in traditional church life with basic Christian concepts of justice, love and equality before god. To be sure, the ideological linkages were obvious once pointed out. The denominational hierarchies virtually had to respond to the women's demands in good faith. As a result, today there is movement toward a variety of reforms, i.e., ordination of clergywomen, liturgical change, modifications of church literature and church school curricula, new Biblical translations and interpretations, hymnals without sexist language, etc. Some denominations (e.g., United Presbyterian, American Baptist, United Methodist) are responding to religious feminism more positively than others (e.g., Roman Catholic, Southern Baptist), and people feel differently about the pace at which the churches are responding. To some feminists, change is coming too slowly. To some traditionalists, any change in sex roles in religion is coming too fast. Perhaps the gradual shifts currently under way in many churches constitute the most prudent pace for the present.

The Question for the Churches

Hardly a major denomination in North America is untouched by pressures from the women-in-ministry movement. Most main-line denominations are responding positively, especially at the national level (Jacquet, 1973, 1978). However, with the exception of a few perceptive "news hounds" among the laity, *most members of local churches have been basically unaware of any of these changes*. If one thinks about it a little, it would be surprising to observe otherwise. Most members have little reason to know about increased female enrollments in theological seminaries. Consequently, they have no way of perceiving the dramatic increase in the number of clergywomen entering the pool of candidates for pastoral positions in local churches. Denominational pronouncements about such matters would make little difference, for they tend to be remote—to be "somebody else's business." Most members are also sufficiently removed from the denominational offices per se that they are similarly unaware of the incorporation of feminism into the organizational structure of the denomination—implementation of feminist values.

There are also psychological reasons for most church members not being "tuned in" to developments like these. Perhaps chief among them is the fact that such things are not what "church" is about to most people. Participating in church life is a very *local* matter to them. It is *this* church in *this* community. It is *their* worship service, their music program, their budget and their cemetery. They are aware of denominational alignments, however, and they place sufficient importance on them to take them seriously. They are willing to support the denomination financially. They are usually glad to use the programmatic resources the denomination provides for them. But for most church members the denomination is remote. It is more "them" than "us." It is a very distant priority compared to their local church. Most members simply do not pay much attention to what is going on at that level.

For many church members, the first time they encounter the concept of clergywomen in any salient way is when a denominational official suggests that they should consider a woman minister for a position in their church. More than likely the administrator has one or more clergywomen's dossiers in hand at that time, and those women are depending on him/her to advocate their candidacy to the churches. How will the members respond? Suddenly they find themselves thrust into a decision-making situation for which they do not feel prepared. The issue requires a major change in their understanding of church leadership. They have not really thought about it before. What will they do?

It is this situation that is confronting the churches as a whole. The clergywomen are in the system. They are graduating from theological seminaries in record numbers. They are seeking placement in jobs in the ministry previously held amost exclusively by men. Many of them aspire to be pastors of local churches. *How will the churches respond to them?* That question is the focus of this book.

Organization of Things to Come

The primary purpose of this volume is to report the results of a study of the reactions of church members to women in ministry. The material is organized in terms of the various ways in which members are likely to relate to the concept, the extent to which members have encountered women clergy and the position the members occupy in the church. Specifically, Chapter 2 indicates the various ways in which people are likely to manifest varying degrees of acceptance or rejection of women in ministry—the structure of attitudes. It also describes the way in which we measured those attitudes among members of a particular denomination. Chapter 3 compares the ways in which laypersons, clergy and denominational officials relate to the issue.

In Chapter 4 we examine differences in members' acceptance of women in ministry more closely by investigating why some people are open to the idea while others are opposed. We explain some of these differences in terms of other ways in which those people differ, i.e., variations in the members' individual characteristics, the nature of their religious commitment and the type of the local church to which they belong.

Chapter 5 examines receptivity to clergywomen from the perspective of a particular kind of problem some members have with the idea. That is, since the introduction of women into the pool of candidates for pastoral positions is controversial for some people, there is concern that dealing with the issue openly will lead to some kind of conflict or even schism in their church. This part of the analysis outlines some dimensions of this kind of problem, and it indicates the role these concerns play in members' attitudes toward women in ministry.

The focus of Chapters 6 and 7 is on the impact that having direct experiences with women clergy has had on members' attitudes toward them—the "contact hypothesis." They describe an evaluation of a church program designed to reduce resistance to women in ministry by placing clergywomen in selected churches as interim ministers. They also compare the effects of these experiences on those members' receptivity to the effects of having a woman as permanently installed pastor in some other churches. After outlining the kinds of changes that occurred, Chapter 8 seeks to identify the reasons why contact with clergywomen as pastor affects people's orientations in the way that it did.

The ninth chapter takes a different approach to the problem. Instead of reviewing data from the members, it looks at information obtained from the clergywomen themselves. It presents the outcome of a study of the placement experiences of women seeking positions in the ministry, focusing primarily on ways of conceptualizing the process, the kinds of actions by clergywomen that are most likely (and least likely) to lead to success in finding a job, and some reasons why such strategies do or do not make a difference.

The final chapter ties the rest of the book together. It presents some corroborating evidence obtained from interviews with the clergywomen who served as ministers-at-large and as installed pastors in the churches where we interviewed the lay members. It then sets forth several basic conclusions derived from the preceding analysis—what it all seems to mean. Finally, this chapter ventures a few predictions as to what the situation for women in ministry is likely to be over the next few years, along with an indication of what the consequences of that situation are likely to be.

Suggestions for Additional Reading

Colman, Penelope Morgan and Ann Dubois Conrad
1978 *Resource Book for Placement, Acceptance and Support of Clergywomen.*
Office for Women in Ministry, The Vocation Agency, United Presbyterian
Church, USA, 406 Interchurch Center, 475 Riverside Drive, New York,
New York 10115

A volume of guidelines for clergywomen and church members to address the range of issues associated with the entry of women into
ministry. Contains programs for dealing with the concept, research
results, models of strategies and bibliography associated with women in
ministry.

Commission on Women in Ministry
1976 *A Resource Guide for Women in Seminary.* Task Force on Women in
Theological Education, National Council of Churches, 475 Riverside
Drive, New York, New York 10027

A source book of printed materials available on women in ministry. Lists
organizations, caucuses, task forces and women's centers. Extensive
bibliography on the subjects of feminist theology, women and religion,
linguistic sexism, etc.

Daly, Mary
1975 *The Church and the Second Sex.* New York: Harper and Row.

A classic statement of feminist concerns about traditional forms of Christian belief and practice and the explicit and implicit sexism imbedded
within them. This printing also contains what the author calls "a new
feminist post-Christian introduction," a reassessment of the book itself
after several years of additional experiences since it first appeared.

Department of Labor, U.S. Bureau of Labor Statistics
1980 *Perspectives on Working Women: A Databook.* U.S. Government Printing
Office, Washington, D.C. 20402

A book of tables indicating national figures concerning women in the
labor force. Breakdowns by a variety of factors, e.g., marital status,
family size, age of children, etc.

Freeman, Jo
1975 *The Politics of Women's Liberation.* (New York: Longman, Inc.)

A study of the development of the women's liberation movement. Looks
at its roots and origins, the conditions necessary for it to take hold, its impact on national policy, etc.

Stromberg, A.H. and Shirley Harkess, editors
1978 *Women Working: Theories and Facts in Perspective.* Palo Alto, California:
Mayfield.

A collection of essays dealing with women in the labor force. Documents statistical descriptions, occupational experiences of women workers, ways of explaining patterns observed in women's work, and suggests implications for policy and the situation in the future.

Taylor, Marvin J.
1982 *Fact Book on Theological Education*. American Association of Theological Schools, Vandalia, Ohio 45377.

An annual publication listing current statistics on students, faculty, and administrations of seminaries in the United States and Canada. Includes interpretations of the tables and discussions of apparent trends in theological education.

CHAPTER 2

How Will the Churches Respond?

How are local church members likely to respond to women as clergy? Will they accept them as routinely as they accept men? Or will they manifest some forms of resistance to women in ministry? Will they accept them in some clergy roles but not in others? To ask such questions is ultimately to ask how church members will act overtly toward clergywomen—to accept or reject them. That outcome is certainly the "bottom line" for the woman minister. Will she find a job in which she can work out her call to ministry, or will she be frustrated and in the final analysis be rejected?

To ask these questions is also to inquire about people's *attitudes*, for most individuals act toward various objects around them (other people, institutions, clergywomen) on the basis of their attitudes toward those objects (see Petty and Cacioppo, 1981). We act toward other people one way if we like them, and we behave quite differently if we do not like them. Liking and disliking—approving and disapproving—are largely what we mean by "attitudes." These orientations tend to guide our actions toward others in ways that are often highly consistent across a variety of situations.

This is not to argue that our attitudes are the only factors underlying our actions toward things around us. There are other explanations for what we do (Deutscher, 1973). One of them is simply how we happen to feel at the moment. If we are feeling happy, we act differently than if we are feeling sad. Similarly, it makes a difference whether we are feeling confident or insecure, accepted or rejected, "up" or "down." Another determinant of our behavior toward others is the social role we occupy in that situation. The fact that we are someone's "employee" usually determines quite a number of things that we will or will not do—especially if we want to keep the job! People behave toward others in typical and predictable ways when acting in particular social roles, e.g., physician, teacher, policeman, parent or customer. These external realities determine a great deal of what we do, virtually regardless of our attitudes.

We also tend to behave toward others in ways that are typical and predictable on the basis of our attitudes toward those others. A person who is prejudiced (an attitude) against blacks, for example, will be motivated to act consistently in some ways toward a black person regardless of the role occupied at the time. So if we want to have some idea of the kinds of actions we can expect from people toward some object of interest, it is helpful to know their attitudes toward that object. *We are interested in knowing what kind of responses we can expect from church members as they confront the idea of relating to women in clergy roles. It will be helpful to know their attitudes toward women in ministry.*

The Structure of Attitudes

What do we mean by "attitudes"? They are really quite complex. Research into attitudes typically deals with them in terms of three "dimensions," aspects referred to as the "cognitive," "affective" and "behavioral" dimensions (Newcomb, et al, 1965: Ch. 3). The cognitive component—sometimes also called the "perceptual" dimension—consists of a person's understanding or definition of the object. It is reflected, for example, in the description one would get from a white person cataloguing the characteristics of a black person or of an Oriental. It is seen in a young person's description of an "old man" and a middle-class, small-town shop owner's description of an "urban welfare mother." The cognitive dimension is the way in which most of us think of prejudice—"prejudge"—to think of a member of some group via an image we have in mind ahead of time. This mode of thinking becomes labelled "prejudice" when a *priori* judgments seem inaccurate, unfair and somehow damaging to the person in question. It is especially frowned upon when it leads to actions that are discriminatory against an individual or an entire group (see Allport, 1958).

The judgments need not be negative, however. They may treat the object very positively such as when one thinks of one's lover. The definition of the object also may or may not be accurate. A young person's description of an "old man" may range from being right on the mark to being unrealistic. But whether correct or incorrect, whether flattering or debasing, the cognitive dimension constitutes an important element of the attitudes behind our actions. It amounts to our definition of the object. *We need to ask people what they think of "clergywomen."*

The "affective" dimension, on the other hand, is more a matter of how we *feel* than of how we think. It consists of our likes and dislikes, preferences, attractions and aversions. It is reflected in the statement often heard during the push for school desegregation. "Sure, I know they're just as good as anybody else, but I just *don't like them*, and nothing you say is going to make me change my mind!" On a romantic note, it is intrinsic to the Hollywood (and sometimes real) way of relating to a lover in which one confesses, "Oh, yes, I know she has faults, but I just can't help loving her!" In relation to the concept of "prejudice," the affective dimension is the point of emphasis for those who argue that prejudice is irrational—not a matter of thought but of *emotion*. Feelings—mere emotions—underlie many of our actions toward others. They are the hatred that fuels lynchings, the love that produces self-sacrifice and the despair that leads to suicide. To many observers it is the affective dimension that is most central to attitudes. *We will find out the extent to which people like and dislike the idea of women in ministry.*

The third dimension—the "behavioral"—simply refers to what we *do* rather than what we think or feel. If the cognitive and affective dimensions of a negative sort connote "prejudice," the behavioral component represents "discrimination." We are motivated to behave toward the object of the attitude from our perceptions and feelings. The behavioral dimension is reflected in the restaurant owner's refusal to seat a black couple in the early days of the Civil Rights Movement. It is reflected in the commercial airline's reneging on hiring a qualified pilot who happens to be female. Yet we must remember that affectively charged action may also be positive. It is the parent's rushing to the aid of a hurt child. It is one's persistent campaigning for his/her favorite political candidate.

One must also bear in mind that people are not always aware that they are engaging in discrimination. People in fact discriminate against others unknowingly in many ways, as when they support government policies that function to the disadvantage of a particular segment of society or when they unquestioningly conform to cultural patterns that serve the interest of some people more than others—such as traditional family roles and child-care customs. While it is the more blatant forms of discrimination that are the more obvious, the subtle forms are no less actually matters of discrimination. In their consequences it is often hard to tell them apart!

Normally, these three dimensions of attitudes are interrelated. People are more inclined to discriminate against members of some group (behavioral) if they do not like the group (affective), and they feel such aversions toward people from that group (affective) if they perceive negative traits in them (cognitive). Individuals normally seem to function this way. However, it is important to consider each dimension separately, because they are not always linked in this way. For example, "undesirable" traits in some people come to be defined as "cute" and thus acceptable, and as such they do not lead to disapproval of that person. Moreover, sometimes we are personally not prejudiced against a certain group, but we discriminate against them nonetheless along with the prejudiced majority, because to do otherwise would result in social criticism or some other negative consequences. (As we will see, this pattern is prevalent in relation to clergywomen.)

Dimensions of Receptivity to Clergywomen

The attitudes underlying church members' responses to women in ministry are what will be called "receptivity" and "resistance." The concepts receptivity and resistance represent opposite ends of an attitudinal continuum of acceptance and rejection, respectively. Like other attitudes, acceptance of women in ministry has at least three dimensions. It involves cognitions—what are clergywomen like? It manifests affect—is having female ministers desirable or undesirable? It incorporates motivation to act in some way—will I go along with it or not? We shall examine each of these dimensions in this study.

We researched the cognitive dimension of receptivity to women in ministry in two ways. First was the simple matter of what members think of clergywomen. Are they perceived in traditional stereotyped sex roles or in more flexible ways? Among individuals who define women in ministry as *women first*, the primary female reference is an unflattering traditional image of women as weak, dependent, emotional and indecisive. At the other extreme, some think of clergywomen as *ministers first* and as females only secondarily, taking them as they are, as individuals without imposing uncomplimentary traits upon them. Secondly we anticipated the judgment that would likely follow these perceptions, i.e., whether the member trusts clergywomen can perform in the role of minister to his/her expectations. These are two ways in which the cognitive dimension manifests itself in attitudes toward women in ministry.

The affective component of receptivity to women in ministry involves church members' liking or disliking the prospect of having a woman as a minister, especially in the role of pastor. We inquired whether or not members would *prefer to have a man* functioning in these roles. Preferring a man in clerical roles represents the negative side of this affect, and being open to either men or women performing clerical functions represents the positive feelings. As you will see below, some of these feelings—especially the negative ones—were expressed very strongly, although the positive feelings were clearly more widespread.

The behavioral aspect of receptivity to women in ministry is a matter of how members act toward clergywomen. The range of such overt action runs from interacting with female clergy in the same way as one would relate to male ministers at one extreme, to rejecting women as ministers and refusing to interact with them in that role at the other. Specific manifestations of negative responses on this dimension would include the radical act of withdrawing from the church when a clergywoman is installed as pastor, as well as lesser actions such as staying home from church, withholding financial contributions and opposing specific acts of ministerial leadership by the woman. At the point of a church's considering the possibility of hiring (or calling) a clergywoman, the negative response would take the forms of being unwilling to consider female candidates, voting against their installation and otherwise opposing their being seriously considered.

When we deal with church members' response to women in ministry, we do so in terms of these three dimensions of receptivity/resistance. We wanted to know how church members differed in each of these ways. How many tend to stereotype? How many really have no preference for a man? How many would vote to install a clergywoman as pastor? Then, once these differences are apparent, how can we explain these variations? What kind of persons tend to be more receptive to women in ministry? On which dimensions? Why?

A National Survey

To pursue these issues, we conducted a national-sample survey of the membership of one Protestant denomination, the United Presbyterian Church, U.S.A. The data were collected in April, 1980, from a source known as the "Presbyterian Panel." The "Panel" consists of approximately 3,800 persons in that denomination who agreed to participate in an ongoing mail survey for a three-year period (this one having begun in January, 1979). It consists of national samples of four sub-groups within the denomination, i.e., lay church members, elders (lay leaders), pastors and clergy in specialized ministries. Each was selected by simple random sampling within each Synod (geographical unit) of the denomination. These individuals completed about six questionnaires each year, and the April, 1980, survey came approximately in the middle of their service on the panel.

The descriptions and explanations set forth in the analysis of these data apply in the strictest sense only to the membership of the United Presbyterian Church, U.S.A. While most observers may regard this body as typical of many other "mainline" Protestant denominations, any generalizations or applications to other bodies should be made with caution. The Presbyterian polity (church governance structure) is somewhat unique, and some patterns in the study may be applicable only to churches with that type of structure. It is also said that some Presbyterians consider themselves more "sophisticated" than members of many other denominations. (Whether this be true or not I shall leave to more reckless sages than I.) It does seem accurate to say that on the socio-political spectrum as a group the United Presbyterians as a whole are positioned to the "left" of most Methodists, Baptists and members of small sects, and they are positioned to the "right" of most Quakers and Unitarians. Again, whether these differences are of sufficient magnitude to rule out generalizations or application of these data to those other denominations must be determined by persons considering making such extensions.

Nevertheless, we can be certain that the data are representative of the national membership of the United Presbyterian Church, and this allows us to make judgments about quite a large number of church members. The overall response to the April, 1980, questionnaire was quite high. Of 2263 elders and other laypersons contacted in that survey, 1720 responded with usable, completed questionnaires. This amounts to a response rate of about 75% which is quite high by most survey standards. Of the 1414 pastors and special clergy contacted, 1143 responded, for a response rate of 81%—again, quite high. Accordingly, we may be satisfied that the data analyzed are sufficiently representative of the total denomination to make generalizations about the issues as they apply to that body. The persons administering the details of the survey also indicated that very few panel surveys receive more open-ended comments at the end than this one did, indicating a high level of interest in the issues being considered.

Images of Clergywomen:
The Cognitive Dimension

We measured the cognitive dimension of receptivity to clergywomen in terms of the members' tendency to view women in ministry according to traditional sex-role stereotypes (Basow, 1980). Some previous research (Epstein, 1970) has identified a set of such sterotypes that seems to emerge repeatedly to characterize women who have moved into professions formerly dominated by men. Women who enter medicine, dentistry, and law, for example, become perceived as pushy, emotional under pressure, unreliable, etc. Descriptions of these stereotypes are contained in the questions shown in Table 2.1. They focus on beliefs that women professionals cannot balance demands of work and home, have high levels of absenteeism from work, are weak leaders etc. We constructed each of these questions to determine the extent to which each of these stereotypes comes to be applied to clergywomen.

The set of items was preceded on the questionnaire by the following statement:

> "The following list of statements represents a series of opinions some person have about women in ministry. After you read each statement, please indicate. . .the extent to which you think each statement is correct or incorrect." "If you have no opinion on a statement, please leave that item blank."

The patterns of response in Table 2.1 indicate wide variations in the extent to which lay church members view women in ministry in stereotypical ways. Some members participate in the stereotypes very much, while others apply them to clergywomen relatively little. (The data in this chapter deal with elders and other lay members only. The data from the clergy will be described in the next chapter.)

A significant number of people perceive problems in dealing with the cross-pressures of home and job. Many lay members expect clergywomen to develop emotional problems in this situation and anticipate that their children will suffer because of their absence from the home while attending to pastoral responsibilities. Among the open-ended comments, this theme was one of the most prevalent. It was the subject of widespread ambivalence on the part of many members who appear to be in favor of women in ministry in principle but have reservations about these pragmatic problems. One person stated, for example, "For many years the family role of 'letting mother do it' in regard to children's religious training did in fact become mother's role. So why the apprehension about women ministers? Women have always ministered in many roles—wife, mother and friend. Women are educable and so (are) called and would make good ministers. My only hesitation is if they could be good wives and mothers as well as ministers to their congregation. I would dislike

TABLE 2.1   DISTRIBUTION OF RESPONSES TO INDICATORS OF STEREOTYPING CLERGYWOMEN (percent)

Opinion Statement	Definitely Correct	Probably Correct	Probably Incorrect	Definitely Incorrect
*A woman minister who is married can fulfill her responsibilities as wife and mother just as well as if she were not working full-time.	11	36	33	20
Women ministers are likely to have higher levels of absenteeism from work than are men.	4	23	45	29
Women ministers are likely to change jobs more often than are men.	2	16	54	28
Women who try to be both full-time ministers and wives and mothers are likely to have emotional problems due to all the demands placed on them by both jobs.	12	41	35	11
The children of women who are full-time ministers are likely to have personal problems due to lack of adequate care and attention.	6	24	48	22
Since most churches today are competing with each other for members, they need the strong leadership that mostly men can give.	13	24	35	28
*A woman's temperament is just as suited for the pastoral ministry as a man's.	39	43	12	6

*Agreement with this item indicates a *non*-stereotyped response. Agreement with all other items indicates the stereotyped response.

31

seeing the burden of sole pastorship fall upon a woman who has a young family to raise. Perhaps an associate (first) and in later years when children are older a full pastorship (could be assumed) with all the demands it places upon the individual and her family." Yet not everyone thought these pressures would be a problem. Said one member, "Women can do it! Just as a man would, they would rely heavily on a helping hand from their mate."

It is also important to note that these expectations of clergywomen having role conflicts of job and home are not based on widespread assumptions about women being constitutionally unfit for the work. Fully 82 per cent of the members indicated that they thought women's temperament is just as suited for the pastoral ministry as men's temperament. One member said, for example, "Women have as much to give as men. Women have been relegated to caretaker and KP roles too long. They have just as much ability to handle the tough problems. . .as men." In a similar vein, relatively few people think that the stresses of the job are likely to lead to high levels of absenteeism or job turnover.

Again, the point in these statistics and quotes is not to argue that clergywomen either are or are not actually suited for the pastoral ministry. Rather they are set forth to indicate *what people think*. In relation to most issues, there is clear evidence that *some church members do think of women in ministry in very stereotypical terms*. The number who think that way varies depending upon the particular stereotype involved. The types of stereotypes parallel those of other professions. The most widespread dimension of the stereotyping seems to involve the image of women as incapable of juggling the cross-pressures of job and home.

For the sake of parsimony, we deal with the answers to these stereotyping questions in combinations. To do this we constructed an "index" (see Babbie, 1983: Ch. 15) of tendency to stereotype women in ministry. We constructed the index by counting the number of questions to which each member gave a stereotyped response, such as saying that it was either "probably correct" or "definitely correct" to assert that clergywomen with families would experience emotional problems. By adding the number of questions each person answered in the stereotyped way, we assigned the respondent a "stereotyping score" (see Babbie, 1983: pp. 351–355). Persons who gave few stereotyped responses thus have "low" stereotyping scores, and those who answered many of the questions in the stereotyped mode have "high" stereotyping scores. This procedure allows us to deal with individual differences on the cognitive dimension of receptivity/resistance while incorporating all of its facets simultaneously.

The distribution of members' scores on this index is contained in Table 2.2. The clearest trend in this distribution is for most members to have relatively "low" scores. One-fifth of them had a score of "zero"—no stereotyping at all. Fewer than one-half answered more than two of the questions in the stereotyped fashion. Only a very small minority indicated stereotyping tendencies on all counts. Overall this pattern suggests that *most lay church members do not perceive women as unable to function effectively as pastors*. Most members are willing to give clergywomen the benefit of the doubt on this issue.

TABLE 2.2   DISTRIBUTION OF STEREOTYPING SCORES

	low						high
Score	0	1	2	3	4	5	6	7
Percent	20	18	15	15	11	10	8	4

Clergywomen Doing the Important Tasks

A similar pattern emerged in relation to questions dealing with members' opinions about whether or not clergywomen can successfully perform functions which members define as the most important things to be done. The form contained questions asking for the members' indications of the kind of role they wanted most for their pastor to perform. Members' responses were directed toward the specific rather than the general; we inquired what they thought was the most critical task, so that the "personal salience" of the issue they identified would be maximized. This enabled us to determine just what members did consider the most relevant issues. It also allowed us to see whether the members thought a woman could perform these highly valued functions as well as a man.

The specific wording on the questionnaire was as follows:

"If you had to pick the *one* thing you most want *your minister* to do for *you personally*, what would that be?" This question was followed by: "Do you think a woman minister could do that for you as well as a man could?"

To analyze the answers to these questions, we first performed a "content analysis" on the question designed to evoke their preferences (see Holst, 1969). Content analysis is a series of techniques for classifying the substance of human communications—books, letters, diaries, motion pictures, etc. (see Babbie, 1983: pp. 272–290). It is also applicable to open-ended questions such as the one about what members most want their pastor to do for them personally. Such a content analysis can systematically identify "themes" or "types" of answers in the total set of responses.

This process was initiated by reviewing the actual answers repeatedly. In this manner we gradually identified commonalities in the responses. Once those themes were identified, each respondent's answer was classified according to theme or type of answer it represented.

Table 2.3 contains the results of the content analysis of the question dealing with members' statements about what they most want their minister to do for them personally. Three major themes and three minor ones emerged from the review of the answers. The type of answer given by most members indicated a desire for *help in dealing with their problems*. Thirty-eight percent preferred this role for their pastor. The theme is illustrated by statements such as: "Be there when I need him (sic)." "Help me deal with the problems of living." "Guide me through this crisis." The theme that emerged second in order of frequency relates to the first, yet is sufficiently different so as to be classified as distinctive. It dealt with members' desire to *become better persons and better Christians*. It was found in 21 percent of the responses. This theme is illustrated by statements like: "Help me to grow." "Lead me to become a better follower of Christ." "Make me a stronger individual." When combined these two predominant types of response comprise nearly 60 percent of the panel members' preferences concerning their pastor's activities in their behalf.

A theme dealing with Sunday morning activities was next in order of prevalence. About 19 percent said that they wanted their pastor to perform mainly *worship-related functions*, usually specifically a matter of good preaching. This ranking of the preaching function is interesting in view of what most pastor nominating committees look for the most—not pastoral care and guidance, but rather preaching.

The minor themes that recurred in these answers dealt with providing general leadership, idiosyncratic traits of the pastor (e.g., "be an example"), and pastoral visitation. None of these types of answer was selected by even 10 percent of the respondents, yet they were frequent enough to merit being noted.

TABLE 2.3 PANEL MEMBERS' ROLE PREFERENCES FOR THEIR PASTOR: "FOR ME PERSONALLY"

ROLE PREFERENCE FOR ME	Percent
provide help to deal with problems and crises	38
help me develop and grow as a person	21
provide good worship experiences/preaching	19
provide general leadership in church	5
idiosyncratic: "be" something	7
visit members, the sick, new people	4
other	6

PERCENT SAYING WOMAN CAN DO AS WELL AS MAN
Role preferences

	Help in crises	Help me grow	Worship	General leader	Idio-syncratic	Visit	Other
percent*	82	83	84	87	86	83	94

*Differences in these percentages are statistically non-significant.

The next question concerned whether members perceived a clergywoman as capable of performing these functions for them. Overall *about 84 percent of the members indicated that a clergywoman could perform the one personal function they wanted the most as well as a man*. This figure is higher than that found on any other indicator of receptivity to women in pastoral roles. It is especially noteworthy, because the issue of personal salience is maximized. It deals not with "just anything" clergywomen might do, but rather it concerns the one thing the member most wants the minister to do for him/her. It is also significant conceptually in that it asks what the member thinks a female minister "can do," i.e., it deals directly with perceptions of clergywomen's *abilities* to perform in the role. In general the members of UPCUSA are saying that *they are satisfied that women can do most clerical functions as well as a man*. (Whether they still *prefer* a man doing those things is another matter.)

We also compared the members' responses to this question

(whether women can perform as well as men) to the specific preferences they indicated. The results of those comparisons are also contained in Table 2.3. The differences in members' responding that women can or cannot perform as well as men in one type of function or another were so slight that they were statistically nonsignificant (i.e., easily due to chance alone) (see Kerlinger, 1979: Ch. 5). Accordingly, we cannot say that members were any more or less willing to grant that women can perform particular functions any better than others. In other words, members tend to indicate that women *can* perform pastoral roles as well as men *regardless of the type of role they personally want the minister to perform for them*. (This is the same pattern as that observed in a similar study among American Baptists, i.e., Lehman, 1979.)

We also asked members what they most wanted their pastor to do, not for them personally, but *for their church collectively*. The wording of the question is as follows:

"If you had to pick the *one* thing you most want *your minister* to do for *your church*, what would that be?" As previously, we then also asked, "Do you think a woman minister could do that for your church as well as a man could?"

We performed a content analysis on the answers to the former question in the same manner as described above. This analysis revealed four major themes and two minor ones. The four major themes were reflected in the responses of nearly equal numbers of respondents. As can be seen in Table 2.4, 21 percent indicated that they most wanted their pastor to *provide good worship experiences*—again, mostly good preaching—for their church. The phrases that illustrate this type of preference include: "preach good sermons," "proclaim the truth," "lift up the Lord," "good church service," and "uplifting" and "inspiring." Another 21 percent preferred their pastor to *provide good general church leadership*. Words that typify this preference include: "provide leadership," "give direction," "lead the staff," and "administer the church."

Responses to this question in two other modes were but slightly fewer than those above. About 19 percent said they wanted the pastor to *pay attention mainly to organizational problems*. They wanted the pastor to develop the church organization—to unify and to build. Phrases typically found in this regard were: "get more youth," "get new members," "bring members

TABLE 2.4 PANEL MEMBERS' ROLE PREFERENCES FOR THEIR PASTOR:
"FOR MY CHURCH"

ROLE PREFERENCE FOR MY CHURCH	Percent
mission outreach into the community/world	6
develop/train/guide the members	18
develop/unify/build the church organization	19
pastoral care/counselling/help with problems	9
provide good worship experiences/preaching	21
provide general church leadership	21
other	6

PERCENT SAYING WOMAN CAN DO AS WELL AS MAN
Role preferences

	Outreach	Develop members	Develop organization	Pastoral	Worship	General leader	Other
percent	84	83	80	90	72	78	78

back in," "make us like a family," "cohesiveness of the congregation," and "church growth." The fourth major theme dealt with *developing the members as individuals* (rather than as a congregation). It was found in the replies of about 18 percent of the members. This theme can be illustrated in terms such as: "train leaders," "inspire people to grow," "get members to work," "enable members to do ministry," "strengthen members," and "get members to follow Christ."

Roughly one-fifth of the respondents answered this preference question in terms of each of these four major themes. No single theme appears to dominate the answers (in contrast to the more personal preference question). Expressed in at least three of them is *a clear concern for the viability of the overall church as an organization*—the need for administrative leadership, unity, members, leaders, etc. If we eliminate the "worship" theme from the four, we still have nearly 60 percent of the members manifesting a concern for these kinds of organizational issues.

The fact that various themes emerged in the two sets of answers and that the rankings differed in each case also indicates that the members were actually making distinctions in responding to the two questions. "What I want for myself" was articulated in a different set of categories from "what I want for my church."

The dominance of "personal problem-solving" and "personal growth" in the first question makes sense in response to the specific directive of that item, and the dominance of "organizational concerns" in the second question is also appropriate.

The number of members who said that they thought a woman could perform these functions specifically for the church is almost as great as those who indicated a woman could perform the more personal functions. Fully 80 percent indicated that a woman could do as good a job as a man in these more organization-related roles. This pattern is important, because it indicates that *four-fifths of the denomination perceives clergywomen as equally capable as men of dealing with the organizational needs of the church*. The consensus is that women *can* do it here too. (Whether members think they *ought to*, again, remains another issue.)

The bottom half of Table 2.4 indicates that *the extent to which members thought a woman could perform these church-related functions as well as a man depended somewhat on the type of function they preferred*. In the case of these two variables, the differences *are* statistically significant. At one extreme, more members who preferred "pastoral" functions for the church as a whole than members who indicated other role preferences tended to say that a woman could do as well as a man. At the other extreme, fewer members who emphasized the "worship" functions thought that a woman could do those things as well as a man. There is also a slight tendency for fewer persons who emphasized the "general leadership" and "organizational development" functions than those who stressed other functions to perceive women as equally capable as men, but those differences are less dramatic. In general, these patterns seem to indicate that *when the organizational viability of the church is at issue, church members are less inclined to perceive a woman as being as competent as a man in dealing with what needs to be done*. (We shall deal with that issue more fully below.) Nevertheless, even in relation to organizational concerns, a *majority of members (75 percent or more) perceive that women can perform as well as men*.

The Cognitive Dimension: A Summary

What do the members' answers about their perceptions of women in ministry mean? Two patterns are clear. (1) Most lay church members are not given to defining women in ministry in stereotyped terms. While some of the stereotypes associated with women in male-dominated professions are applied to clergy-women by a few members (an average of about 21 percent), most members are willing to view female clergy primarily as ministers without imposing traditionally feminine traits where they do not necessarily apply. This is especially true concerning members' assumptions about women's temperament. Over four-fifths view women as sufficiently similar to men temperamentally as to basically reject the idea that women may not be able to function as pastors as well as men can. (2) Even though church members differ widely in terms of what they want most for their pastor to do for them personally and for their church collectively, more than four out of five think a woman can perform that function as well as a man. The point on which there is the most dissension has to do with females performing tasks associated with maintaining the organizational viability of the congregation. A few more people question women's abilities in that function than in others, although even here more than 75 percent think that a woman can perform as well as a man. *No matter how the question is posed, then, most church members think clergywomen have the ability to function effectively as pastors.*

Preferences for Men: The Affective Dimension

Ideally one would think that persons who are satisfied that women can perform in clerical roles as effectively as men would also be satisfied with having a woman in the position of their minister. In a purely rational sense, the one idea would follow from the other. Unfortunately, reality seems to be more com-plicated than that. While, as we shall see below, most people are consistent in this way, a significant number are not. One member summed up this orientation in saying, "I believe a woman could minister to the needs of a congregation and to myself personally. I just don't feel I would prefer a woman. Some woman pastors are far better than many male pastors, but as a personal preference I would choose a man."

Others couch their reservations in pragmatic terms. Wrote one elder, "I have no objection to women in the ministry, but I feel they will definitely have a tough row to hoe. Not all men make good ministers, and this would certainly be true of women.

A good woman minister would be better than a poor man minister, but not as good as a good man minister. Right now I would say 'bless those women who are interested in the ministry', but let them be aware of the problems which exist. . ." Yet others related their reservations to perceived role conflicts between job and family, as in the comment, "Theologically I favor women in the ordained ministry. I believe they have always been in ministry in one form or another. However, pragmatically I see great difficulty with or for ordained women ministers who are newly married and also want to be mothers. The dual role, as I have seen it in one particular instance, is difficult for the ordained minister and not satisfying for the congregation. . . ."

Accordingly, members' *feelings* about whether they will accept clergywomen may be different from their rationale of women in ministry. What they like and want may or may not be consistent with their understanding of what women can do. So we need to look at indications of the affective dimension separately.

Measuring the Affective Dimension

To disclose members' feelings about accepting clergywomen, we focused on their *preferences* for men or women occupying various positions in the church and performing a variety of clerical roles. To introduce these questions, the questionnaire contained the following instructions:

"Listed below are several parish positions and several activities typically associated with the pastoral ministry. Please indicate below whether—given the choice—you would prefer to have a man or woman serving in each of these pastoral positions or performing each of these activities, or if it would make no difference to you."

The specific positions and functions are contained in Table 2.5, together with the percentages of lay members who indicated various preferences on each item. On nearly every question, *the major distinction turned out to be between preferring a man and having no preference*. Very few people indicated an actual preference for a woman on any of the questions. The only exceptions to this pattern were the 15 and 9 percent preferring a woman for the positions of Minister of Education and Minister of Music respectively, areas in which some women have worked for many years.

TABLE 2.5   DISTRIBUTION OF RESPONSES TO INDICATORS OF THE
ATTITUDINAL DIMENSION OF RECEPTIVITY TO CLERGYWOMEN (percent)

	Prefer a man	No difference	Prefer a woman
I. PARISH POSITIONS			
Senior or sole pastor	60	39	1
Associate or assistant pastor	21	76	3
Minister of Education	7	78	15
Minister of Music	7	85	9
Youth Minister	21	75	4
II. PASTORAL ACTIVITIES			
performing a baptism	27	72	1
administering the Lord's Supper	27	73	1
preaching a sermon	33	66	1
conducting a funeral	33	67	1
advising about a personal problem	25	71	4
moderating the session meeting	21	78	1
coordinating church staff as senior minister	39	60	1
working with a contractor to renovate the church	45	54	1
planning your congregation's annual budget	17	81	2
pronouncing the congregational call to worship	13	86	1
reading the Scripture lesson	9	90	1
leading a pastor prayer	14	86	1
pronouncing the benediction	16	83	1
visiting you in the hospital	13	84	3
developing your church's programs	14	84	1

Another pattern is probably consistent with what one might expect. The position for which there is clear preference for a man is "senior or sole pastor." Nearly two-thirds of the members indicated that they wanted a man in that post. "Pastor" should be a man. While this observation is in line with common sense, it is not consistent with some other preferences, i.e., those dealing with specific things pastors typically do. Between two-thirds and three-fourths of the respondents also said that they would have *no* preference for a man when it comes to preaching sermons, administering the sacraments, and conducting weddings and funerals. Nearly four-fifths had no preference for a man serving as moderator of the session. The proportion indicating no preference is between 80 and 90 percent on those ritualistic activities pastors usually perform which laypersons also do occasionally, e.g., reading scripture, public prayer, etc.

The point of inconsistency appears to be between the general and the specific. The general title "pastor" must be associated with a male in the minds of most church members, but the specific functions which pastors uniquely perform may be associated with either a man or a woman. The incongruity is also apparent when these preferences are contrasted with members' perceptions of clergywomen and what they can do (above). The clear majority of members appear to have informed and non-stereotypical impressions of the characteristics of women in ministry, and they assert even more overwhelmingly that women can perform the religious functions they consider the most critical for themselves and for their church. Yet they tend to want a man in the position of "pastor."

It is interesting to speculate about possible reasons for these differences. One which appears plausible is that members' preferences concerning the identity of their pastor rest on other than rational criteria, grounds which embody their understandings of the skills and insights ministers must have to be effective. Their preferences also touch upon areas of a great deal of symbolism, an area of life which is not always amenable to rational thought—to linking appropriate means and ends. Even though most church members "know" that clergywomen have the same seminary training and consequently the same knowledge and repertoire of abilities as male clergy, there still seems to be something about having a woman as pastor that does not suit them. "Pastor" symbolizes the church to them. It also symbolizes millennia of traditional male leadership in the church and in society in general. Seeing a man in the pulpit and hearing a male voice evokes a response that everything is "normal" in this area of life. Things are as they "should be" according to tradition. Whether this concept is consistent with either their understanding of what clergywomen are capable of or their sense of justice may be somewhat irrelevant. Our feelings—our likes and wants—are often quite non-rational, and this seemingly inconsistent set of church members' indications of their receptivity to women in ministry appears to be no exception.

Dimensions of Gender Preferences

There is also some evidence that the church members were making yet other distinctions in their responses to the "preference" questions. That is, they appeared to be varying criteria of preference as they proceeded from one question to another. It seems that they applied a small number of criteria to specific subsets of questions. The questions members appear to have answered on the basis of a common criterion can be described as one "dimension" of their gender preferences in relation to the ministry. There are at least three such dimensions (see also Blizzard, 1958).

These dimensions of gender preference were determined by subjecting the members' answers on the preference questions to a "factor analysis" (Kerlinger, 1979: Ch. 12). Factor analysis separates out dimensions of people's answers to a set of questions in a way roughly analogous to the way a prism separates out different frequencies of light. Light emanating from an ordinary light bulb— sometimes called "white light"—is undifferentiated light. The rays of the color spectrum are all mixed together, and the result is that we perceive no colors when looking at the light coming directly from the bulb. However, when that undifferentiated light is passed through a prism as illustrated in Figure 1, the prism "refracts" (bends) some frequencies (colors) of light more than others, and we are able to perceive the various shades of refracted light in a color spectrum. The various frequencies are present in the white light all along, but we are unable to detect them without the aid of the prism's refracting properties.

Factor analysis takes the seemingly "undifferentiated" set of preference questions and identifies subsets. This differentiation is accomplished by the application of a series of mathematic formulas (most easily done by a computer) which sort out the answers to the questions much as the prism organizes the undifferentiated light. The procedure identifies "factors" (clusters) that appear to belong together on the basis of the way people actually responded to the questions. The underlying theme (or dimension) common to the questions in each cluster (factor) usually can be ascertained fairly easily by reviewing the contents of the questions comprising each grouping.

The results of the factor analysis performed on the gender preference items are portrayed in the bottom of Figure 1. The specific questions included in the analysis were those that pertain primarily to actions engaged in almost exclusively by ordained clergy. *Not* included were activities in which laypersons often participate—call to worship, reading Scripture, benediction,

Prism refracting undifferentiated light

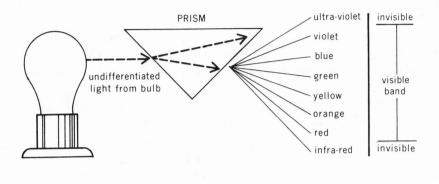

Computer factoring dimensions of gender preferences

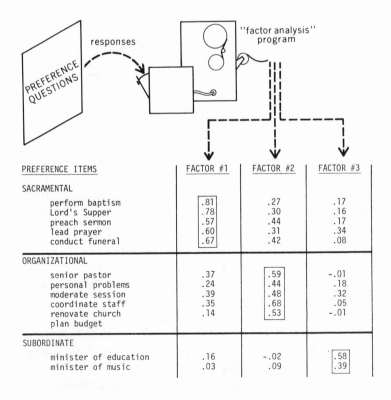

PREFERENCE ITEMS	FACTOR #1	FACTOR #2	FACTOR #3
SACRAMENTAL			
perform baptism	.81	.27	.17
Lord's Supper	.78	.30	.16
preach sermon	.57	.44	.17
lead prayer	.60	.31	.34
conduct funeral	.67	.42	.08
ORGANIZATIONAL			
senior pastor	.37	.59	-.01
personal problems	.24	.44	.18
moderate session	.39	.48	.32
coordinate staff	.35	.68	.05
renovate church	.14	.53	-.01
plan budget			
SUBORDINATE			
minister of education	.16	-.02	.58
minister of music	.03	.09	.39

Figure 1. Factor analysis compared to refracton of light

hospital visitation and church program planning. This restriction narrows the analysis to issues associated most centrally with the concept of women in *ordained* ministries.

Members' preferences for men or women in the ministry appeared to group themselves into three factors. This grouping is determined by examining the "loadings" (numbers) of each item on each factor. The higher the loading, the more a particular item belongs in a particular cluster. The first factor included the items dealing with baptism, the Lord's Supper, preaching sermons, leading congregational prayers and conducting funerals. Common to these items is that they are all concerned with some form of liturgical ritual. They reflect the sacramental/priestly role of the ministry. We call this factor the "sacramental" dimension.

The second factor included preference items dealing with administrative tasks that must be done to keep the organized congregation functioning—working on the budget, church renovations, coordinating church staff, moderating the session, helping solve personal problems and the position of senior pastor. These are very different activities from those that loaded on the sacramental dimension. We call this factor the "organizational" dimension.

It is noteworthy that the position of "pastor" *per se* loaded on the organizational dimension and not on the sacramental one. This result suggests that church members indicated their preferences for men in the pastoral ministry in general—as it is symbolized in the pastorate itself—more strongly according to church organizational criteria than sacramental criteria. If preferences for a man as pastor were mainly a theological issue, one would expect the choice concerning pastor *per se* to load with the more theologically salient items, i.e., on the sacramental dimension. But it did not. Instead, the position of pastor loaded with the choices associated with running the church as an organization. As we see more fully below, this pattern is consistent with the idea that one of church members' major concerns when thinking about recruiting a pastor is keeping the local congregation alive and well. Members typically prefer to avoid issues and arrangements that threaten the solidarity of that community. Since clergywomen are viewed by some church members as objects of controversy—and hence to be avoided—this dynamic could be an important factor in those members' preferences for male pastors.

The third cluster of members' gender preferences consists of but two questions—preferences for Minister of Education and Minister of Music. These are positions in which women have served for several decades, although today women are more numerous than they once were in these positions too. Churches where these positions exist are also typically large churches. In terms of the overall authority structure of these organizations, the music and education posts are almost always subordinate to the pastorate. (In a few instances, they are even subordinate to the associate pastorate, although this arrangement is more rare). Some feminists argue that it is precisely *because* these positions are less powerful than the pastorate that women have been more welcome in them than in senior posts (see Colwill, 1982). Accordingly, we shall call this dimension the "subordinate" factor—preferences for men in ministry roles that are subordinate ones in most churches where they are found.

Two questions did not load clearly on any of the three factors. The position of associate pastor responses loaded equally on all three. The associate pastor role is, in fact, open to women in some churches but not in others. Its status as a position "for males only" is questionable. This general ambiguity is probably responsible for the factor loadings involving that item. The question about the Minister for Youth loaded equally on factors "2" and "3" and is therefore also ambiguous. For these reasons, these two positions were eliminated from the subsets of the affective dimension.

What does all of this tell us? By looking at the members' preferences for men or women in clerical roles through the factor analysis, we can deal with their feelings about clergywomen in more precise terms. We have evidence that *laypersons apply variable criteria when indicating their preferences for people in these positions depending upon the type of position considered.* The particular criteria they apply give some indication of how they group the roles in their mind. Functions that are largely ritual/liturgical in nature are "one thing," and members feel receptive or resistant to the idea of having a woman performing them on a specific set of grounds. Functions that are associated with keeping the organizational machinery of the church running smoothly are "another thing," and members apply other specific criteria when confronted with choices associated with keeping the church community alive. Finally, having women as Ministers of Education or Music is yet another issue, and members react to that concept differently from the other two. In order to benefit from possible insights associated with these differences, we treat these three dimensions of affective receptivity to clergywomen separately in the rest of the analysis.

Indexes of the Affective Dimensions

As with the stereotyping items (above), we constructed an "index" (see Babbie, 1983: Ch. 15) to measure each of these dimensions of receptivity. We combined the preference items that clustered in each factor to form a composite measure of receptivity differences on each dimension. We thus created a "sacramental score" for each member by adding the number of questions from factor # 1 on which he/she indicated a preference for a man (usually in contrast to "no preference"). Low scores indicate that those members preferred a man for few of the sacramental functions, and a high score indicates the opposite, i.e., preferring a man for most of them. In the same manner, we created an "organizational score" and a "subordinate score" for each respondent using the items that loaded on factors "2" and "3" respectively.

The distribution of scores (see Babbie, 1983: pp. 351–355) on these three indexes is contained in Table 2.6. At least two potentially meaningful patterns are apparent. First, the distribution of scores on all three indexes are skewed (bunched up) toward the low end. On the sacramental dimension, little more than one-third of the members had a score greater than zero. Less than one-half preferred a man for more than one item on the organizational index. Over 90 percent had subordinate scores of zero. These low scores reinforce the earlier perceptions that *most church members are willing to consider having clergywomen function in a wide range of ministerial activities.*

Also of note in the distributions of scores in Table 2.6 is that proportionately more members have preferences for male clergy when it comes to organizational concerns than on the other two dimensions. (The highly skewed subordinate scores suggest that just a very few conservative die-hards would resist women in those positions. The sacramental scores fall somewhere in between). The appearance of relatively high resistance associated with female organizational leadership *per se* lends further support to

TABLE 2.6   DISTRIBUTION OF SCORES ON INDEXES OF SACRAMENTAL, ORGANIZATIONAL AND SUBORDINATE DIMENSIONS OF RECEPTIVITY TO CLERGYWOMEN

	SACRAMENTAL SCORES					
	low					*high*
Score	0	1	2	3	4	5
Percent	63	11	6	5	8	8

	ORGANIZATIONAL SCORES						
	low						*high*
Score	0	1	2	3	4	5	6
Percent	38	16	13	12	9	6	7

	SUBORDINATE SCORES		
	low		*high*
Score	0	1	2
Percent	91	7	2

the interpretation (above) that these concerns are more salient to lay church members than are theological matters. To put it another way, some members consider the potential implications of having a woman minister more grave in relation to local church viability than in consideration of theological matters.

Such an interpretation appears to be consistent with observations made in the context of sex-role research in other settings. One such pattern involves the idea of having women in positions of authority (especially over men) in general. Having women in top leadership posts is a clear departure from tradition. Many people are simply uncomfortable in work situations where women make the critical decisions and otherwise wield power. It seems "unnatural" to them. They seem to think it is "too manly" a thing for women to be doing—ceratinly not "lady-like." The idea of having a woman as pastor clearly introduces this dynamic to the local church scene. Stated slightly differently, one member asked, "If women become pastors, then what will men do?" We examine other facets of this issue in detail in Chapter 5.

Willingness to Discriminate: The Behavioral Dimension

The survey of church members employed a simple indicator of members' tendencies to overtly behave differently toward clergywomen than clergymen (see Feagin and Feagin, 1978). Since it is not possible to obtain a direct measure of overt behavior through mail surveys, we conceptualized the behavioral dimension in terms of relative *willingness* to discriminate against a clergy-woman (see also Liska, 1974; 1975). In the context of a series of questions about whether there would be tension or conflict in the congregation in response to having a woman as a candidate for a pastoral position (or in response to a decision to install a woman as pastor), the respondents were asked the following question:

"If in fact there were conflicts and tensions in a congregation because a woman had been recommended, which of the following actions do you think the pastor nominating committee (search committee) should take? Do you think they should:

1. try to convince the congregation to call the woman they recommended,
2. take a neutral position and let the congregation decide, or
3. withdraw the woman's name and recommend a man?"

The question was intended to evoke responses indicating either that the committee should: (a) "back off" from their recommendation (answer # 3) and thus show clear readiness to discriminate against the female candidate, (b) take a "safe middle ground" (answer # 2) and in effect say that they were willing to discriminate against her in the name of majority rule, or (c) assert that the committee should "stick to their guns" (answer # 1), signifying that they were *not* prepared to discriminate.

The pattern of answers to the question is as follows:

support the candidate 37%
defer to the church 52%
withdraw her name 11%

Perhaps the most noteworthy finding here is that but one in ten members is prepared to flagrantly discriminate against the woman candidate. More than one-third appear prepared to be willing to support her even in the face of internal church conflict. These results should be encouraging to women moving into ministry.

However, the 52 percent who said they would discriminate against the woman if a majority of the congregation voted that way is disquieting. On the one hand, it does represent local democracy at work. Nevertheless, it also defies denominational policy concerning principles of "equal employment opportunity" and decisions to follow a path of "affirmative action." Qualitatively the "middle ground" here is of the same *genre* as discriminatory practices in the recent past so roundly condemned by voices of moral indignation around the world—treatment of Blacks, Jews, Roman Catholics, Hispanics, etc.—all of which were perpetrated in local communities in the name of majority rule. Even in the church, it seems as though some people are prepared to sacrifice principle to pragmatic exigencies.

Some comments associated with this question indicate that a significant number of members took refuge in the middle ground based on their understanding that it would be the "correct procedure." That is, they said that the matter *should be* put to a vote of the congregation, so that is what they would do. In responding in that mode, of course, they were actually avoiding the question asked, i.e., how should the committee react to the fact that their recommendation generated controversy? The middle ground position is also debatable in view of other denominational policy governing equal opportunity. This mode of response has methodological implications. The question was intended to evoke responses indicating members' *willingness to discriminate against clergywomen*. Those who replied in terms of proper procedure were actually answering in ways to show their *readiness to follow rules for local decision making*. To a degree, then, we have a problem of comparing "apples and oranges" in the responses. At this point there is nothing that can be done to determine exactly which mode each person was applying in answering the question. As we use the variable in subsequent analysis below, the reader should simply bear in mind the problem of interpretation associated with it. By retaining the measure of the behavioral dimension in the rest of the analysis, we are asserting that the problem of interpretation is not sufficiently great as to rule out inclusion of the various answers to the question. We are also proceeding with additional analysis of the question based on the assumption that *any* response other than an indication that the committee should stick by its convictions bespeaks a willingness to discriminate against a female candidate.

Summary

Based on these national survey data, we should expect large numbers of church members to respond to women in ministry quite well. Most people have open and healthy images of clergywomen in mind, and they perceive female clergy as being capable (on a par with men) of performing the church-related functions on which they place the greatest value. Receptivity is relatively high on the cognitive dimension.

The picture is also positive on the affective dimension—people's likes and dislikes. However, it is not as clear as the cognitive component. While most members indicate no real preference for having a man or a woman doing the basic jobs pastors are typically called upon to perform, they do say that for the incumbent of the pastorate *per se* they prefer to have a man. The grounds for this apparent contradiction are not entirely clear, but they seem to involve influences other than rational choice. Affectively charged symbols probably underlie this resistance. Of particular significance is members' regard for of the reactions of others in their congregations, especially as those responses may generate a rift in the church community.

The findings are most foreboding in the area of church members' apparent willingness to discriminate against female candidates for church positions. Nearly two-thirds of the respondents indicated that in the face of some local church resistance to calling a woman as pastor, it is acceptable to set the woman's candidacy aside in preference for a man. While this inclination to avoid internal church conflict is understandable, it does go counter to the denomination's policy specifying equal employment opportunity and implementation of affirmative action guidelines.

The basic picture in these data is that *most people are fundamentally and philosophically open to women in ministry, including specifically the ordained ministry.* Yet many of them do have reservations. It is a "mixed bag." How can we explain these differences in receptivity to clergywomen? What factors seem to go into determining whether a member will be in favor of or opposed to the idea? We address that question systematically in Chapters 4 and 5. First, however, it is instructive to review the levels of receptivity to women in ministry manifested in the data from the pastors and other clergy in the survey. These individuals often set the tone of opinion on various issues in the denomination, so their influence on lay church members concerning this issue can be significant. We turn to these questions in the next chapter.

Suggestions for Additional Reading

Allport, Gordon W.
1958 *The Nature of Prejudice.* Garden City, New York: Doubleday & Co.

A classic statement of the origins and characteristics of prejudistic attitudes. While somewhat dated, the book is still considered a seminal work on attitude formation and change, as it contains many important insights into human functioning.

Blizzard, Samuel W.
1958 "The Protestant Parish Minister's Integrating Roles," *Religious Education* 53 (July), 374–80.

Blizzard was one of the first social scientists to identify the oft competing and contradictory demands placed upon clergypersons. This article is one of his early attempts to articulate the nature of the role conflicts and the ways in which clergy try to cope with them.

Deutscher, Irwin
1973 *What We Say/What We Do.* Glenview, Illinois: Scott-Foresman.

A study of the complex relationships between attitudes and overt behavior. Takes a position that behavior is not consistently predictable from attitudes. Also argues that in many instances overt behavior is antecedent to attitudes.

Epstein, Cynthia Fuchs
1970 *Woman's Place.* Berkeley: University of California Press.

A study of the circumstances women find themselves in when they try to move into fields formerly the exclusive province of men. Contains discussions of the kinds of stereotypes that are applied to women moving into the professions such as law and medicine.

Feagin, Joe R. and Clarice Booker Feagin
1978 *Discrimination, American Style: Institutional Racism and Sexism.* Englewood Cliffs, New Jersey: Prentice-Hall

A discussion of the various forms in which discrimination manifests itself in American society. Outlines the subtleties of "institutional" patterns of discrimination, many of which we participate in virtually unknowingly.

Hacker, Helen M.
1951 "Women as a Minority Group," *Social Forces* 30 (October), 60–69.

One of the earliest statements concerning the status of women in the United States. Argues that structurally women constitute a "minority group" on the basis of their subordination socially, economically and legally. In these ways the identity of "female" is qualitatively the same as that of "Black."

Holsti, Ole
1969 *Content Analysis for the Social Sciences and Humanities.* Reading, Massachusetts: Addison-Wesley.

An overview of content analysis as a method of analysing human communications. Describes the various techniques employed, giving illustrations of their applications and results. A "thorough" introduction.

Kerlinger, Fred N.
1979 *Behavioral Research: A Conceptual Approach.* New York: Holt, Rinehart, Winston.

A presentation of the logic of behavioral science research without worrying about formulas and techniques of application. Ideal for the person who doesn't want to know too much about it. Contains clear descriptions of the basic logic underlying survey research and factor analysis.

Petty, Richard and John T. Cacioppo
1981 *Attitudes and Persuasion: Classic and Contemporary Approaches.* Dubuque, Iowa: William C. Brown.

An overview of the literature dealing with the concepts of attitude and attitude change. Outlines various theories and the research evidence associated with them. Exhaustive bibliography.

Ruether, Rosemary R.
1974 *Religion and Sexism: Images of Women in the Jewish and Christian Tradition.* New York: Simon and Schuster.

Traces the subordinate status of women in these two religious systems which have dominated religious life in the United States. An early and forceful statement from a pioneer in contemporary religious feminism.

CHAPTER 3

Where Do the Clergy Stand?

In Chapter 2 we indicated that the survey had gathered data from both lay persons and clergy. From the analysis in that chapter, we have a basic picture of the levels of receptivity to clergywomen among the laity. Now we want to turn to the pastors and special clergy to determine where they stand on the issues. To what extent do clergy view women in ministry in stereotyped terms? How much do they prefer a male in clerical roles? How likely are they to discriminate against a female candidate for a church position? On each of these dimensions of receptivity, how do pastors and special clergy compare to lay persons? We shall try to answer these questions in this chapter.

Before we examine the clergy data, however, it will be useful to note the composition of this segment of the sample. In the survey, the data classified as being from "pastors" actually were gathered from three types of ministers. Senior pastors/co-pastors comprised 75 percent of the people in this category, associate/assistant pastors made up 16 percent, and supply pastors were the remaining 9 percent. The subsampling is heterogeneous. Nevertheless, it is clearly dominated by senior pastors, most of whom are also solo pastors. Thus any unique patterns of receptivity associated with the "pastor" category will be attributable mostly to those ministers who have primary responsibility for the ordained leadership role in the local churches.

We cannot make the same kind of statement about the category "special ministries," for the clergy classified this way in the survey were even more variegated than the pastors. The breakdown of types of ministries in this subsample is:

national/synod/presbytery staff 11%
institutional chaplains. 11%
missionaries/at-large clergy 7%
non-UPC professional (secular) 26%
unclassified ministers 46%

With so many types of vocations included in the special clergy category, what can be said about patterns in their responses? Probably the most distinctive characteristic shared by these persons, in addition to the fact that they are clergy, is that—unlike the pastors—they are occupationally removed from the local church scene. They do not have direct responsibility for local church affairs. Their work is either in other segments of the denominational structure or outside of the church organization entirely. An exception would be some of the "non-UPC professionals" who are serving churches in other denominations, but they are distinctly a minority. Contrasted with the pastors, therefore, the special clergy are mostly in positions from which they can relate to issues associated with clergywomen with greater detachment. The possible implications of positions they take on women in ministry can easily remain relatively objective, indirect and devoid of immediate local consequences. Whatever differences might exist between pastors' and special clergy's levels of receptivity to women in ministry may be attributable to these uniquenesses of their respective work roles.

The Importance of Clergy Support

Even though it is the laity who ultimately decide whether or not to accept women in the role of pastor, the position the clergy take on the issue is quite important. This is true for three fundamental reasons. *First, the clergy function as "opinion leaders" in the local churches and most other segments of the denomination.* Opinion leaders are persons whose ideas on issues relevant to a group or community tend to be adopted by other members (see Katz, 1957). They are typically persons of relatively high status in the group. They also are usually better educated in relevant areas than other members, and they tend to have social ties with persons outside the group who are sources of potentially important information. With resources such as these, opinion leaders are typically able to bring more complete, accurate and up-to-date information into the arenas of discussion. When this set of resources is coupled with a relatively charismatic personality, the force of their opinions can be highly influential. Add to this combination one's occupying a position of formal leadership in the group—being the mayor, for example, or being the chairperson of a committee or an academic department—and the influence of one's opinions is enhanced still further.

Clergy—particularly pastors, national and judicatory staff, and seminary and college faculty—characteristically possess most of these attributes. They occupy formal leadership positions, they are highly educated, their positions place them in contact with important sources of information and more often than not they manifest some personal charisma. With these traits they usually set the tone of opinion among others with whom they work, i.e., in the congregation, among subordinate staff and in the classroom. Clergy establish these ideological climates both by precept, utilizing sacred authority to legitimize their teachings, and by percept with their actions viewed as reflecting the aura of sacred traditions.

Some clergy would argue with these assertions. They perceive themselves as having little impact on their constituencies. Complaining that few people listen to what they preach and teach, they define themselves as basically powerless before the onslaught of secular forces and a materialistic culture. It is true that secularization has eroded the influence of religious institutions. However, it is also verifiable that there are limits on the extent to which secular values can disrupt the relationship between pastor and laity. In situations where ministers have done both their homework and their job, a strong measure of influence remains. When clergy are informed and develop ways to inform their people—about facts, about religious tradition and about implications of the latter for issues of the day—the members will usually take heed. Especially when pastors develop relationships of honesty and love between themselves and their members, and when they genuinely share the vicissitudes of their people's lives, they have a "currency" of lasting value with which they may purchase credibility and social influence when dealing with both innocuous and controversial issues. One must approach contentious matters cautiously, of course. But doing so can be successful, and exceptions are probably fewer than one might suspect. Even when clergy fail to persuade their members, the attempt to exercise influence almost invariably restrains actions contrary to the path they advocate, and this outcome in itself is a form of social influence.

For these reasons clergy can have important input into their members' consideration of utilizing women in ministry. Like it or not, they are opinion leaders on the issue. The stance which pastors and special clergy adopt in what they preach and teach will get their members' attention and in most instances will also influence their members' position. Pastors can relate Biblical and theological scholarship to the concept of clergywomen, and in the process they can either promote women's acceptance in the ministry or establish more barriers for women to overcome. Clergy in other positions can similarly either promote or retard the cause of clergywomen by their words and actions.

Failure on the part of clergy to deal with the issue amounts to a statement to the members. Ignoring the women-in-ministry movement communicates the attitude that the issue is not important, that the church need not think about it and that nothing is likely to happen in the future to make them confront it. Not dealing with the matter further legitimizes an all-male ministry by default. It also separates religion from this and other social issues. So either way, by action or inaction, the clergy influence the way church members respond to women in ministry.

The second reason why the position the clergy take in relation to women in ministry is important is that they exert significant influence on members' consideration of the ministry as a vocation. This has long been recognized as an important step for the entry of men into the ministry. It now appears as though the same principle applies to women's vocational choices. For both men and women, the pastor's actions are an important determinant of whether they will experience a sense of call to full-time Christian service.

The influence of clergy on decisions to enter the ministry will be felt in at least two ways. First, what ministers say and do may be a *major source of inspiration* to consider the possibility of religious vocations. Through dynamic and thoughtful preaching and teaching, as well as by means of exemplary performance in other pastoral functions, ministers lead other church members— especially young people—to want to emulate them. Conversely, the words and deeds of clergy can fail to inspire others to consider a call to ministry. Furthermore, they can make other members actively avoid religious vocations.

The implications for women of this inspirational function seem fairly obvious. If clergy do not deal with the issue of women in ministry, especially as advocates of clergywomen, the possibility of many women entering full-time Christian service will be very slight. The ministry will not appear as a viable option to them. Women who otherwise could have made important contributions to the lives of others through the ministry will move into other occupations. Their ministry will remain a potentiality unfulfilled.

The second way in which clergy influence members' decisions to prepare for professional ministry is through *validation of the sense of calling*. At times the vehicle through which one experiences a desire to enter the ministry is someone other than a minister. The impulse can result from interaction with parents, spouse or close friends. Sometimes the impetus is not another person at all, but is instead a dramatic struggle or a personal crisis. (Nevertheless, even in these situations, the influence of clergy is probably a latent factor reflecting the slow influence of years of exposure.)

Whatever the direct source of inspiration, once a member has this kind of experience, the first person whose advice is sought upon the matter is typically a minister—usually the person's pastor. Such a procedure is hardly surprising. Persons with a level of religious commitment that could lead to entry into full-time ministry usually also have a vital relationship with a minister. The association also is most likely one of longstanding. Even if such relations are tenuous, it is entirely appropriate to consult a member of the profession one wants to enter for advice on a wide variety of topics. In the case of the ministry, the move is all the more fitting, because entry into religious vocations involves an ideology that goes beyond pragmatic issues of occupational choice. The decision embodies transcendent values associated with a theological system. Clergy persons symbolize and to some extent embody such values. A pastor's opinion concerning the advisability of one's pursuing the ministry is important to most members considering the step.

Validation of the sense of call by a minister is probably a major factor in a woman's decision to enter the ministry. It is listed by clergywomen as an important influence in their commitment more often than any other single element. Since opting for the ministry is a relatively new choice for women, when most of them first reflect on the idea they have serious doubts. They question the validity of the call. They question their own motives. They anticipate resistance to the idea from friends and family. The inner conflicts can be severe.

The response they get from the minister they consult can be decisive. Clergy who are in favor of women in ministry are likely to react to a woman's request for advice quite differently from those who are opposed. Ministers who are open to clergywomen need to deal only with the issue of whether the particular individual they are confronting should pursue the call to ministry, not an easy task but one uncomplicated by extraneous issues. Those who are philosophically opposed to women in ministry, however, may never actually deal with the question of whether this particular person should continue preparation for ministry, because essentially they are dealing with a separate issue, i.e., they are operating from the assumption that no one but a man should consider the call seriously. In effect the two types of ministers are addressing very different issues in their response to the woman's request for validation. In the first case, validation is plausible. In the second, it is a logical impossibility.

There is a third reason why the opinions of pastors and special clergy are important. In addition to being significant sources of inspiration and validation for clergywomen, *male ministers are also usually strategically placed in various networks of social relationships in the denomination within which policy is created, codified and implemented.* It is true that in this denomination (UPCUSA) the representative political structure is designed to reflect the collective will of the membership, both lay and clerical. But it is also true that it is the clergy who are most directly and pervasively involved in matters of policy and that they occupy the key leadership positions in most segments of the denominational structure where policy is implemented. Lay leaders usually defer to the clergy. Why should we expect it to be otherwise? The clergy are the "professionals," and most lay members respect that.

The significance of this observation resides not in some notion that the clergy in any way abuse their positions of power. There is really no evidence of such action. Similarly there are no indications of any desire to manipulate their status for self-aggrandizement. Rather to make a point of the clergy's position of power is to say that their opinion does make a difference. As human beings the clergy argue their consciences and press for policies consistent with them. If some of those personal convictions are in favor of women in ministry, the clergy will press for policies that promote clergywomen's interests, but if they are persuaded that women in ministry is not a good idea they will also act accordingly. Once denominational and church policy is set, if they agree with it they usually implement it vigorously. However, if they find policy repugnant, they conform to it half-heartedly at best.

For all of these reasons (and more), *it is important to know what pastors and other clergy think about women in ministry.* Lay persons determine the final outcome at the level of the local church, but ministers have important influence on what they do. The clergy are in fact the leaders denominationally, and they truly lead only in directions they really want to go. The ways in which they relate to both the spirit and letter of denominational policy concerning women in ministry have significant consequences for the interests of clergywomen. Accordingly, let us look now at the stance the pastors and special clergy took on the three dimensions of receptivity to women in ministry.

The Cognitive Dimension

How do pastors and special clergy view women in ministry? Are clergy significantly different from the lay members in this regard? How much do they differ among themselves? The distribution of clergy responses to the stereotyping questions are contained in Table 3.1. Like the data from the lay members, these patterns indicate considerable variations in tendency for clergy to impose traditional images on clergywomen.

Some dimensions enjoy more consensus than others. Clergy are in relatively strong agreement that clergywomen are no more likely than men to manifest high levels of absenteeism from work or high rates of job turnover. There is also strong agreement that women's temperament is just as suited for the pastoral ministry as men's. There is slightly less agreement that women can provide just as strong church leadership as men and that clergywomen's children will not necessarily suffer because of their mothers' working outside the home.

The major area of disagreement among clergy concerns the clergywoman's ability to juggle the competing demands of church and family. About one-half of the pastors and special clergy indicated that in their opinion the woman minister could not fulfill both sets of responsibilities adequately. Slightly fewer than one-half said they thought the female pastor would have emotional problems because of those cross-pressures. One pastor commented, for example, "My responses regarding the difficulty of a woman being a full-time pastor and mother revolve around child care and whether or not the husband is willing to really help and also stay home from his job if the child is sick. My experience so far is negative; that is, the men have not adjusted *their* roles." This focus on role conflicts (see Smith, 1973) between job and home is also a major point of concern among the lay members.

The responses in Table 3.1 also indicate that the pastors are more inclined to think of clergywomen in stereotypical terms than are the special clergy. On every question a higher percentage of the pastors gave the stereotyped response than did the other clergy. The differences are not great on some of the items, e.g., concerning job turnover, absenteeism and providing strong leadership, but they are completely consistent and statistically significant. As noted above, these differences may be attributable to the fact that the pastors are professionally involved in the local church scene, while the special clergy as a group are not. This difference in involvement could produce a variety of dynamics. First, the pastors are probably more sensitive to the possibility of

TABLE 3.1   CLERGY RESPONSES TO QUESTIONS INDICATING TENDENCY
TO STEREOTYPE WOMEN IN MINISTRY (percent)

Questions	Percent** responding "definitely" or "probably" correct	
	Pastors	Special Clergy
*1. A woman minister who is married can fulfill her responsibilities as wife and mother just as well as if she were not working full-time.	45	58
2. Women ministers are likely to have higher levels of absenteeism from work than men.	19	14
3. Women ministers are likely to change jobs more often than are men.	12	10
4. Women who try to be both full-time ministers and wives and mothers are likely to have emotional problems due to all the demands placed on them by both jobs.	46	38
5. The children of women who are full-time ministers are likely to have personal problems due to the lack of adequate care and attention.	28	17
6. Since most churches today are competing with each other for members, they need the strong leadership that mostly men can give.	20	14
*7. A woman's temperament is just as suited for the pastoral ministry as a man's.	86	90

*Agreeing with this item indicates the non-stereotyped response. Assenting to the other items indicates the stereotyped response.
**All of the differences between pastors and special clergy are statistically significant.

controversy in the local church in response to a woman's candidacy. Second, pastors are more likely to feel a sense of competition with clergywomen, since it is widely known that most of those women in seminary at least consider the pastorate a vocational goal if indeed they are not aiming directly for it. Third, as persons caught up in the multiple demands of parish life, pastors may honestly think that women cannot cope with those pressures as well as men, particularly if they are married and have young children. All of these factors are consistent with the pastors' being more conservative than are most special clergy on the issue of women in ministry, as the patterns in Table 3.1 show.

A comparison of the responses in Table 3.1 to those of the laity (Table 2.1) also reveals some consistent differences. On almost every type of stereotype, the pastors and special clergy tend to be more flexible in their perceptions of women in ministry than do the lay members. Lay persons are the more inclined to stereotype. The one exception to this pattern is in response to the first item, i.e., concerning fulfilling her responsibilities as wife and mother. In that case the response of the laity lies between that of the pastors and special clergy. The pastors are more inclined to see problems in this area than are the lay members. Again, this result may be attributable to the intense involvement of pastors in the day-to-day demands of the pastoral ministry, leading them more than the others to expect women to experience conflicts. (However, this interpretation is not entirely supported by the pastors' answers to the "emotional problems" question and the item about children's problems, although the lay responses to those questions closely resemble those of the pastors.) Nevertheless, on every other perceptual dimension, the group of clergy tends to be more open to clergywomen than does the laity.

Dimensions of Clergy Stereotyping

The concern of the clergy about whether female pastors can successfully handle the role conflicts stemming from the demands of job and home also appears in the results of a factor analysis of these questions. Just as was done with the lay members' answers to the preference questions in the previous chapter, we subjected the clergy's responses on the stereotyping items to a factor analysis in order to see if they cluster into identifiable categories. Those clusters are seen in Table 3.2

The factor analysis indicates whether the clergy stereotype women in ministry in terms of three criteria. Factor #1, the major cluster, contains the questions dealing with the possible role conflicts experienced by clergywomen and their families—wife and mother tasks, emotional problems, children's problems and husband's adjustment. Clergy who answered one of these questions in a way that anticipated problems also tended to answer each of the other three in the same mode and vice versa. This pattern reinforces our earlier interpretations that this theme is an important one in the clergy's thinking about women in ministry. This factor was the dominant one, i.e., these concerns are more clearly salient to the clergy than are any other concerns reflected in the questions.

TABLE 3.2   FACTOR ANALYSIS OF INDICATORS OF STEREOTYPING CLERGYWOMEN AMONG PASTORS AND SPECIAL CLERGY

	Factor 1*	Factor 2
wife and mother tasks	.57	.25
tasks being emotional problems	.63	.30
children's personal problems	.62	.38
husband's role adjustment	.49	.27
absenteeism from work	.32	.68
change jobs often	.18	.73
churches need stronger leaders	.44	.55

*Factor #1 accounted for 90 percent of the variance, and factor #2 explained the remaining 10 percent.

The second factor which emerged focuses more narrowly on job performance per se, i.e., absenteeism from work, job turnover and strength of leadership. If the clergy indicated some apprehension about one of these issues, they also showed concern on the other two. The fact that these questions loaded together and separately from the role-conflict items indicates that the clergy related to this theme as a separate issue. The fact that they clustered as the second factor implies that the issue is of less concern to them than is the problem of role conflicts.

The question about whether women's temperament renders them constitutionally fit for the pastorate did not load with any of the other items. It stands alone. This solitary nature of the issue in the clergy's mind is noteworthy for at least two reasons. First, it implies that any assumption that women are or are not fit for the job by nature does not necessarily lead to a perception that they can or cannot handle the cross-pressures they may experience. Problems of dealing with multiple demands are seen as purely situational and not constitutional. The difficulty is attributed to the demands themselves and not with womanhood per se. Second, a similar idea applies to dependability on the job. The clergy do not translate their perceptions of women's temperament automatically into notions that clergywomen will or will not be reliable and steady workers. Among the clergy, these issues are kept separate.

The results of this factor analysis were used to construct indexes (see Babbie, 1983: Ch. 15) of clergy perceptions of women in ministry. Instead of creating one index of the cognitive dimension (as was done with responses of the laity), for the clergy we created three—one for each sub-dimension as defined by the factor analysis. To measure the extent to which the ministers view women as rendered ineffective by role conflicts associated with job and home, we created a "family stereotyping" index. Each respondent was given one point for each indication that clergywomen would have a problem in this area—wife-and-mother problems, emotional stress, children's adjustment and spouse adjustment. Similarly, we constructed a "job-role stereotyping" index by combining answers on the items dealing with absenteeism, job turnover and strength of leadership. The question dealing with women's temperament stands alone as the indicator of differences on that dimension.

The relative centrality of the role conflict issue to clergy is also demonstrated in the distribution of the scores on these indexes. Those scores are contained in Table 3.3. The "family stereotyping" scores are more uniformly distributed than are the other two sets. Fully ten percent of the clergy perceive women in ministry as having problems juggling the cross-pressures of job and home on all four items. Only 25 percent view these role conflicts as no problem at all. On the "job-role stereotyping" index, however, 3 percent see clergy-women as unreliable on all counts, whereas 70 percent see them as fully dependable workers and leaders. The temperament stereotyping scores also are low.

Clergy Perceptions of Women's Abilities

We know from the above that the clergy as a group tend to have open and non-stereotyped conceptions of women in ministry. We now ask whether these perceptions lead the clergy to say that women can perform critical clergy roles as well as men. *As was the case with the laity, the answer is clearly predominantly affirmative.*

TABLE 3.3   DISTRIBUTION OF CLERGY SCORES ON INDEXES OF RECEPTIVITY
TO CLERGYWOMEN (percent)

	Family stereotyping				
	low				*high*
score	0	1	2	3	4
percent	25	28	19	18	10

	Job role stereotyping			
	low			*high*
score	0	1	2	3
percent	70	19	8	3

	Temperament stereotyping			
	low			*high*
score	1	2	3	4
percent	53	35	9	3

	General preference									
	low									*high*
score	0	1	2	3	4	5	6	7	8	9	10
percent	51	11	8	7	5	4	3	2	3	2	4

	Subordinates preference			
	low			*high*
score	0	1	2	3
percent	83	12	3	2

	Willingness to discriminate		
	low		*high*
score	1	2	3
percent	64	29	7

Given the same questionnaire as were the lay members, the clergy were asked to identify the most important functions their pastor could perform for them personally and for their church collectively. These questions were followed by the question of whether a woman can perform those functions as well as a man. The pattern of their answers is shown in Table 3.4. Both types of clergy responded to both questions overwhelmingly positively. About 90 percent said "yes," a woman can perform the functions they considered the most important ones as well as a man.

TABLE 3.4   PERCENTAGE OF CLERGY INDICATING A WOMAN CAN
PERFORM CLERICAL FUNCTIONS AS WELL AS A MAN

	Percent* responding affirmatively	
	Pastors	Special clergy
Can a woman do the one thing you most want a minister to do *for you personally* as well as a man?	89	93
Can a woman do the one thing you most want a minister to do *for your church* as well as a man?	87	92

*Differences between pastors and special clergy are statistically significant.

Two other patterns are worth noting. First, as was the case
with clergy stereotyping, the pastors tend to have less favorable
images of clergywomen than do the people in special ministries.
The pastors are less likely than the other clergy to say that a
woman can perform important ministerial roles as well as a man.
This applies to both personal and congregational functions. The
differences are not great, but they are not likely due to chance.
The reason for this pattern is probably the same as that discussed
above in relation to stereotyping, i.e., a series of consequences of
the fact that the special clergy are less directly involved than are
the pastors in shouldering responsibility for the structures and
programs of the local congregation.

As was also observed in relation to stereotyping, as a group
the clergy are more inclined than the laity to assert that women
can perform the important clergy roles. More clergy than lay
members (see Tables 2.3 and 2.4) said "yes," the women are as
capable as men. Again, the differences are not great, but they are
real.

Summary of Clergy Perceptions

Even more so than among the laity, *there is relatively little inclination of the clergy to have biased opinions about women in
ministry.* Ministers already in the denominational structure tend
to have open and flexible perceptions of clergywomen rather
than stereotyped ones. Where they do share traditional images of
women in ministry, the questionable perceptions deal more with
problems associated with cross-pressures between home and job

than with other issues. The clergy also overwhelmingly take the position that clergywomen can perform important personal and congregational functions just as well as male ministers can. Finally, the clergy in special ministries tend to be more open to women in ministry in these ways than do the pastors. These differences between pastors and special clergy are probably attributable to variations in specific responsibilities they have for the life of the church

Clergy and the Affective Dimension: Preference for Men

Even though most clergy perceive women in ministry in very positive rational terms, sometimes their logic clashes with their feelings. It is one thing to say clergywomen are capable of functioning in the ministry just as well as men. Often it is quite another thing to *feel comfortable* with the idea of departing from the traditional patterns which appear so "natural," i.e., not to prefer to have men as ministers, especially as pastors of congregations. One pastor revealed this type of inner conflict when he remarked, "As a man, I have culturally related hesitancy (in relation) to females as the sole minister of a congregation, more specifically (of) those church congregations (which are) larger than average. I have no hesitancy whatever to women in any other role in the church or in performing any of the rites of our church. In time I am sure even my present hesitancy will disappear. *My mind tells me that women should have equal opportunities—my cultural bias hesitates*" (italics added). Another clergyman in a special ministry said, "Emotionally, I see the ministry as a role which is exclusively male. Intellectually, I think this is nonsense. I am working on my ambivalence . . . ." What we think of an idea is sometimes at odds with how we react emotionally. How widespread are these conflicts about women in ministry among the clergy? What is the level of clergy receptivity to clergywomen emotionally?

To measure the clergy's feelings about females occupying church positions and performing ministerial roles, we asked the same set of questions as those posed to the laity. That is, we asked them whether they would prefer a male, a female, or if sex would make no difference.

Table 3.5 shows the percent of clergy who indicated a

preference for a male (in contrast to either "no difference" or "female") in response to each question. (Again, activities in which laypersons often participate are omitted in order to focus primarily on the ordained clergy.) A few patterns in the responses parallel those of the lay members. The questions on which clergy indicated preference for a man are the same as those indicated by the laity. Very few clergy preferred a male for either Minister of Education or Minister of Music. The same applies to preference for males' leading pastoral prayer. Slightly more, but still very few, preferred males for associate pastor, budget planning, and several other functions. The position for which most preference for males

TABLE 3.5   RESPONSES TO QUESTIONS INDICATING PREFERENCE FOR MEN
IN MINISTERIAL POSITIONS AND ACTIVITIES (percent)

| | Percent indicating preference for a man | |
Questions	Pastors	Special Clergy
PARISH POSITIONS		
senior or sole pastor	46	32
associate or assistant pastor	13	7
Minister of Education	4*	3
Minister of Music	7*	3
Youth Minister	18	10
PASTORAL ACTIVITIES		
performing baptism	16	10
administering the Lord's supper	16	11
preaching a sermon	24	16
leading a pastoral prayer	8	6
conducting a funeral	16	10
advising you about a personal problem	16*	13
moderating the session meeting	17	10
coordinating church staff as senior minister	38	23
working with a contractor to renovate the church	34	24
planning your congregation's annual budget	14	7

*The differences between pastors and special clergy marked with an asterisk (*) are statistically non-significant. All other differences in the table are statistically significant.

was indicated is senior or sole pastor. High levels of preference for males were expressed for those performing the functions of preaching sermons, working with contractors and coordinating church staff. As occurred with the laity, the positions involving the most power are those for which males are preferred most often.

The table also indicates that the pastors differed from the special clergy in their preferences for men or women. On all but three of the items, the pastors preferred men for ministerial positions and roles more than did the special clergy. Even on the three items wherein the differences are not statistically significant, they tend to be in the same direction—pastors' having greater preference for males. The range of magnitudes of the differences in preferences between the pastors and other clergy are also about the same as on the stereotyping differences. They were the greatest in relation to the senior pastorate and the least in relation to the subordinate church positions. The reasons for pastors' indicating more preference for males than did the special clergy probably also parallel those associated with stereotyping. That is, because of the pastors' direct vocational involvement in local church affairs, they are probably more sensitive to local feelings and pressures, more conservative about introducing potentially controversial candidates for local church positions and potentially more competitive in relation to women in ministry.

Dimensions of Clergy Preferences

Lay members' preferences for men or women in ministerial roles clustered into three categories—"sacramental," "organizational" and "subordinate" roles. These clusters comprised subsets of preference questions that the laity answered according to one of those three kinds of considerations. The nature of the clusters was identified by performing factor analysis on those items.

We performed a factor analysis (see Kerlinger, 1979: Ch. 12) of the clergy responses to the preference questions as well. That analysis indicates that the clergy also dealt with preferences for men or women in clergy roles on peculiar bases. However, the structure of the sub-dimensions of clergy preferences is different from that of the lay members. As shown in Table 3.6, the clergy's preferences factor in but two clusters. The second of the two factors is the same as the third cluster found in the lay members' responses, i.e., a "subordinate" dimension. The clergy apparently applied similar preferences for males or females in relation to these positions according to their common status.

However, the main factor of clergy preferences combines into one dimension the roles with which the lay members dealt in terms of two criteria—the sacramental and organizational dimensions. The clergy related to these roles as though they were all of the same status. To some readers, this pattern may seem curious. One might expect the clergy to make fine distinctions in the work of pastors, because after all they are (have been) in the role and are supposedly more familiar with the complexities of church life than are the laity. They are the trained professionals. However, on the basis of familiarity with the complexities of ministerial work, what the clergy may be saying instead is that all of the functions that loaded on the first (and dominant) factor are of equal importance and are interrelated—are equal aspects of the role of "pastor." For whatever reason, the clergy appear to apply the

TABLE 3.6   FACTOR ANALYSIS OF PREFERENCES FOR MEN IN CLERGY ROLES AMONG PASTORS AND SPECIAL CLERGY

	Factor 1*	Factor 2
senior or sole pastor	.67	.14
performing baptism	.74	.35
administer Lord's Supper	.73	.37
preaching a sermon	.72	.33
conducting a funeral	.76	.28
advice re: personal problem	.51	.35
moderating the session	.62	.45
coordinate church staff	.72	.20
working on church renovation	.58	.19
planning annual budget	.56	.39
Minister of Education	.13	.63
Minister of Music	.15	.56
Youth Minister	.31	.50

*Factor #1 accounted for 91 percent of the variance, and factor #2 explained the remaining 9 percent.

same criteria in stating male/female preferences for the roles in the first factor. Their preferences associated with pastoral positions and activities are relatively generalized.

As with the responses of the lay members, we created indexes (see Babbie, 1983: Ch. 15) to measure differences in degree of preference for men on each of these sub-dimensions. The clergy were given scores on the basis of one point for each role in relation to which they preferred a male, with one set of scores computed for each factor. This gave each person a "general preference" score (factor #1) and a "subordinate" score (#2). The higher the score, the greater the person's preference for a male in that type of clergy role.

The distribution of these clergy preference scores is contained in Table 3.3 (above). The subordinate scores, first of all, tend to be quite low. More than four-fifths of the clergy showed no preference for a man in any of the subordinate positions. The scores on the general preference index, on the other hand, are not as consistently low. Nearly 50 percent of the clergy preferred a male for one or more ministerial roles other than the subordinate ones. The role for which the male preference is expressed most consistently, of course, is the senior pastorate. However, once one gets beyond the position of pastor per se, the number of preferences for males diminishes markedly. No more than roughly one-third of the clergy feel that they wanted a male for any position other than that of senior minister.

Nevertheless, one-third of the clergy's feeling some aversion for females performing several clerical roles is potentially quite important. The number implies that a significant proportion of the clergy experience conflicts between logic and emotions as illustrated in the quotes noted above. With about 90 percent of them asserting that women can perform as effectively as men, and yet one-third of them saying that they really prefer a male in ministerial roles, we have evidence of ambivalence that could turn into resistance under certain circumstances. In effect these clergy are saying, "Yes, a woman can perform clergy roles as well as a man, but I am not ready to fully accept a woman in that way." *The situation represents a "soft spot" in the denomination's support for women in ministry.* Clergy are important spokespersons for most causes in the church. If a significant number of them are personally ambivalent toward women in ministry, then the clear advocacy the women need to break through traditional barriers will not be forthcoming. *The equivocal advocacy typically associated with ambivalence often amounts to no effective advocacy at all.*

Clergy Willingness to Discriminate

The third major dimension of receptivity to women in ministry is behavioral—how people are likely to act toward them. Again, the question used to measure clergy tendencies to act positively or negatively toward clergywomen is the same as that posed to the lay members. We asked them, "If . . . there were conflicts and tensions in a congregation because a woman had been recommended (for the position of pastor), which of the following actions do you think the pastor nominating committee should take? Do you think they should:

1. try to convince the congregation to call the woman they recommended,
2. take a neutral position and let the congregation decide, or
3. withdraw the woman's name and recommend a man?"

How did the clergy responses compare to those of the laity? How did the pastors' compare to those of the special clergy?

The positions the clergy took in response to the discrimination question are shown in Table 3.7. The patterns of response closely-parallel those noted on other dimensions above. As a group the clergy appeared much less willing to discriminate against women in ministry than did the laity. About two-thirds of the ministers took the position that in this kind of situation the committee should stick to its guns and stay with the original recommendation—stand behind the woman candidate. Less than one-third were willing even to defer to the church, thereby being unwilling to discriminate in the name of majority rule. Less than one in ten were prepared to discriminate outright and have the committee withdraw the woman's name in favor of a man. The major difference between these responses and those of the lay members is in the category indicating clear affirmation—sticking with the initial recommendation. Proportionally nearly twice as many clergy as lay members categorically rejected the discriminatory stance. At the opposite extreme, nearly the same proportion of clergy as laity did take the discriminatory stance. The percentage of true conservatives in the situation is about the same for both groups.

TABLE 3.7   WILLINGNESS TO DISCRIMINATE
AGAINST FEMALE CANDIDATES: PASTORS
AND OTHER CLERGY (percent)*

	Pastors	Special Clergy
support the candidate	59	70
defer to the church	31	26
withdraw her name	10	4

*Differences between pastors and special clergy are statistically significant.

The differences between pastors and special clergy also parallel those noted on the dimensions discussed previously. Just as appeared on the cognitive and attitudinal dimensions, the pastors took a more conservative stand than did the special clergy on the issue of discrimation against women in ministry. More special clergy than pastors indicated that the pastor nominating committee should stick with its initial recommendation in the face of potential challenge. More pastors than special clergy asserted that the committee should withdraw the woman's name and recommend a man instead. The reasons for the greater conservatism of pastors than of special clergy are probably the same as those discussed earlier in this chapter, i.e., differences in involvement of these two types of ministers in the affairs of local congregations.

Summary

On the basis of the data collected from the clergy, what can be said about their orientations to women in ministry? The question is an important one, for the position clergy take on the issue can greatly influence the relative success or failure women will experience in their efforts to move into this field so clearly dominated by men in the past. In most religious bodies, at both the denominational and congregational levels, the clergy tend to be opinion leaders. The positions they take on a variety of issues influence the thinking of the rest of the members. They can help establish a climate of opinion either favorable or in opposition to women in ministry. The clergy also play important roles in inspiring women to consider the ministry as a vocation, and they can help validate a sense of call for women who entertain the idea seriously. Finally, the clergy are strategically more involved than are lay members in those church structures where church policy is made and implemented. As the actors in these situations, their actions will heavily impact the fate of women in ministry.

In general the analysis of the clergy's responses indicates that *they tend to take a very positive stance in relation to women in ministry.* This pattern is observed on all three dimensions of receptivity/resistance—their perceptions of clergywomen, their preferences for men in clergy roles and their willingness to discriminate against female candidates. On all counts the clergy were more receptive than were the lay members, although among the clergy the pastors were more resistant than were special clergy. The greater conservatism of pastors is probably due to their direct involvement in the daily life of the congregation and the perceptions of the members that result from it. On balance, then, one would expect the clergy to play a significant, positive role in relation to women in ministry.

Nevertheless, just as was the case among the laity, there were real discrepancies in receptivity among them. Why is this so? What factors go into making one person in favor of women in ministry and another person opposed? We pursue this question systematically in the next two chapters.

Suggestions for Additional Reading

Carroll, Jackson W., and Robert L. Wilson
  1978 *The Clergy Job Market: Over-Supply and/or Opportunity.* Hartford: Hartford Seminary Foundation.

   A study of the current situation in several denominations concerning the supply of clergy in relation to the demand for their services. Documents the situation in which parish ministers feel threatened by a growing sense of competition for a shrinking number of jobs, one of the factors underlying some of the resistance of pastors to women in ministry.

Harrison, Paul M.
  1959 *Authority and Power in the Free Church Tradition.* Princeton: Princeton University Press.

  A classic study of the centralization of power in the hands of clergy even in a denomination whose polity is officially congregational in nature. Identifies ways in which formal democratic or representational structures can be subverted or circumnavigated in order to control the content of denominational policy.

Smith, Donald P.
  1973 *Clergy in the Cross Fire: Coping With Role Conflicts in the Ministry.* Philadelphia: Westminster Press.

  A book which systematically reviews the literature dealing with role conflicts experienced by clergy. Identifies several types of role conflicts and their sources. Presents several modes of dealing with role conflict, including manipulation of both self and social system, as well as programmatic suggestions for clergy and churches to follow.

Stark, Rodney, et al.
  1971 *Wayward Shepherd: Prejudice and the Protestant Clergy.* New York: Harper and Row.

  A study of the evidence of prejudice among the clergy, focusing on anti-Semitism. Chapter 5 analyses the gap between the potential the clergy have for influencing their congregations on social issues and the actual low amount of effort clergy exert to have such influence. Identifies factors that explain differences in the extent to which clergy take the opportunity to deal with social issues from the pulpit.

CHAPTER 4

Explaining Differences in Receptivity

The measures of receptivity to women in ministry reviewed in the previous two chapters indicate clearly that the overall attitudes toward clergywomen among lay church members and clergy tend to be positive. There is rather little stereotyping of female clergy, there is near unanimity that women can perform important clergy roles as well as men (the majority have no preference for men in those roles), and there are few who would discriminate outright against women candidates for church positions. These orientations speak well for the chances of women seeking to enter ordained vocations. Most members are apt to support them.

However, it is equally obvious that there is some resistance to women in ministry among the members on every dimension. This evidence of hesitancy to accept female clergy is particularly apparent among those who perceived problems in women's trying to juggle the demands of both job and home. It is present in those who indicated that they really prefer a man in the position of pastor. It is manifested in the course of action some members would take in response to controversy engendered by a woman's candidacy for a local pastorate. Not everyone is prepared to accept women clergy.

How can we account for these differences? What is it that makes one person ready to cooperate with women in ministry and another inclined to resist the idea (see also Lehman, 1979)? This chapter and the next deal with this question. We actually already have one possible answer in the patterns noted in the previous two chapters, i.e., the distinction between clergy and laity. On every dimension of receptivity, the clergy demonstrated higher levels of readiness to accept women in ministry than did the lay members. These differences are probably due to several factors, e.g., the greater prevalence of theological sophistication among the clergy, the greater contact clergymen have with clergy-women, the heightened awareness clergy are likely to have of a variety of ethical issues including feminism. But what about the differences observed *within* the ranks of the laity alone—and variations just *among* the clergy themselves? How can we explain those differences?

Factors Related to Attitude Differences

We are hardly without theories of sexist attitudes. They range from sympathetic references to the effects of socialization to quixotic perceptions of communist (or fascist) plots, from carefully constructed explanations to untested folk wisdom. Which approach is most useful? If we err in any way in this study, it will be in the direction of considering theories more like the former than the latter, i.e., we shall ignore untested modes of explanation, and instead we shall use some ideas from social science to better understand the attitudes. Specifically, we shall assess the explanatory power of three types of theories in this chapter, i.e., that resistance to women in ministry is but a manifestation of prejudice in general (see Peek and Brown, 1980), that such resistance is uniquely a religious matter, and that it is a consequence of the type of church and local community in which members are involved. A fourth theory (dealing with organizational viability) will be addressed in the next chapter.

To some, sexist attitudes toward clergywomen are not fundamentally religious issues at all. To them the phenomenon of resistance to women in ministry is but one dimension of tendencies to be prejudiced in general and to dislike departures from traditional sex roles in particular (see Dempewolff, 1974; Henley and Pincus, 1978; and Tedin, 1978). It is symptomatic of conservatism in general (see also Beck, 1978). Sometimes it is viewed as a component of a personality type—it helps define a "kind of person."

We have measures of a number of variables involved in this kind of thinking, i.e., the members' age, sex, race, education, occupation, income and marital status. Several of these variables have been found related to differences in levels of prejudice involving other types of persons, such as race, ethnicity, religion and sexism in general. We shall try to determine the extent to which these factors are also predictive of differences in receptivity to women in ministry.

Another approach to explaining attitudes toward clergywomen is to emphasize the importance of the religious factor rather than to play it down. "Clergypersons are, after all," says this mode of thinking, "fundamentally religious leaders." They represent important cultural symbols dealing with transcendent values and concepts, they represent the religious community in the minds of other participants in social gatherings where they are present, and they are expected to embody religious ethics and values in their own deportment. There at least ought to be a religious dimension to church members' relative willingness to accept women as religious leaders if the religion *per se* makes any difference (see Driedger, 1974). We have measures of differences in the members' religious involvement for use in pursuing this type of thinking. We shall try to determine whether those measures are predictive of the measures of receptivity. This step will involve looking at differences in members' religious ideology, church attendance, financial contributions, church office-holding and praying before meals.

The third type of theory focuses on characteristics of the congregation rather than the individual member. One factor in this approach deals with size—number of members as well as size of community. Another dimension is the budget. Others are the size of the church staff and the denominational alignment of the congregation. Common to all of these factors is the belief that members of churches with different congregational characteristics will react to various issues—including the idea of women in ministry—in predictable ways (see also Lehman, 1981a). These attributes of the collectivity (rather than the individual) are expected to have an impact on attitudes toward clergywomen regardless of the effects of individual traits and levels of individual religious involvement. In this theory, type of church is the important variable.

Which of these theories is (are) useful in explaining differences in attitudes toward women in ministry? Let's look at them one at a time. Before we do, however, let us look briefly at an analytical device we will use in showing the relationships between attitudes and each of the variables involved in the theories.

The Concept of "Correlation"

Since we are dealing with a large number of measures of receptivity on the one hand, and even larger numbers of factors that might influence receptivity on the other, presenting a table to show the relationships between each pair of variables would be very cumbersome. It could conceivably double the physical size of this volume. Fortunately, it is not necessary to present each relationship in tabular form. Instead we can use coefficients to summarize the nature of the relationship in each table and still communicate parsimoniously but with sufficient clarity the ways in which various factors seem to influence levels of receptivity. These coefficients that will represent the relationships otherwise shown in tables are called "correlation coefficients" (see Babbie, 1983: pp 408–414). Let us digress for a moment to indicate how the coefficients work and how they are interpreted.

A correlation coefficient is a single number that summarizes the information in a table in which one compares two variables (such as member's age and stereotyping score). Correlation coefficients tell us the "direction" in which the variables are related to each other as well as the "strength" of that relationship. By "direction" we mean that as one factor increases the other one also increases, or as one variable increases the other one decreases—the variables are "directly" related or they are "inversely" related respectively. By "strength" of the relationship, we mean the extent to which one variable may be predicted if we know the value of the other variable, e.g., if we know a person's age, to what extent can we predict that person's stereotyping score? Figure 4.1 illustrates the basic principles involved. Look at section "A" at the top of the table. Suppose we took ten identical glasses and filled each one with different amounts of water. Suppose we then weighed each glass. If we plotted the weight and volume of the water for each glass on a graph as in Figure 4.1-A, we would get a plot of points that approximate a straight line across the table. The line would be an indication that the two events are "related," i.e., as volume increases weight also increases. If we apply this information to a mathematical formula that produces a "correlation coefficient," the coefficient resulting from Figure 4.1-A would have a value of "1.0." A coefficient of 1.0 indicates a perfect direct relationship—a one-to-one relationship. Each variable increases and decreases directly with the other variable.

Now look at Figure 4.1-B. Suppose we counted the number of leaves on all of our neighbors' trees, and then counted the number of hairs on the heads of all of the members of each neighbor's family. If we plotted these values on a graph as we did above the pattern in Figure 4.1-B would result. It is like a random set of dots from a shotgun blast. There is no "line." This is as it should be, for the two factors—number of leaves and number of hairs—are unrelated; they are "independent" of each other. If we now apply this information to our correlation formula, the result will be a coefficient of "0.0." This says the same thing. The strength of the relationship between these two variables is "zero"—no relationship at all.

Now look at Figure 4.1-C. This graph illustrates the kind of relationship we usually get in social science (and often in natural science as well). This pattern is the kind we would obtain if we cross-tabulated measures of: (1) the extent to which each person considered religious conversion to be an important purpose of the church and (2) the extent to which each person would be willing to accept a clergywoman as pastor. Here we have neither the straight line of dots that appeared in "A" nor the random pattern that emerged in "B." Instead we have the dots following a line along one diagonal rather than the other. This pattern says that the two factors are related, but they are not related perfectly.

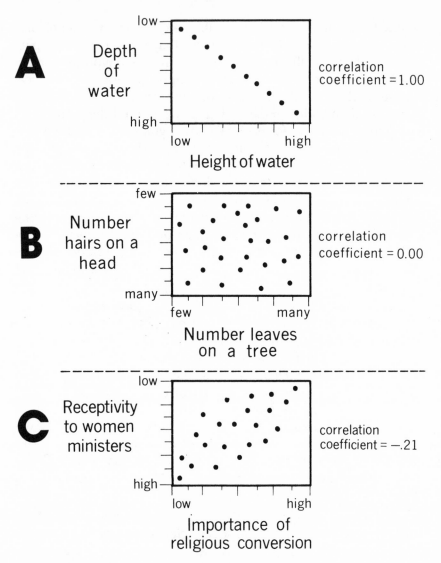

Figure 4.1 The Concept of Correlation

There is a "tendency" for them to be "inversely", related. As the subjective importance of religious conversion increases, the willingness to accept a clergywoman tends to decrease. Incorporating the formula for correlation in this case would yield a number somewhere between "1.0" and "0.0." In this case it would result in a value of something like "– .21."

It is in these ways that a single number—a correlation coefficient—can represent the relationship between two variables. It indicates how strongly they are related and in what direction without having to portray the entire table. Since we are going to deal with a large number of relationships in the balance of this report, one of the devices we shall use to present them is the correlation coefficient. In interpreting them, simply remember that the rule of thumb is this: *the closer the number is to "1.0," the stronger the relationship. The closer the number is to "0.0," the weaker the relationship.* Most of the time (almost always) the coefficient is going to be somewhere between these two extremes and should be understood in relative terms, i.e., as "weak" or "strong." Finally, coefficients that are so small as to occur easily by chance alone are labeled "statistically non-significant" and are interpreted as indicating that there is *no* relationship between the variables in question (see Babbie, 1983: pp. 414–427).

Effects of Individual Characteristics

In order to assess the extent to which differences in individual characteristics are related to differences in receptivity to women in ministry, we cross-tabulated the measures of those variables and calculated correlations to represent the results. (The specific correlation coefficient employed is "gamma.") The values of the resulting coefficients are contained in Table 4.1. The patterns of relationships in the table indicate that some individual characteristics are consistently predictive of attitudes toward clergywomen, while others are either less so or not predictive at all. (Note that the values are small—nowhere near 1.0—thus indicating patterns of relationships analogous to that in Figure 4.1-"C" above.)

Sex is a favorite topic of speculation in relation to attitudes toward women in ministry. There are numerous arguments attributing malevolent attitudes to males. One person said, "The basic problem is that a number of men are not prepared to respond to women as pastors. To push the issue is to sacrifice the men." Another complained similarly that accepting women as pastors would "feminize" the church and drive the men away. Yet others argue exactly the opposite. They say that resistance is greatest among females. Said one pastor, for example, "Women

TABLE 4.1 CORRELATIONS BETWEEN RECEPTIVITY AND PERSONAL CHARACTERISTICS: BY SUB-POPULATION

Lay members	Sex	Age	Race	Marital status	Education	Income	Occupation
stereotyping	.26	.21	ns	.10	.08	ns	ns
can do for me	.56	.16	ns	.18	ns	ns	ns
can do for church	.39	.13	ns	.27	ns	.12	ns
sacramental	.12	.17	ns	ns	.17	.09	ns
organizational	.27	.22	ns	ns	.07	ns	ns
subordinate	.20	.09	ns	ns	.12	ns	ns
willingness to discriminate	ns*	.10	ns	ns	.17	.16	ns

Clergy	Age	Race	Marital status
family role stereotyping	.21	ns	.23
job role stereotyping	.37	ns	.33
temperament stereotyping	.27	ns	.27
can do for me	.20	ns	.39
can do for church	.17	ns	.68
general preference	.23	ns	.20
subordinate	.19	ns	.22
willingness to discriminate	.10	ns	ns

*"ns" indicates a statistically non-significant correlation.

86

in our congregation on the session have refused to serve communion (or) to assist in worship. For reasons beyond my understanding, *women* in the area are the ones who resist women in ministry more than men." What do the data from the members in the survey tell us about this?

The data involving sex as a correlate of receptivity support the argument that *women tend to be more hospitable to women in ministry than men.* More men than women have high stereotyping scores, perceive that women cannot perform important church functions as well as men, and prefer to have men performing sacramental, organizational and subordinate roles. However, sex is not predictive of willingness to discriminate against women, the behavioral dimension. Women are as likely as men to be willing to reject a female candidate for a church position in the face of controversy in the congregation.

Age is another factor that many people use to predict which members are likely to have positive or negative attitudes. There seems to be a nearly universal expectation that older members will be more prejudiced than younger ones. Said one person, "Ours is an old established "First" church full of elderly and conservative people. While I personally believe that a woman. . .will probably do as good a job as a man. . ., I do not see this coming about very quickly." Many people see resistance in others, and one "kind" of other to whom they attribute it is "older" people who are described as "set in their ways." However, there are some dissenters from this view, as revealed in the following remark, "As more women are successful as junior pastors, they will become qualified for senior roles. . . . Personally I believe this to be a good thing, although *my daughter* disagrees, based on her reading of Scripture."

The data in Table 4.1 clearly support the view that *older members tend to be more resistant to women in ministry than younger people.* On every dimension of receptivity, more older members than younger ones had high resistance scores. Older persons are also more likely than younger ones to discriminate against female candidates. Furthermore, the same pattern applies to the clergy. On every dimension of receptivity, older clergy tend to be less receptive to women in ministry than do younger ones. To the extent that older clergy are the more likely to be in positions of influence in the denomination, this pattern could portend less firm denominational support for women in ministry than clergywomen would like to see.

Race has also been put forth as an important variable in explaining differences in receptivity to women in ministry. It has been suggested that resistance is higher among non-whites than among whites. Especially among black congregations, the ministry has been described as "a bastion of male dominance," partly because of the ascendancy of females in some black families. However, the results of the analysis in Table 4.1 do not support such an image. Among both the lay members and the clergy, there are no significant differences between members of racial groups concerning receptivity to women in ministry. We cannot say that non-whites are less likely than whites to favor the women-in-ministry movement.

Marital status, however, is predictive of receptivity to women in ministry. *Especially among the clergy, being married is associated with acceptance of clergywomen.* An exception to the pattern is the behavioral dimension. Whether one is married or not is unrelated to whether or not one will discriminate against female candidates. Correlations do exist on the other dimensions. There is less stereotyping and less preference for a man in clergy roles by those who are married than by those who are not. Among the lay members, marital status appears to make a difference only on the cognitive dimension—tendency to stereotype and to perceive women as less capable than men to perform important pastoral functions. Those who are not married are more inclined to manifest these opinions than those who are married.

The final individual characteristic to consider is a set of attributes associated with socio-economic status. The three indicators typically used to measure such status differences are education, income and occupation. As the correlations in Table 4.1 indicate, differences in receptivity are related to some of these factors and not to others. Occupational differences (other than the clergy/non-clergy distinction noted above) are not predictive of receptivity to clergywomen on any dimension. Income is associated with some but not others. More people with relatively high incomes than low tend to be accepting of women in ministry in terms of being unwilling to discriminate against female candidates for local church positions. The higher income members also tend to perceive women as being just as capable as men in performing important tasks in behalf of the congregation as a whole. They also tend to have few preferences for men performing sacramental functions.

Of the three indicators of social status, education is clearly the most predictive of receptivity to women in ministry. *On all three major dimensions, persons with high levels of education are more favorably disposed to clergywomen than are those with less education.* The more highly educated hold few stereotypes, have few preferences for men in clerical roles and tend to act supportively toward female candidates. This pattern is consistent with what one would expect to find if the effects of education are what they are designed to be, i.e., to liberate from parochial and simplistic images of the world and toward more universalistic and analytical perspectives. However—lest we beat our drum too loudly—the relationships are not very strong, so formal education is also no panacea.

So what can we make of all of this? These patterns would seem to have positive implications for the theory that *resistance to women in ministry is epiphenomenal of more general tendencies to be prejudiced toward minorities.* This applies especially to factors found to be correlates of sexism in general (see Tavris and Offir, 1977). Other research has demonstrated that opposition to feminist objectives tends to be more prevalent among males, older people, the less educated and the unmarried. These are precisely the variables found to be correlated with differences in receptivity to women in ministry in the analysis above. Accordingly, such variations in receptivity may not be unique to the issue of women in ministry at all. They may be expressions of differences in "sexism in general." Nevertheless, the correlations are not terribly strong to say the least, so sexism in general is most likely not the entire story. Apparently other factors are operating too.

Effects of Differences in Religiosity

Another line of thought argues that attitudes toward women in ministry involve more than just prejudice or sexism in general. After all, it says, the vocation in question is specifically religious in nature, and it partakes of a particular religious tradition. Some segments of the tradition have been interpreted historically as postulating male dominance within the organized collective religious life. People who participate in this ideology (see Stark and Glock, 1970), should have different orientations toward women in ministry than those who do not. Recently others have been emphasizing other segments of the tradition, as well as reinterpreting the traditional portions alluding to gender-based distinction in power and authority emphasizing universalistic norms concerning gender. Immersion in this revisionist perspective should also have consequences for one's orientation toward the women-in-ministry concept. The nature of one's involvement in the religious sub-culture, then, should be associated with his/her attitudes toward female clergy (see also Garsuch and Aleshire, 1974).

Contemporary theology involves numerous schools of thought, each of which places emphasis on unique sets of concepts, symbols and values. It would be virtually impossible to capture the essence of any of them within the limitations of a study such as this. Accordingly, in an effort to measure differences in members' religious ideological orientations, we made no pretense at trying to capture the richness of theological diversity that actually exists. Instead we focused on obtaining a relatively simple indication of what the members considered important as a guiding ideological theme for the church to follow. We asked about one aspect of their ecclesiology, hoping the differences we would obtain would also reflect differences in what they thought was important in the religious life generally. The questionnaire contained the following question.

"People often differ regarding the relative importance of various aspects of congregational life. Four such aspects are listed below. We recognize that all of these aspects may be important; nevertheless, we would like for you to think about their relative importance to you. Please indicate which aspect is *most* important to *you* by writing the number "1" beside it. Then write the number "2" by the next most important aspect, the number "3" by the third, and the number "4" by the fourth in importance.

_____ worshipping God as a community of people seeking to follow Christ
_____ trying to convert people to faith in Christ
_____ seeking to help individuals who cannot help themselves
_____ trying to solve social problems outside the church through social reforms."

The four answer categories represent a set of crude indications (see Babbie, 1983: Ch. 5) of one's position on a theological continuum from "evangelical" (the "convert" item), to "conservative" (the "worship" item), to "liberal" (the "helping" item) and to "radical" (the "reform" item). (As a group the members tended to rank the "worship" item first in importance, the "helping" item second, the "reform" item third and the "convert" item last.) We placed each individual respondent on the theological continuum in terms of the item he/she ranked "first."

Table 4.2 contains the results of comparing this measure of religious ideology to the measures of receptivity to clergywomen. The coefficients indicate that the *theological differences are predictive of receptivity to women in ministry on all dimensions.* The closer members' theological position was to the evangelical/ conservative end of the continuum, the more they held biased views of clergywomen, preferred men in clergy roles and would discriminate against female candidates for church positions. This pattern is consistent with what one would predict on the basis of the nature of those theological orientations.

The results were dramatically different among the clergy, however. For them, differences in ideology were predictive only of the behavioral dimension. Clergy with conservative ideology were more likely to discriminate against clergywomen than were those with other views. None of the other dimensions of receptivity related to ideological differences. The reason for this result in the analysis of the clergy data may be the greater ideological homogeneity among clergy than among the laity (see Stark, et al, 1971).

Another aspect of religious involvement is ritual behavior. Not only do members differ in terms of the ideology they hold, but they also diverge when it comes to their overt church participation, financial contributions and devotional behavior. We measured level of church participation by asking members whether they attended worship services:

> every week,
> nearly every week,
> once or twice a month,
> about six times a year,
> once or twice a year, or
> rarely or never.

TABLE 4.2 CORRELATIONS BETWEEN RECEPTIVITY AND INDIVIDUAL RELIGIOSITY: BY SUB-POPULATION

Lay Members	Attendance	Contributions	Grace	Officer	Ideology
stereotyping	.15	.08	.05	ns*	.22
can do for me	.28	.17	.12	ns	.10
can do for church	.26	.15	.14	.12	.14
sacramental	.21	.06	.11	ns	.33
organizational	.22	.10	.11	ns	.25
subordinate	.29	.12	.12	.18	.35
willingness to discriminate	.15	.05	.05	ns	.20

Clergy	Attendance	Contributions	Grace	Officer	Ideology
family stereotyping	.20	—	.27	.09	ns
job role stereotyping	.20	—	.31	.17	ns
temperament stereotyping	ns	—	.33	ns	ns
can do for me	ns	—	.47	ns	ns
can do for church	ns	—	.57	ns	ns
general preference	.15	—	.31	ns	ns
subordinate	ns	—	.52	.17	ns
willingness to discriminate	ns	—	.30	.18	.13

*indicates a statistically non-significant correlation.

Modally the respondents presented themselves as fairly frequent attenders, although there were significant numbers of people reporting each level of involvement.

The differences in church participation are consistently related to the variations in receptivity to women in ministry. Members who are relatively *high* in church attendance also tend to stereotype clergywomen, perceive that women are less capable than men to perform ministerial roles, prefer men in church positions and discriminate against female candidates more than do those who are low in attendance. (The reason for this pattern may be the difference to which the members identify with and/or have personal investment in the local congregation, a point to which we shall return in detail in the next chapter.) Religious participation is less consistently predictive of the clergy's levels of receptivity, however. Attendance is related to some clergy stereotyping and to clergy preferences for men in most church roles, but it is unrelated to the other dimensions. Again, the reason for an absence of many of these relationships is probably the relative homogeneity of most clergy.

Members' financial contributions are also predictive of receptivity to women in ministry. The *more* lay members give to the church, the more resistant they are toward clergywomen on all dimensions—more stereotyping, more male preferences, more discrimination.

The indicator of devotional religious involvement we used in the survey is the frequency with which members say grace before meals, i.e., whether it was daily, weekly, only on special occacions or never. The results of the analysis (Table 4.2) indicate that this type of religious commitment is also related to receptivity to clergywomen. *The more frequently members engaged in prayer before meals, the more resistant they were toward women in ministry,* a pattern which held across all dimensions of receptivity. The correlations between devotional commitment and receptivity among lay members were consistently weak. However, they were considerably stronger among the clergy. For the ministers, being involved in this form of devotionalism apparently makes more difference in the levels of their receptivity than it does for the laity.

The final aspect of religious involvement considered in this phase of the study is holding an office in the church organizational structure. The members were asked whether they had held an office or been on a committee in their congregation at any time within the last year. About twice as many members had held such positions as had not. The results of comparing office-holding to measures of receptivity were quite mixed. Among lay members, there was a slight tendency for office holders to be the more resistant toward women in subordinate positions and to feel that women cannot perform functions for the congregation as well as a man. Office holding was unrelated to the other dimensions of receptivity. Among clergy there were a few more relationships involving holding office in the congregation. These related to stereotyping, preferring men in subordinate roles and willingness to discriminate against women applying for pastoral positions. In each case office holders were more resistant to women in ministry than were non-office holders. Again the correlations are not strong.

What conclusions can we make about the relationship between the religiosity factor and receptivity to women in ministry? Several patterns are clear. In the most general sense, the results support the idea that *the more members are traditionally involved in the religious system, the more they are resistant to women in ministry.* Among lay members, as their theology was conservative, their church participation high, their involvement in devotionalism high and their financial contributions much—the more they were opposed to clergywomen. Traditional involvements engender or reinforce preferences for traditional patterns of male leadership. Among the clergy the infuence of differences in religiosity shows up clearly only when considering variations in devotional practice—saying grace at meals. The relative absence of an association between the other dimensions of religiosity and receptivity is probably a reflection of the high degree of similarity among clergy person in those other modes of commitment.

Is there a uniquely religious dimension to the question of receptivity to clergywomen? Yes, there seems to be one, and its name seems to be "traditionalism." The more traditional one is in one's religious commitments, the more traditional one is likely to be in relation to the question of women in ministry. However, as we shall see in the next chapter, these patterns involving religious commitment may be indicative of a factor other than traditionalism too. Just as resistance to clergywomen is more than a reflection of sexism in general, it is also more than an effect of traditionalism.

Effects of Type of Church

The third type of theory we considered focuses on the type of church in which the members were involved—city churches versus rural churches, growing congregations versus declining ones, etc. Comments volunteered by the members suggest that there may be no other approach to identifying where women clergy will and will not be accepted which enjoys a wider variety of explanations. To some it is the size of the congregation that makes the most difference. One member said, for example, "Women may have a place in large churches; however, small churches like ours are better off with a male minister." One of the special clergy made a similar comment, "I am convinced that women have a place in the full ministry of the church. However, I also recognize that at the present (time) there are some congregations that could be destroyed over this issue. The church I attend is a small, southern, country church. . .(where) the backbone of the church is still thinking conservatively. Women ministers for another church, OK—*but not at home.*"

However, there are others who are equally convinced of the opposite. Women belong not in large churches but in small ones. Said one member, "It takes a significant amount of . . . work to produce a pastor parish relationship if the pastor is male and even more so if the pastor is female. This can happen easier in a smaller parish than a large one." In a more cynical mode, another person said, "Other denominations have women ministers in this area. They seem to be doing well. This may help small churches that can't pay the salary nor expenses (men) need and highly educated men demand."

Other comments made analogous points concerning the fact that theirs is a small town, a rural area, a large city or an area of primary industry, each implying that the key variable is the size of community rather than size of church. In each case the argument was that there are characteristics of their community which militate against clergywomen's succeeding there. This last point seems to be the theme which actually ties most of these comments together. "*Clergywomen can function someplace but not in this kind of setting." "Women in ministry constitute a good idea—for somebody else's church!"*

We can use the survey data to determine the truth of some of these allegations, but we must be cautious about doing so. We can compare levels of receptivity to women in ministry with variations in the characteristics of members' churches along a variety of dimensions—community size, congregation size, trends in membership and budget, denominational alignment and size of staff. Such comparisons will tell us whether there is any tendency for receptive or resistant *attitudes* to be associated with some of these attributes of congregations more than others. However, such data will *not* answer the question of whether there is some objective characteristic of one or more of these congregational types which does *actually* make it easier or harder for clergy-women to succeed in them. We can speak of the distribution of *attitudes* (receptivity) toward women in ministry in different types of churches. We cannot address (with these data) the distribution of other situational barriers which a type of congregation may actually involve.

With that caveat before us, let us review the results of correlating church characteristics with levels of receptivity. Those results are shown in Table 4.3. Looking first at the factor of community size (see Warren, 1972), we see that it has some effect on the behavioral dimension but is inconsistent on the others. Among both clergy and lay members, people in small communities were more ready to discriminate against female candidates than were people in large places. The greater pervasiveness in urban places of equal-opportunity and affirmative-action norms appears to influence persons living there as to what they will do in recruiting clergy. The relative absence of such guidelines in small towns and rural areas, where there typically exists a traditional preference for applying personal and particularistic orientations to the market place, allows for the possibility of more frequent discrimination against candidates for a variety of jobs—apparently including the ministry.

The results of comparing other dimensions of receptivity to community size are less conclusive. Among the lay members, some concern about women's ability to perform sacramental roles appears to exist more in smaller places than in larger ones, although it is not clear why this pattern exists. Among the clergy,

TABLE 4.3 CORRELATIONS BETWEEN RECEPTIVITY AND CHURCH CHARACTERISTICS: BY SUB-POPULATION

Lay Members	Church size	Community size	Member trend	Budget trend	Dual align	Multiple staff
stereotyping	.06	ns*	ns	-.05	.16	ns
can do for me	.16	ns	ns	-.16	ns	ns
can do for church	.20	.10	ns	-.18	ns	.14
sacramental	.05	.06	ns	-.12	.19	ns
organizational	.12	ns	ns	-.07	.17	.08
subordinate	.16	ns	ns	-.10	.25	.17
willingness to discriminate	ns	.09	ns	-.12	.24	.12

Clergy	Church size	Community size	Member trend	Budget trend	Dual align	Multiple staff
family stereotyping	ns	.09	ns	-.12	ns	.10
job role stereotyping	ns	ns	ns	-.13	ns	ns
temperament stereotyping	ns	.10	-.07	-.14	ns	.09
can do for me	ns	ns	ns	-.18	ns	ns
can do for church	ns	ns	ns	-.27	ns	ns
general preference	ns	ns	ns	-.16	ns	ns
subordinate	.13	ns	ns	-.21	ns	ns
willingness to discriminate	ns	.12	ns	-.12	ns	.19

*indicates a statistically non-significant correlation.

on the other hand, the point of divergence seems to be stereotyping. There is a slight tendency for clergy from small communities to be the more given to perceiving women as temperamentally unfit for the pastorate and as unable to juggle the demands of both job and home. Perhaps this pattern is but a reflection of the traditional division of labor in the home which is more characteristic of small communities than large ones.

When the point of comparison is the size of the congregation itself (rather than the community), a different pattern emerges. Evidently this distinction reflects meaningful differences in the thinking of the lay members but not the clergy. First of all, there is no identifiable tendency for members of large or small churches to behave differently toward women as candidates for church positions. Large churches are as likely as small ones to discriminate against clergywomen in the face of controversy. This applies to both clergy and laity. Beyond this point, however, there is but one relationship of receptivity to church size among the clergy. Ministers in large churches tend to have more preferences for men in subordinates roles than do those in smaller congregations.

Church size is more consistently predictive of receptivity among the lay members. Size apparently influences both stereotyping and gender preferences. More members of *large* churches than small ones had high stereotyping scores, felt that women could not perform important pastoral functions as well as men, and preferred men in ministerial roles. None of the coefficients representing these relationships are large, indicating that the associations are relatively weak. Nevertheless, the pattern of relationships is highly consistent and probably meaningful. Since large churches typically have more resources with which to undertake new ventures, especially undertakings that their members think might involve some risk, one would expect that the larger congregations would be the more receptive to new directions in ministry. They have larger budgets, more human resources, larger church plants and often multiple staffs. These attributes would give larger churches room to maneuver and adapt, a flexibility small congregations do not have. However, the data in Table 4.3 indicate that *just the opposite is the case.* Members of congregations with few such resources are the ones where *positive* attitudes toward women in ministry are the more prevalent. We shall return to this point below.

Another approach to the organizational characteristics of the church is to look at the *trends* in its organizational strength over time. Is membership growing or declining? Is the budget increasing or decreasing? Regardless of absolute size, are these trends associated with different levels of receptivity to women in ministry? The answer in Table 4.3 is clear. Members of congregations whose numbers are growing are neither more nor less likely to be positively disposed toward clergywomen. Growth and decline in size of membership are basically unrelated to receptivity.

However, it is a different matter altogether when one considers *budget* trends. Whether or not the church budget is growing in relation to inflation is consistently predictive of members' attitudes toward women in ministry. Again the association between this indicator of organizational strength and receptivity is in the opposite direction from what one would expect. Members of churches whose budgets are *declining* are more *open* to clergywomen than are those in healthy churches. Congregations with *declining* budgets are associated with little stereotyping, few preferences for men and little readiness to discriminate against female candidates for pastoral positions. The consistency and magnitude of the relationships hold for both lay members and clergy. We shall consider some possible reasons for this pattern. Before we do, however, let us look at two more organizational characteristics, denominational alignment and size of church staff.

Some congregations are aligned with only one denomination—they are strictly labelled "Presbyterian," for example, or "Baptist." Others cooperate with more than one parent body, such as both Presbyterian and Baptist. Another common form of dual alignment is regional, as in affiliation with both UPCUSA and PCUS, north and south. Dually aligned churches are sometimes called "union" churches, uniting two or more denominations within one congregation. In this study, about one congregation in ten were dually aligned in some way.

Since affiliation with more than one denomination virtually *de facto* reflects a greater liberality of spirit than does single alignment, it is possible that such cosmopolitanism extends to other issues. Accordingly, it is likely that members of dually aligned churches are similarly more receptive to women in ministry than are those in congregations with but one denominational affilia-

within one congregation. In this study, about one congregation in ten were dually aligned in some way.

Since affiliation with more than one denomination virtually *de facto* reflects a greater liberality of spirit than does single alignment, it is possible that such cosmopolitanism extends to other issues. Accordingly, it is likely that members of dually aligned churches are similarly more receptive to women in ministry than are those in congregations with but one denominational affiliation. Table 4.3 indicates that among the lay members such is indeed the case. Members of congregations with multiple alignments manifested less stereotyping, less preference for men in clergy roles and less willingness to discriminate against female candidates than those in churches with single alignments. However, this pattern is not observed among the clergy. It seems to be exclusive to lay members.

Finally there is the issue of the size of the staff serving the congregation. While most congregations are served by a "solo" pastor, simply because they cannot afford more than one paid professional, others are fortunate enough to have more than one minister on the staff. Very large churches often have several clergy serving in a variety of roles. Some have thought that churches with multiple staff enjoy a flexibility and/or specialization of function that would make it easier for them to incorporate women into ministry in their organizational structure. If this is so, members of churches with multiple staff should manifest more receptivity to clergywomen than those in churches with solo pastorates. Is this correct?

The data in Table 4.3 show that the results do not permit much generalization. Neverthelesss, the relationships that do exist indicate that members of churches with multiple staff tend to be more *opposed* to women in ministry than do those in solo situations. This is just the opposite of what one would expect. The pattern also does not apply across all dimensions. The point on which there is consensus between lay members and clergy concerns the behavioral dimension. In both groups, members of congregations served by multiple staff are *more* prepared to discriminate against female candidates than are those in churches without multiple staff. The congregations with the greatest flexibility show the least inclination to use it.

Considering the other dimensions of receptivity, one observes no such similarity. Among the lay members, the problem is not one of stereotyping but role preferences. Lay members in multiple-staff churches prefer men in ministerial roles, apparently because they question the woman's ability to perform important functions that impact on the congregation as a whole. The situation is just the opposite for the clergy. More clergy in multiple-staff congregations than in solo pastorates perceive clergywomen stereotypically. They view them as incapable of handling role conflicts and as being temperamentally less fit for the pastorate than men.

By way of summary, the data indicate that the type of congregation does make a difference in one's receptivity to women in ministry. However, it is clear that both the criteria used in classifying types of congregations and the population referred to are important considerations. Not all congregational differences are relevant. Some factors appear to make little difference, e.g., trend in size of membership and community size. Other differences in congregations are related to variations in receptivity, but only (or primarily) among the laity—church size and dual alignment. Only one congregational characteristic is predictive of level of receptivity to women in ministry in an unambiguous fashion in both populations, and that is budget trend. Churches in growing fiscal situations have more members who are opposed to clergywomen than do churches experiencing financial declines.

It is important to note also that wherever a congregational characteristic that reflected on the organizational health of the church was found to be associated with differences in receptivity, the members of the healthier congregations were the more resistant. *Members of large, affluent churches tended to be opposed to women in ministry, whereas persons in small, struggling congregations tended to be in favor of clergywomen.* Perhaps, as has been observed elsewhere, the healthy churches tend to shun clergywomen because they don't "have to" consider them seriously, while the struggling congregations (seriously) consider women as pastors simply because they "have to." We shall pursue this line of reasoning in the next chapter.

Simultaneous Effects on Receptivity

We know from the analysis above that there are verifiable ways of explaining some of the variations in receptivity to women in ministry. Differences in receptivity appear to be partly indicative of general attitudes toward sex roles, partly influenced by type of religious commitment and partly a consequence of type of church. Several of the specific factors incorporated in those theories consistently correlated with the measures of receptivity when considered separately.

The next question to ask is which of the correlates turn out to be predictive when the effects of all of them are occurring simultaneously. In reality the influences do not operate separately or sequentially. When an individual is confronted with the possibility of having a woman as pastor, the person does not respond *either* on the basis of his/her education *or* age *or* religious participation *or* type of church. All of these forces (and more, of course) are operating in the person's experience simultaneously.

In this congeries of inputs, some reinforce others, while others cancel each other out. Being both female and highly educated, for example, would lead one to accept women in ministry, while being both male and theologically conservative would lead one to be opposed. However, being both male and highly educated would be indeterminate, for those attributes are associated with conflicting reactions to clergywomen.

Furthermore, reality is more complicated than even the above description. Not only do various attributes press for similar or different responses, but they also vary strength of impact. Some of the correlations in this chapter are stronger than others, indicating that the influence of some variables is probably greater than that of others. In this mix of cross-pressures, with many attributes pulling in different directions and with varying degrees of force, *which influences are the more pervasive ones?* When we consider all of the variables related to receptivity, *which ones make the most difference?*

There is an analytical procedure available for addressing this question. It is called "multiple regression" analysis (see Kerlinger, 1979: Ch. 11). Regression analysis works in roughly the following way. Figure 4.2 contains two lines, each representing a relationship between two variables. One variable is something we want to explain—a "dependent variable"—such as amount of stereotyping of clergywomen or willingness to discriminate against them. Its values (scores) are represented by the vertical axis or the left-hand edge of the graph. The other variable is one which we think will explain differences in the dependent variable—a "predictor variable"—such as amount of education or size of congregation. It is represented by the horizontal axis.

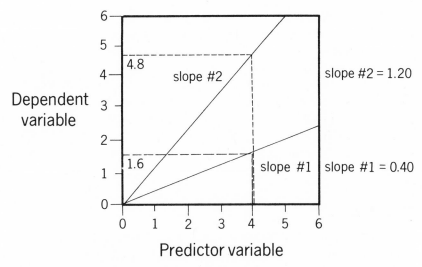

Figure 4.2 Linear regression lines of one dependent variable with two independent (predictor) variables.

The question the graph (regression analysis) answers is *how much change occurs in the dependent variable for each unit of change in the predictor variable.* For example, how much change is there in stereotyping score for each unit of change in education, or how much change is there in willingness to discriminate for each increment in size of congregation? The steepness of the "slope" line represents the answer to that question. The steeper the slope, the more the dependent variable changes with a given amount of change in the predictor variable. The steeper the slope, the more changes in the dependent variable are associated with changes in the predictor variable—the more the latter variable "predicts" the one whose variations we want to explain. When using regression analysis, the basic procedure is to compare the "slope coefficients" of several predictor variables to see which relationships are the strongest. Numerically *the larger the value of the coefficient that represents the slope, the stronger the relationship between the two variables in question.*

By way of illustration, if stereotyping score were the dependent variable and education were the predictor variable, the two slopes (and their coefficients) in Figure 4.2 would represent dramatic effects of education on stereotyping. In the case of slope # 1—which is calculated using the respondents' answers to questions such as those in the survey—a difference of four years' education would be associated with a shift of 1.6 units (of score) in stereotyping. The value of the slope coefficient would be 0.40. Slope # 2, on the other hand, represents a much stronger relationship between stereotyping and education. In this case a shift of 4 years' education is related to a difference of 4.8 in stereotyping score, with a slope coefficient of 1.20.

In *multiple* regression analysis, the values of the slope coefficients of several simultaneous predictors can be calculated. The relative size of each coefficient represents *the contribution of that predictor variable to the variations in the dependent variable when the effects of all others are taken into account.* The procedure lets us determine which variables are the more important ones.

The Laity

The data contained in Table 4.4 represent the results of a regression analysis of the members' receptivity scores and ten variables found (above) to be relatively consistent correlates of those scores. Those selected correlates include three individual characteristics—sex, age and education; four measures of religious involvement—attendance, financial contributions, devotionalism and ideology; and three church characteristics—size of congregation, budget trend and denominational alignment. Each column of the table represents the relative effects of each of those factors on a particular dimension of receptivity. Each coefficient in a given column should be read as an indication of *the effect of that predictor variable on that dimension of receptivity after the effects of the other predictor variables have been taken into account.* For example, the top figure in the left-hand column (".19") is a slope coefficient representing the effect of sex differences on stereotyping score after the influence of all the other variables (e.g., age, education, etc.) has been accounted for. Thus the figure of ".19" is an indication of the amount of difference in stereotyping score uniquely attributable to differences in sex. Finally, since these coefficients are standardized to a common base of 100, the figure of ".19" also shows that sex makes "more" difference in stereotyping score than do any other predictor variables in the analysis.

What generalizations can we make from the regression analysis shown in Table 4.4? Several patterns are relatively clear. First, two variables turn out to be *not* very important at all, i.e., financial contributions and religious ideology. They contribute little or nothing compared to the other variables. Others are quite marginal, contributing to the differences in but a few aspects of receptivity. Age contributes to stereotyping score and to preferences for men in sacramental and organizational roles—which can be important. Devotionalism is also associated with gender preferences in the same two types of roles. Budget trend appears to be a factor in perceiving women as capable of performing important functions for the congregation. Budget trend also affects preference for men in sacramental roles and willingness to discriminate against female candidates. Declining churches are the more receptive of women in ministry. Being in a dually-aligned church contributes to low stereotyping, little preference for men in sacramental and organizational roles, and little readiness to discriminate against women as candidates.

The *major* determinants of differences in receptivity—from the standpoint of *consistency* across many dimensions—are clearly church attendance, sex, education and size of congregation. Church attendance is predictive of differences in every dimension of receptivity even when the effects of other variables are taken into account. Sex, education and church size are predictive of all but one dimension. A similar pattern emerges in response to a slightly different question, i.e., which predictor variables show the *largest coefficients* (indicating the greatest impact) when the influence of others is held constant? Sex clearly makes the most difference in receptivity, followed by church size, church attendance and education. Age also tends to be a stronger determinant where it plays a part, even though it is not consistent.

The table also indicates that some *dimensions* of receptivity are more amenable than others to explanation by these variables. Members' preferences for men in sacramental roles are related to more of these influences than any other dimension. Preferences for men in organizational roles are related to more of these influences than any other dimension. Preferences for men in organizational roles are related to almost as many, followed by amount of stereotyping, willingness to discriminate and then the other dimensions. When we modify this question and ask which dimensions are influenced the *strongest,* the picture changes a bit. This set of variables influences preferences for men in organizational roles the most strongly. Tendency to stereotype is explained by these variables almost as well. Preferences for men in subordinate roles and willingness to discriminate are accounted for the least. Accordingly, *the theories underlying the analysis are the most applicable to preferences for men in organizational roles and*

TABLE 4.4 MULTIPLE REGRESSION COEFFICIENTS (BETA) OF RECEPTIVITY SCORES WITH SELECTED CORRELATES

Laity correlates	Stereotyping score	Can do for me	Can do for church	Sacramental score	Organizational score	Subordinate score	Willing to discriminate
sex	.19	.22	.15	.08	.20	.08	—*
age	.15	—	—	.08	.15	—	—
education	.10	.08	—	.13	.09	.07	.09
church attendance	.06	.09	.08	.09	.13	.08	.09
financial contributions	—*	—	—	—	—	—	—
say grace	—	—	—	.08	.07	—	—
ideology	—	—	—	—	—	—	.08
church size	-.09	-.10	-.11	-.07	-.14	-.10	—
budget trend	—	—	-.06	-.07	—	—	-.07
dually aligned	.05	—	—	.06	.06	—	.07
R^2	.09	.08	.06	.06	.12	.03	.04

Clergy correlates	Family stereo	Job role stereo	Temperament	Can do for me	Can do for church	General preference	Subordinate preference	Willing to discriminate
marital status	—*	—	—	—	—	—	—	—
age	.19	.24	.18	.07	—	.17	—	.07
budget trend	-.09	-.08	-.10	—	-.10	-.14	-.08	-.08
say grace	.14	.10	.13	.09	.10	.14	.08	.12
R^2	.07	.08	.07	.02	.03	.08	.02	.03

*indicates a statistically non-significant coefficient

to tendencies to stereotype. The theories are least useful for explaining differences in preferences for men in subordinate roles and in relative willingness to discriminate against female candidates for pastoral positions.

The Clergy

The lower portion of Table 4.4 contains the results of a regression analysis of selected correlates of receptivity among the clergy. Fewer variables were significantly related to receptivity among the clergy than the laity. In the case of the clergy, the predictor variables incorporated in the regression analysis were age, marital status, devotionalism and budget trend.

A few patterns are evident in the results. First, marital status turns out to be of little predictive value in comparison to the other three variables. Whatever effect marital status seemed to have on receptivity is clearly overshadowed by other factors. Second, in terms of *consistency,* devotionalism is more predictive of receptivity than is either of other two remaining items. The more clergy practice devotional prayer at meal time, the more they are opposed to women in ministry. The correlate which turns out to have the *strongest* set of coefficients is age. While age is unrelated to two aspects of receptivity—performing church functions and preferences for men in subordinate roles—age is more strongly predictive of stereotyping and general preferences for men in clergy roles than is any other variable.

As was the case with the lay members responses, some dimensions of receptivity are more susceptible to explanation with these theoretical approaches than are others. Willingness to discriminate and perceiving women as capable of performing important functions are explained relatively little by these theories. General preferences for men in clergy roles and tendencies to stereotype clergywomen, on the other hand, are explained as functions of these factors.

Summary: Correlates of Receptivity

Having observed wide variations in receptivity to women in ministry among lay members and clergy, we sought explanations of those differences. Why are some people in favor of having clergywomen serve their churches while others are opposed? To address that question, we looked to three theoretical approaches, i.e., that prejudice against clergywomen is: a feature of sexism in general, a consequence of persons' religious commitments and a derivative of the type of church in which they were involved.

Each of these theories successfully accounted for some of the differences in receptivity but by no means all of them. There was evidence that level of receptivity/resistance is partly a matter of more general inclinations to either favor or oppose changes in sex roles, primarily among the laity rather than the clergy. The variables that constitute correlates of sexism in other research were also found to be correlates of attitudes toward women in ministry—age, sex, education and marital status.

The second theory also received partial support. Especially among the laity, the more the members were traditionally involved in the religious system, the more they tended to oppose women in ministry. This pattern was quite consistent across various dimensions of religiosity. It involved members' religious ideology, ritual participation, financial contributions and practice of devotionalism. Among the clergy devotionalism was the only consistent predictor of receptivity.

The third approach also successfully explained differences in receptivity. Especially among the lay members again, the larger and more affluent the church to which the person belonged, the more likely that member was to be opposed to women in ministry.

The results of multiple regression analysis provided additional insights into the effects of these variables on receptivity. Three points may be noted here. First, some variables turn out to be more predictive of differences in receptivity than others. For the lay members, the strongest predictor was sex. With the influence of all other variables held constant, being male or female made more difference in receptivity than did the other influences. Among the clergy, the most important predictor was age. Second, the factors that predicted differences in every dimension of receptivity for both lay and ordained respondents were religiosity variables. How frequently lay members attended church affected every dimension of their receptivity, and how often clergy engaged in prayer at meals was a determinant of every dimension of clergy receptivity. The more one is involved in traditional ritual behavior, the more one tends to be opposed to women in ministry.

Finally, some dimensions of receptivity/resistance are most susceptible to these explanatory factors than others. The three theories appear to be most applicable to differences in tendency to stereotype clergywomen and in preferences for men in clergy roles, especially roles dealing with the organizational functioning of the church. Preferences for men in subordinate roles, willingness to discriminate and perceptions of women as incapable of performing ministerial roles adequately were less amenable to these explanations.

Some of these factors that influence persons' receptivity appear to involve a common thread—involvement in and concern for the viability of the local congregation. Such concern may be a major determinant of the fate of women seeking to enter this traditional realm of men. We look into this possibility systematically in the next chapter.

Suggestions for Additional Reading

Babbie, Earl R.
  1979 *The Practice of Social Research* (2nd. ed.). Belmont, California: Wadsworth Publishing Co.

  A widely used general text in social science research methods. Chapter 18 contains a basic introduction to statistical procedures used in this chapter—measuring relationships with correlation coefficients and testing their statistical significance. The basic logic of multiple regression is discussed in Chapter 19.

Basow, Susan A.
  1980 *Sex-Role Stereotypes: Traditions and Alternatives.* Monterey, California: Brooks/Cole Publishing Co.

  A review of the literature dealing with sex-role stereotyping. Covers theories of stereotyping behavior. Includes discussions of the sources of stereotypes and their consequences. A chapter is devoted to the consequences of stereotypes in the world of work.

Chalfant, H. Paul, Robert Beckley and C. Eddie Palmer
  1981 *Religion in Contemporary Society.* Sherman Oaks, California: Alfred Publishing Co.

  A general introduction to the sociology of religion. Contains a chapter dealing with types of religious groups in American society. Also contains a discussion of the effects of social stratification on religious belief and behavior. Some brief treatment of women in ministry.

Kerlinger, Fred N.
1979 *Behavioral Research: A Conceptual Approach.* New York: Holt, Rinehart and Winston.

A non-technical treatment of issues and methods in social science research. Chapter 5 explains procedures for dealing with "relations" between variables. Chapter 11 presents a clear and concise explanation of multiple regression techniques—again, a good treatment for someone who does not want to know a great deal about it.

Stark, Rodney and Charles Y. Glock
1970 *American Piety: The Nature of Religious Commitment* (vol. 1). Berkeley, California: University of California Press.

A classic study of patterns of religious involvement in the United States. Contains a pioneering exploration of the "dimensions" of relgious commitment, a treatment which led to the more recent flurry of activity in relation to those issues.

Tavris, Carol, and Carole Offir
1977 *The Longest War: Sex Differences in Perspective.* New York: Harcourt, Brace, Jovanovich.

A study of differences between the sexes, comparing the modes by which a variety of disciplines seek to document and explain such differences. The book assumes the existence of misogyny. Indicates how social, cultural and psychological factors contribute to the kinds of attitudes we develop toward men and women.

Warren, Roland I.
1972 *The Community in America* (2nd ed.). Chicago: Rand Mcnally & Co.

A thorough discussion of the nature of "community" in America. Reviews several classic treatments of community. Focuses primarily on different types of community as they have existed historically in the United States. Explains the nature of the significant transformations communities have undergone in the 19th and 20th centuries.

CHAPTER 5

Clergywomen and Local Church Stability

There is some evidence that attitudes toward women in ministry are related to church members' concerns about the impact that female church leadership will have on their congregations. Specifically, some members are concerned that calling a woman, especially as pastor, will create enough controversy in the congregation to jeopardize its viability.

Several previous observations (above) treated this theme. Some members felt, for instance, that recruiting female church leadership would "drive the men away" and transform the church into a "feminine" institution. Some of the correlates of receptivity discussed in the previous chapter imply similar motivations. For example, the more members were personally involved in the ritual life of the congregation, the more they tended to be opposed to calling a woman as pastor. Such opposition to women as ordained church leaders was also associated with contributing money to the church, placing emphasis on the importance of evangelism and corporate worship, being indigenous to the local community (lay versus clergy) and being in a large, affluent church. What links these characteristics with tendencies to reject women in ministry rather than to accept them may be concern for the welfare of the congregration as a corporate entity in and of itself.

Churches as Organizations

The pattern is probably a manifestation of what some sociologists call the "maintenance motif" found in formal organizations (see Etzioni, 1964; Hall, 1977; and Katz and Kahn, 1970). Once an organization has been created, it nearly always develops ways of generating concern for its own maintenance. It has a "life of its own." It strives to maintain its own viability, at times to the detriment of its own participants. Certain corporate policies and/or actions will be either established or abolished "for the good of the company," for example, and the interests of individuals or entire classes of participants will be sacrificed "for the common good." The organization generates patterns of thought and action which place the value of maintaining the organizational structure itself higher than that of protecting other kinds of interest.

The maintenance dynamic also takes another form. In many organizations, issues fraught with controversy and divisiveness are either avoided altogether or approached with extreme caution lest they decimate the ranks of the participants. Eschewing dissension and schism is assumed to be beneficial for the maintenance of group loyalty and continued participation. Such assumptions often dominate the thinking of members of political parties, extended families, international organizations, fraternal groups, consortiums of many kinds—and churches. The tendency for organizations to engender concerns about organizational solidarity and to develop patterns of behavior to promote organizational maintenance seems to be universal.

This motif is especially pervasive in "expressive" organizations, i.e., groups in which social participation *per se* is the major goal. People immerse themselves in such groups not to produce some product or to tender some service. Instead, being involved is the primary purpose. Just *being in the group* is the outcome individual participants seek in the first place. *Participating in the group's activities* is its own reward. Its product is sheer enjoyment.

Examples of this kind of social participation would include playing on the community softball team, bowling in the company league, singing in the local chorale and playing cards with the neighborhood bridge club—and attending church.

By way of contrast, other groups are formed as but a means of achieving some other goal. These are called "instrumental" groups. Organizations such as General Motors exist almost entirely to produce and market manufactured goods. Service organizations like the International Red Cross exist primarily to offer humanitarian services. The New York Stock Exchange has its *raison d' etre* in providing investment services. If the extrinsic outcomes of involvement in these kinds of organizations do not follow participation in them with some level of predictability, that participation is quite likely to cease. The participation itself is not its own reward. Being in the organization *per se* is not the purpose.

The maintenance motif is present in both kinds of organizations, of course, but it is much more critical in expressive ones. The task of maintaining the viability of expressive organizations is largely a matter of retaining realistic access to people. Having people participate in the organization is both its end "product" or "service" and its means of accomplishing it. The central task is to motivate people to become involved. By definition, then, if the expressive organization attracts and motivates people to participate, it has largely succeeded. Without access to members, the organization fails. Its effectiveness is also questionable without the participants' conformity to the norms specifying what its members are expected to do as participants. The role of group member normally involves attending meetings, promoting group-morale and enhancing the enjoyment of other members. Especially in modern complex societies, having access to these human resources is not always easy, because numerous other organizations are also striving to obtain the loyalty and time of a finite supply of people and their energy.

Religious groups are not immune to these problems. Congregations and denominations are classic examples of expressive organizations. They are competing with numerous secular structures and their subcultures for the time and allegiance of people in the community (see also Hoge and Roozen, 1974). Moreover, the problems of organizational maintenance are more difficult for churches to overcome than for many secular groups. Churches are "voluntary" organizations. Virtually by definition, organizational maintenance is more difficult in voluntary organizations than in other types. Unlike work organizations and some political structures, voluntary organizations are unable to effectively coerce members into complying with norms specifying acceptable member participation. Voluntary organizations must convince and persuade members to conform to group values and to pursue group goals. Members who are not convinced or persuaded can easily withdraw their participation in favor of some other body which is presumably either more persuasive or actually able to coerce. Since there are few immediate negative consequences associated with deciding to withhold one's participation in religious groups in most communities today, in contrast with the results of avoiding other affiliations, denominations and congregations have had to be increasingly concerned with problems of maintaining adequate church participation.

In this sense, not only do religious organizations have little coercive power over their members today, but the members actually have some such power over their churches (see also Harrison, 1959). The congregations and denominations depend for their viability on members' voluntary participation. The leaders know it, and the members do too. The influence and position of church leaders are actually quite precarious, for there are narrow limits within which people can maneuver and still retain the allegiance of rank-and-file members. This issue is typically in the forefront of their thinking when making decisions about controversial issues such as civil rights, war, distribution of wealth, community health care and other issues with ethical and/or political dimensions. Make the wrong decision—the one that will eliminate members—and the flock may be lost (see also Westhues, 1976; Wood, 1970; and Wood, 1981).

Clergywomen and Organizational Viability

Unfortunately, women in ministry symbolize an issue that is charged with this potential controversy. The women-in-ministry movement participates in the broader feminist movement, representing the concept of women's liberation before the churches.

Some members fear the issue will hurt church viability (Lehman, 1981b). Just as the encroachment of contemporary feminism upon vocations in secular institutions has generated conflict—labelling, litigation, demonstrations, suspicion—the move to alter the roles of men and women in the churches has also created hard feelings there. When the General Assembly met in 1980, for example, and decided that every church in the denomination must open the ranks of lay leaders to women, many churches rebelled. Several congregations withdrew from the denomination. Some withheld financial contributions.

This negative reaction to changing sex roles is likely to be even more intense when the issue involves not lay leadership but the ordained ministry. Many members relate to the question of calling a woman as pastor as intrinsically controversial. They fear it will become an issue that will inevitably generate controversy within congregations and within the denomination. They are concerned that the result of that conflict will be erosion of membership and financial contributions. One member commented, "Many men consider religion somewhat feminine. Having a female pastor would only reinforce that notion. Many women have to go to church without their husbands for the most part (already), and they fear a woman in the pulpit would increase the problem. The knowledge that men usually control the money at home (makes me think that) they might be inclined to reduce that pledge."

Some members link the attempts women are making to enter the ministry with campaigns to get the Equal Rights Amendment ratified. Those who oppose the broader feminist push also resist the move in the church. One woman said, for example, "I am a college graduate with 36 hours past my degree . . . I am extremely opposed to ERA and *everything* (italics in original) it stands for. It is doing more to bring about the destruction of this country than anything I know. And now the very existence of this questionnaire (shows that ERA) seems to be creeping into the churches as well."

There is some evidence that the clergywomen issue has already brought about schism in a few communities. One member reported a major split in his/her church. "Our church split four years ago over the issue of ordination of women (although other liberal attitudes within the denomination were factors). About 100 went with the minister to form a new independent church, another 150 became inactive, (and) the remaining 500 have lost considerable enthusiasm; (they think that) the ordination of women is not Biblical but not to the point of leaving the local church. Most would much more readily leave the denomination.''

It is a fear of such consequences that led one pastor to say, ''Probably the most stupid thing the UPCUSA has done is to force the issue in Overture L (on women as lay leaders). It is bowing to a pressure group and giving in like this that is apt to split the church. Like the liberalism of the '60's and '70's, the proponents don't give a damn what happens as long as they get their way. In a letter to (the) Chairman of the Council on Women and the Church, I said, 'I realize my feelings make little difference . . . , but you gals go ahead, and after you have what you want and have driven home your point, and all the men are out of the Church, congratulate yourselves; you've won—you've been able to accomplish (your goal) regardless of the rules of the denomination or the ethical implications of getting your own way . . . Keep it up, stick with it . . . , and you will be stuck with it. May God in all Her Glory bless all of you. Have pity on the poor emasculari'.''

However, these sentiments are not shared by everyone by any means. There are some members who think that women in ministry will have the opposite effects—will bolster church viability. Said one person, ''I would expect to see a 15–20% increase in members' participation and financial contributions as a result of having a woman pastor.''

A significant variant in the perceptions of the situation is the position that there may be conflict over the issue of women in ministry, but that such controversy is alright. An elder stated, ''Women have been discriminated against, but that is changing. There are those who have real trouble with this—e.g., the (name) Presbytery. I say let the conflict come and then let's get on with other things.'' Another elder asserted that the innovation would not necessarily even result in conflict. ''I believe in women's rights in a moderate way as most of our congregation does to my knowledge. I think only the radical thinkers pro and con equal rights would cause any great conflict in this matter. . . . I will say that to have a woman pastor would cause some deep thought and prayer for us, but not necessarily opposition."

A third way of viewing the potential for conflict over women in ministry is to perceive it as a proverbial "red herring." A number of people have argued that the issue may be intrinsically important to some—even threatening—but the way individuals and congregations have reacted to it with such alarm may also be misleading. The real problem is an underlying discontent with a series of "liberal" policy decisions the UPCUSA has taken, not just women in ministry *per se*. The clergywomen controversy is possibly but a symptom of broader underlying divisions in the house. One pastor put it this way, "The current controversy regarding service of women in the church is to split the church, USA and US. Had this (issue) not been handy to use, another excuse probably would have been invented." Some potential shift in the denomination may be already apparent. The issue of women in ministry is but a catalyst for getting it out into the open according to this way of thinking.

Because women in ministry represent an issue that is charged with potential controversy, the "clergywoman problem" is a matter requiring the use of some degree of discretion by church leaders and members who are particularly concerned about the organizational health of their congregations. From the point of view of organizational interests alone, many leaders wish that the issue had never come up, for it is difficult to balance the obvious ethical dimensions of the women-in-ministry movement with the organizational constraints associated with voluntary organizations. Nevertheless, seminary enrollments and denominational policy indicate that clergywomen are in fact on the scene. They cannot be "wished away." The members must adapt. How are they handling these conflicts? Does concern about these organizational problems influence the levels of receptivity/resistance of members who are grappling with them? The analysis of the survey data suggests that indeed it does.

Expecting Negative Reactions by Others

One approach to gauging the effect of possible conflict on attitudes to women in ministry is to determine members' perceptions of what other people in their congregation would do if the issue came up. Do they think the prospect of having a female pastor would make any difference to others in their church? How do they think others would handle the idea?

With this approach in mind, we asked the members a number of questions about how others in their congregation would respond to a woman as a candidate for the pastorate of their church. The questions dealt with both general and specific consequences. The first question simply asked, "If a Pastor Nominating Committee in your church recommended a woman, do you think it would create tension or conflict within the congregation?" The percentage of lay members and clergy who answered positively is shown in Table 5.1. Nearly two thirds of both lay members and clergy answered affirmatively. They perceive a woman's candidacy as likely to create tension.

TABLE 5.1   MEMBERS' PRECEPTIONS OF OTHERS' REACTIONS TO WOMEN IN MINISTRY

	Percentage perceiving problems		
	Lay members	Clergy	Correlation
recommendation of woman would create tension	65	66	—*
recommendation of woman would make others stay home from church	71	61	.21
recommendation of woman would make others reduce financial contributions	63	54	.18
others would be alienated by attempt to change language	86	85	—*

*indicates a statistically non-significant correlation

The second question was more specific. It asked, "If a Pastor Nominating Committee recommended a woman, would you expect some members of your congregation to reduce their church participation?" Similar numbers responded affirmatively to this item, but in this case there were significant differences between the responses of lay persons and the clergy. About 71 percent of the lay members said "yes," a woman's candidacy would make some people stay home from church. Among the clergy the figure was 61 percent. The threat of reduced numbers is a reality for more of the laity than the clergy.

A similar pattern resulted in response to the third question, "If a Pastor Nominating Committee recommended a woman, would you expect some members of your congregation to reduce their financial contributions?" Nearly two-thirds of the lay members and slightly over one-half of the clergy thought this would happen. Some people would expect others to withhold their monetary gifts if it looked like a woman pastor were coming aboard. *According to all three indicators, the members thought others in their congregations would react negatively and predictably to a search committee's recommendation of a woman as their pastor.*

Another approach to the possibility that clergywomen are viewed as sources of controversy, and thus as possible threats to the maintenance of local church viability, is to inquire about members' reactions to the language issue. Participants in the feminist movement within the churches, not unlike their counterparts in the movement in the larger society, have placed a great deal of emphasis on the problem of sexist language in religious literature and liturgy. The basic complaint is that Biblical translations, systematic theology, folk theology, congregational recitations, ritualized prayers, hymns, church school literature and many other items are replete with needless and often inaccurate references to "man" and other masculine images to the exclusion and derrogation of "woman" and feminine images (see Ruether, 1974; Stendahl, 1966; and Russell, 1976). This theme currently constitutes a significant element in the subculture and curriculum of theological seminaries both in scope and intensity. In the recent past it has been a dominant rallying point for women's support groups and coalitions on seminary campuses. It has also been a virtual "litmus test" for a person's sentiments either for or against the women's movement in the churches (as in the larger society).

The desire to implement inclusive language in church life has become so commonplace in circles of clergywomen that those who subscribe to the idea sometimes lose sight of the fact that this preference remains unique to their circle of participants and supporters. The need to change sexist religious symbols is still a very new idea to the vast majority of laypersons in the churches. The theological shifts that non-sexist language imply still surprise members not in the movement, and the typical response to initial confrontation with inclusive language as an issue continues to involve a sense of being threatened.

Accordingly, it is necessary to ask whether the issue of sexist language is related to the members' levels of receptivity to clergywomen. Is the issue a basis for resistance to women in ministry? As it has been a symbol of "right thinking" to participants in the women-in-ministry movement, is it also a symbol of "feminist belligerency" to members who are at best marginal to the movement? How do laypersons and other clergy respond to clergywomen's efforts to make the language of the church sexually inclusive?

In this study we were limited to two questions about sexist language. The first asked, "There are ministers and laypersons today who question the necessity or desirability of using the traditional male language to refer to God. Do you think we should change this language or keep it as it is?" The patterns of preference among lay members is clear. About 95 percent of the lay members indicated a preference for the status quo. The clergy, apparently being more in touch with the issues, tend to be more open to the idea of change, for among them only 55 percent preferred to avoid linguistic reinterpretations.

The second question dealing with the linguistic challenges is the more critical one, for it deals with perceptions of how others would react to pressures to do away with sexually exclusive language. This question asked, "To what extent do you feel that a woman minister who openly questioned the traditional male language about God would be likely to alienate members of her congregation? Do you think that a woman acting this way would 'definitely alienate,' 'probably alienate,' 'probably not alienate' or 'definitely not alienate'?" About 85 percent of both lay members and clergy answered that such linguistic challenges would alienate their congregations either "definitely" or "probably."

Nearly all of the rank-and-file members, along with about half of the clergy, personally prefer not to depart from traditional sexist patterns of language in church liturgy and literature. Perhaps more significantly, nearly as many lay members and an equal proportion of the clergy perceive direct challenges to religious language as a threat to the relationships between minister and people—a source of controversy and conflict. One of the most important components of the women-in-ministry movement has the clear potential of disrupting the harmony of church life. Most proponents of the change no doubt would respond that such reactions are neither new nor surprising and that they should not dissuade anyone from pressing for sexually more inclusive language. By contrast most members probably would question whether the linguistic alterations are important enough to risk intra-church conflict and the reductions in church rolls and budgets that typically accompany it.

Individual Predispositions to Worry

This brings us to yet a third approach to the issue of women in ministry as a potential threat to church viability, i.e., the extent to which individual members differ in their personal predispositions to be concerned about harmony in the congregation. Just as people differ in their church participation, they probably also differ in the degree to which they pay attention to church solidarity. To some members the congregation is an important reference group (see Newcomb, 1965). They feel personally satisfied or dissatisfied as they perceive their church succeeding or failing respectively. They identify with the congregation and view a wide variety of issues from the perspective of their potential impact on the church community. Other members, on the other hand, are much more casual about their identification with the church. They can "take it or leave it," and they do not particularly experience its collective achievements or defeats personally. They do not evaluate issues from the standpoint of their possible impact on the church. It is not very much of a reference group for them. The welfare of the congregation is more important to some members than it is to others.

Assuming that such differences do exist among individual members, a point we shall document below, we may ask whether variations such as this are predictive of members' receptivity to women in ministry. It is plausible that members with general tendencies to identify with the church and to be concerned about its welfare will be more likely to manifest hesitancy about considering clergywomen for pastoral positions than are those for whom the church generally matters less. Since many members view clergywomen's candidacy as relatively controversial, one would expect more members who are generally concerned about the organizational consequences of controversy to oppose the introduction of such conflict into the life of the church than would those who have fewer such concerns.

To measure the extent to which members are concerned about intra-church conflict and its consequences, we asked six questions. The items are listed in Table 5.2. The survey asked the respondents to indicate the extent to which each statement depicts a characteristic which resembled them personally. The response categories were: "very much like me," "somewhat like me," "somewhat *un*like me" and "not at all like me." One-half of the questions were phrased positively, and the other half were worded negatively, in an effort to avoid a "response set," i.e., to elude a simple pattern of either agreeing or disagreeing in general, regardless of the content of the question.

The patterns of response in Table 5.2 indicate that individuals do differ in these ways. The most consensus appears on the last item, i.e., the one dealing with "morally right decisions." More than nine members in ten said that trait resembled them. There was very little such agreement in response to the other questions.

The table also indicates that lay members differ from clergy in the extent to which these traits are seen as characterizing themselves. There are significant linear differences on all items but the first one. Clergy tend to be more willing than lay members to risk a church fight, to let disgruntled members go their way and to stand up for moral principle. Lay members are more inclined than clergy to be concerned that church conflict will result in some members' staying home from church and withholding financial contributions. *In general lay members tend to recoil from controversy more than do clergy.*

We also performed a factor analysis (see Kerlinger, Ch. 12) as a check on the homogeneity of the set of questions. The results are shown in Table 5.3. They indicate that our efforts to avoid a response set by having both positively and negatively worded items succeeded even more than we had planned. Not only was there no apparent general disposition to answer all questions in the same way, but the sets of positively and negatively worded questions turned out to be measuring *different concepts.*

The negatively worded questions clearly loaded on the first factor to form one cluster, and the positively worded items loaded on the second factor to form another. The negatively worded items appear to have more face validity than the positively worded ones as measures of the concept "disposition to be concerned about church viability." Accordingly, we combined the items loading on factor #1 into a composite index of concern over viability. Each respondent received a "viability concern score" based on his/her answers to these questions. The scoring awarded three points for each answer of "very much like me," two points for "somewhat like me" and one point for "somewhat *un*like me." Zero points were added for answers of "not at all like me."

The items which were worded positively, upon closer examination, appear to indicate differences in a general "willingness to risk conflict" in the congregation. Rather than the "concern" measured by the negative items, they gauge differences in "risk taking." So we combined the positively worded items into an index also, this being a composite measure of "willingness to risk conflict." The items were combined and scored in the same manner as with the negative items above.

We correlated (see Babbie, 1983: pp. 408–414) the scores on these two indexes as a final check on the extent to which they were measuring different concepts. The result supported the interpretation that they are distinct. The value of the coefficient in this case was but .054, and a correlation this low was not statistically significant (see Babbie, 1983: pp. 414–427). Evidently there is little relationship between the extent to which church members generally worry about the organizational viability of their local church and the extent to which they are prepared to risk conflict when basic principles are at stake.

The distribution of the scores on these two indexes are contained in Table 5.4. The scores on the index of "concern over viability" tend slightly to be toward the low end, although there are significant numbers across the entire continuum. The median score of both the lay members and the clergy is "4," but the correlation indicates a very slight tendency for lay members to have higher scores than clergy. Predispositions to worry about local church viability is slightly more characteristic of the laity than the clergy.

The distribution of scores on the "willingness to risk conflict" index tend to cluster toward the high end of the continuum. The

TABLE 5.2 LAY MEMBERS' AND CLERGY'S CONCERNS ABOUT INTRA-CHURCH CONTROVERSY (percent)

From time to time, controversial events and decisions take place that intrude upon the time and energies of a local congregation —events such as war and civil rights challenges and the policies created to deal with such issues. Thinking of your role in your own congregation, to what extent does each of the following statements characterize you personally?

	Lay members				Clergy				
	Very much like me	Somewhat like me	Somewhat unlike me	Not at all like me	Very much like me	Somewhat like me	Somewhat unlike me	Not at all like me	Correlation
I worry about my church becoming split over controversial issues.	14	35	21	30	11	36	29	25	—*
I am usually willing to risk a church fight if the issues are important.	28	43	16	13	34	48	14	4	.21
I am concerned that heated discussions of controversial matters will make some people stay away from church.	21	41	21	18	10	46	29	15	−.12
I am satisfied that the church is better off without people who would pull out if things don't go their way.	19	32	24	25	16	37	30	17	.05

I fear that dwelling on controversial issues might hurt our church's budget.	12	33	28	27	6	35	36	24	−.05
I am convinced that making the morally right decision is more important than avoiding conflict in the congregation.	56	35	6	4	60	35	5	1	.09

*indicates a statistically non-significant coefficient.

TABLE 5.3 FACTOR ANALYSIS OF QUESTIONS MEASURING CONCERN OVER INTRA-CHURCH CONFLICT

	Lay members		Clergy	
	Factor 1	Factor 2	Factor 1	Factor 2
worry about church split	.61	.16	.61	−.03
concerned about heated discussion	.75	.09	.73	−.13
fear about controversial issues	.63	.18	.61	−.17
willing to risk a church fight	.12	.64	−.03	.67
church better off without pull-outs	.25	.36	−.06	.20
morally right decision more important	.09	.73	−.10	.58

median score of the lay members was about "6," while that of the clergy was closer to "7." Thus more clergy than laity show a high willingness to risk local church conflict. The correlation of ".17" indicates the same thing.

By way of summary, the patterns of response to the questions discussed to this point support the following generalizations: (1) significant numbers of both laity and clergy perceive internal strife for their congregation in response to the recommendation that a woman be called as pastor, (2) even greater numbers of lay members and clergy think that if a clergywoman were to press the language issue in their congregation, she would become alienated from the members, and (3) significant numbers of lay members and clergy are concerned "in general" about local church viability in the face of controversy, although most of them appear willing to risk intra-church conflict if the situation demands it. In short, the issue of church viability is important to most members, and it is possible, in their opinion, that the introduction of a clergywoman into the life of their congregation could jeopardize the viability.

Correlations With Measures of Receptivity

If these issues are associated with differences in receptivity to women in ministry, then the measures of level of concern should be related to the indicators of receptivity to clergywomen. Is this so?

The results are clear and virtually unequivocal. *The more members perceive that the introduction of clergywomen into the life of their congregation will create tension there, the more they tend to be opposed to women in ministry.* The results of comparing the above measures to the indicators of receptivity to women in ministry are contained in Table 5.5. The most general pattern in the table is one that indicates correlations between every approach to the issue of church viability and every dimension of receptivity.

The more members think that recommendations of clergywomen as pastor will create tension in the congregation, result in some members staying home from church and withholding their financial contributions, the more they also tend to stereotype

TABLE 5.4 DISTRIBUTION OF SCORES ON INDEXES OF "CONCERN OVER VIABILITY" AND "WILLINGNESS TO RISK CONFLICT"

CONCERN OVER VIABILITY

		low concern 0	1	2	3	4	5	6	7	high concern 8	9
laity	score	0	1	2	3	4	5	6	7	8	9
	number	159	106	172	200	249	266	242	140	86	51
	(percent)	(10)	(6)	(10)	(12)	(15)	(16)	(15)	(8)	(5)	(3)
clergy	score	low concern 0	1	2	3	4	5	6	7	high concern 8	9
	number	78	74	108	169	177	191	185	58	27	21
	(percent)	(7)	(7)	(10)	(16)	(16)	(18)	(17)	(5)	(3)	(2)

correlation = − .04

WILLING TO RISK CONFLICT

		low willingness 0	1	2	3	4	5	6	7	high willingness 8	9
laity	score	0	1	2	3	4	5	6	7	8	9
	number	37	29	65	107	180	325	365	252	220	97
	(percent)	(2)	(2)	(4)	(6)	(11)	(19)	(22)	(15)	(13)	(6)
clergy	score	low willingness 0	1	2	3	4	5	6	7	high willingness 8	9
	number	6	5	17	32	101	202	268	208	171	79
	(percent)	(1)	(1)	(2)	(3)	(9)	(19)	(25)	(19)	(16)	(7)

correlation = .17

TABLE 5.5   CORRELATIONS BETWEEN RECEPTIVITY AND PERCEIVED RESPONSES OF OTHERS: BY SUB-POPULATION

LAY MEMBERS	Create tension	Stay home	Reduce contributions	Resent language	Worry	Risk
stereotyping	.29	ns	.27	.27	.15	ns
can do for me	.68	.58	.52	.54	.21	-.11
can do for church	.70	.60	.56	.52	.15	-.11
sacramental	ns	ns	.35	.29	.13	-.09
organizational	.40	ns	ns	.27	.15	-.08
subordinate	.56	.42	.26	.38	ns	ns
willingness to discriminate	.35	.21	.27	.30	.10	-.14

CLERGY	Create tension	Stay home	Reduce contributions	Resent language	Worry	Risk
family stereotyping	.30	.18	.22	.41	.21	-.05
job role stereotyping	.36	.25	.22	.39	.22	-.10
temperament stereotyping	.33	.19	.19	.42	.21	-.15
can do for me	.63	.47	.43	.74	.22	ns
can do for church	.72	.50	.51	.74	.19	-.14
general preference	.42	.31	.30	.48	.20	-.16
subordinate	.41	.18	.16	.53	.18	-.13
willingness to discriminate	.24	.31	.22	.53	.17	-.21

*indicates a statistically non-significant correlation.

clergywomen, perceive that women cannot perform important clergy functions, prefer men in pastoral roles and are willing to discriminate against female candidates. The perception of female candidates generally creating tension tends slightly to be the strongest correlate, and the idea that some members will stay home from church appears to be the weakest.

It is interesting to note that among the lay members these concerns about the impact of female candidates are associated *least* with people's preferences for men in clergy roles. The fear that a clergywoman would lead members to reduce their church participation is unrelated to their preferences for men in either sacramental or organizational roles—two important indicators. It is not clear what this exception might imply other than the idea that there are limits on the extent to which organizational concerns are translated into resistance to women in ministry. However, no such pattern appears among the clergy responses, wherein the relationships are consistent across all dimensions.

The role of the language issue is also consistently related to differences in receptivity. The more members perceive others in their congregation as being alienated by a clergywoman's openly questionning traditional male-God language, the more they tend to be opposed to women in ministry. This pattern applies to both lay members and clergy. Apparently the approach one takes to the language issue can be critical in determining the type of response one gets.

There are also clear differences in the extent to which the above concerns predict attitudes to women in ministry and the effect of members' general predispositions about church viability on those attitudes. Differences in general tendencies to worry about church viability and general willingness to risk conflict in the congregation are related to differences in receptivity, but the correlations between these sets of variables are much weaker than those shown elsewhere in the table. Nevertheless, while the correlations are relatively weak, they are also rather consistent. Among both lay members and clergy, the more people are concerned about the impact of conflict on their congregation, the more they are opposed to women in ministry. The *less* they are willing to risk conflict in their congregation, the more they resist having women in clergy roles.

Simultaneous Effects on Receptivity

As in the previous chapter, we next want to determine which of these factors are the more important ones in their effects on levels of receptivity. For most members all of these considerations operate simultaneously as they consider the possibility of having a woman serve their congregation as pastor. At the same time that people ponder the impact of a woman's candidacy on others' church participation or financial contributions, for example, they already have certain predispositions to be more or less concerned about church viability and to be willing to take risks. All of these factors operate concurrently to influence the way members react. Which variables make the most difference when the influence of all others is taken into account?

We subjected the set of "viability" factors to a multiple regression analysis (see Kerlinger, 1979: Ch. 11), to determine which ones were the better predictors of receptivity. The results of that regression analysis are contained in Table 5.6. Several patterns are worth noting. First, the factor that most consistently predicts levels of receptivity among both lay members and clergy is the issue of sexist language. The more members perceive that a clergywoman's pressing the language issue will alienate the congregation, the more likely they are to manifest high levels of resistance to women in ministry, even with the influence of the other concerns taken into account. The language issue is one of two consistent predictors among the laity and the only consistent one among the clergy.

Second, the predictiveness of the other two specific areas of possible concern—declines in church attendance and budget—turns out to be marginal. When the effects of other factors are taken into account, concerns about participation and contributions specifically have relatively little explanatory power. Among the clergy they become almost irrelevant in comparison to the other areas of concern.

Especially among the lay members, the *general* concern about a woman's candidacy creating tension or conflict in the congregation remains as predictive as the language issue. This general concern about internal stress makes more difference than do the specific concerns about reduced participation and contributions. Evidently members' anticipations of specific reactions to a female candidate have less impact on their receptivity to women in ministry than does the more *general* idea of unsettling whatever good will exists in the congregation.

TABLE 5.6 MULTIPLE REGRESSION COEFFICIENTS (BETA) OF RECEPTIVITY SCORES WITH INDICATORS OF CONCERNS FOR CHURCH VIABILITY

LAY MEMBERS	Stereotyping score	Can do for me	Can do for church	Sacramental score	Organizational score	Subordinate score	Will discriminate
language alienates	.14	.15	.16	.12	.12	.10	.13
create tension	.12	.14	.15	.20	.19	.11	.13
will stay home	—*	—	—	—	.08	—	.08
reduce $	.08	—	.09	.08	—	—	.13
worry	-.12	-.08	-.05	-.07	-.11	—	-.06
will risk	.06	.08	.10	.11	.12	—	.12
R²	.11	.09	.11	.13	.15	.04	.08

CLERGY	Family stereotyping score	Job role score	Woman's temperament	Can do for me	Can do for church	General preference	Subordinate score	Will discriminate
language alienates	.26	.16	.22	.23	.23	.29	.15	.29
create tension	.08	.08	.09	—	.09	.11	—	—
will stay home	—*	—	—	—	—	—	—	.14
reduce $	.10	—	—	—	—	—	—	—
worry	-.15	-.11	-.10	—	—	-.08	—	—
will risk	—	—	.07	—	—	.08	—	.12
R²	.14	.07	.10	.09	.10	.18	.03	.14

For the lay persons in the study, differences in predispositions either to worry about church viability or to take risks involving church conflict were predictive of all dimensions of receptivity except for the attitudes toward subordinate church positions. However, the magnitude of the coefficients involving these dispositions tends to be somewhat smaller than does that of the coefficients associated with the language issue or general tension. The predispositions were even less consistently predictive of receptivity among the clergy.

Finally, shifting the focus of attention from the predictors to the dimensions of receptivity, some dimensions are explained by these kinds of concern better than others. Among the laity the dimension which the viability concerns explain best is preferences for men in organizational roles. For the clergy it is the general preferences dimension. Each of these dimensions contains the question of their preferences for men specifically in the role of pastor, which may be the factor tying them together in this fashion. Conversely, the dimension explained least well by the viability items is preferences for men in subordinate church roles, positions which evidently are non-threatening, with women having served in them for a number of years already.

Interaction Effects on Receptivity

There is yet another way in which the simultaneous effects of various correlates may operate on levels of receptivity toward women in ministry. Some factors reinforce each other's effects on members' attitudes, while others cancel out each other's impact. For example, if a person is very concerned about the disruptive consequences of conflict in the congregation—worries about it and seeks to avoid it—the perception that a clergywoman may create tensions in the congregation is important, and it promotes negative attitudes toward women in ministry. On the other hand, if the person does not particularly care whether the church experiences cleavages, then the perception that a clergywoman might be repugnant to some members is neither likely to be threatening nor to influence the individual's attitude toward women in ministry. In this situation it is the *interaction* (see Kerlinger, 1979: Ch. 7) of concern about church conflict and perceptions of the impact of a woman's candidacy that together influence attitudes.

There is some evidence that such dynamics were affecting the lay members in the study. Focusing on members' preferences for a man specifically as pastor, we sought to determine whether certain predictor variables influenced those preferences primarily in interaction with each other. The correlates we inquired about were: (1) perceiving that a woman's candidacy would create tension in the congregation, (2) degree of overt involvement in church life as revealed in church participation, (3) tendency to worry about church viability in general, and (4) willingness to risk conflict in the church.

The pattern of interaction among these factors ought to be such that members prefer a man as pastor if:

1. they perceive that considering a female candidate for the pastorate will create tension, *and:*
   a. they are personally highly involved in the church,
   b. they tend to worry about local church viability, or
   c. they are relatively unwilling to risk conflict in the church.
2. they are personally highly involved in the church, *and:*
   a. they perceive that considering a female candidate for the pastorate will create tension,
   b. they tend to worry about local church viability, or
   c. they are relatively unwilling to risk conflict in the church.

Personal involvement, tendency to worry about the church and willingness to risk controversy are conditions under which perceiving a woman as creating tension becomes translated into resistance to women in ministry. Similarly, thinking that others will react negatively to a female candidate, tendency to worry about such controversy and willingness to risk conflict are conditions under which differences in church involvement are likely to affect attitudes toward clergywomen.

The data in Table 5.7 indicate that interaction effects such as these did occur. Factors influencing receptivity do not operate in isolation from each other, but instead they either enhance or depress the influence of other correlates and are so influenced by others. Specifically the table indicates that *perceiving a female candidate as creating tension in the church is more closely associated with preferences for a man as pastor if the member also is highly involved in the church, is concerned about church viability or is relatively unwilling to risk conflict.* It also shows that a *high degree* of church involvement is associated with preferring a man as pastor only if the member thinks that a female candidate will create tension. The impact of church involvement on gender preferences is basically unaffected by predispositions to worry about the church or to chance congregational conflict.

TABLE 5.7 CORRELATIONS BETWEEN PREFERENCE FOR A MAN AS PASTOR AND CHURCH INVOLVEMENT AND PERCEIVED TENSION, WITH SELECTED CONTROLS (LAY MEMBERS ONLY)

perceive tension

	church involvement		controlling for: concern for viability		willingness to risk conflict	
	low	high	low	high	low	high
prefer man as pastor	.37	.64	.52	.65	.63	.52

church involvement

	perceive tension		controlling for: concern for viability		willingness to risk conflict	
	yes	no	low	high	low	high
prefer man as pastor	.29	—*	.22	.21	.21	.24

*indicates a statistically non-significant coefficient

Summary and Implications

Churches are human organizations, and as such they manifest many of the same characteristics as those found in other kinds of structures. One of these attributes of organizations that is important to churches is the need *to guard their own viability as organizations.* Churches can remain viable social entities only if they are able to maintain access to members and succeed in motivating those people to contribute their time, energies and finances. The prospect of losing these scarce resources is a serious threat to religious organizations, and they tend to develop patterns of thought and action among their members to guard against such prospects materializing.

Since church members disagree on a variety of grounds about whether women should be accepted as ordained ministers, there is the potential for intra-church conflict over the issue. Among both lay members and clergy, most members would expect controversy to develop in response to a woman's being a candidate for the pastor of their congregation. They would expect some other members to reduce their participation in church and to reduce their level of giving to underwrite the budget. An even greater majority of members would expect clergywomen who press the issue of sexually inclusive language to alienate themselves from the congregration. The women-in-ministry movement and its symbols are potentially threatening to most members, at least partly because it constitutes a possible threat to church viability.

Some members are more prone to worry about these kinds of issues than are others. They differ in the extent to which they are concerned about church viability in general. They also diverge in their willingness to accept conflict as a way of resolving issues in the congregation.

The results of comparing measures of these perceptions and predispositions with the measures of receptivity indicate that *the possibility that clergywomen may disrupt the harmony and cooperation of the congregation is related to attitudes toward women in ministry.* The more members are concerned about this issue along a variety of dimensions, the more they oppose women in ministry. In the final analysis, it appears as though concerns about *conflict in general* are more predictive of attitudes toward clergywomen than are specific fears. The possibility of alienating the congregation or of creating tension or conflict among members is more predictive of different attitudes than are specific concerns about declines in church participation or financial contributions.

Preference for a man as pastor appears most likely to result from a combination of these influences. Thinking that a clergywoman would create conflict in the church most likely results in preferences for men if the member also is highly involved in church activities, prefers to eschew conflict and tends to worry about maintaining church viability.

The significance of these patterns is underscored by the fact that *in circumstances such as these a minority of members can have significant influence on collective decisions about which path to follow—to consider a woman as one's minister or to reject the idea.* We noted in Chapters 2 and 3 that a clear minority of members were personally opposed to women in ministry. Very few engaged in stereotyping clergywomen, few preferred men in specific clergy roles, and few were willing to discriminate against female candidates outright. The majority of members manifested high levels of receptivity. *However,* an equally clear majority of members perceived the introduction of clergywomen into the life of their church as disruptive. If they then follow organizational norms to act in such a way as to protect the viability of the congregation (and denomination) as the first priority, they are likely to have little enthusiasm for seriously considering the clergywoman's candidacy. The interests of the congregation, *as they are perceived by most members,* would most likely be served by sticking with traditional male leadership. The interests of the clergywoman would be subordinated to the value of maintaining organizational viability.

Nevertheless, what members perceive as social reality does not always square with the actual realities. Lest the reader conclude at this point that churches ought not cooperate with the women-in-ministry movement because such actions might jeopardize their congregations, let the reader *read the next three chapters.* They deal with the question of what *actually* happens when a woman becomes a pastor of a church. That reality does not square with what most members expect.

Suggestions for Additional Reading

Hall, Richard H.
1982 *Organizations: Structure and Process* (3rd ed.). Englewood Cliffs, New Jersey: Prentice-Hall.

A general introduction to the study of organizations, especially large, complex structures. Includes discussions of uniquenesses of voluntary organizations and the problem of maintaining organizational viability.

Hertzler, Joyce O.
1965 *A Sociology of Language.* New York: Random House.

A thorough study of the role of language in human societies. Contains chapters dealing with the role language plays in either uniting them into groups and causes or being a divisive factor.

Hoge, Dean R. and David A. Roozen (eds.)
1979 *Understanding Church Growth and Decline, 1950–1978.* New York: Pilgrim Press.

A collection of essays dealing with the problems of accurately describing and explaining patterns of church growth and decline in the United States during the period identified in the title. Contains studies of specific denominations, some of which have grown and others which have declined. Ends with attempts to identify themes which cross denominational and situational boundaries.

Kerlinger, Fred N.
1979 *Behavioral Research: A Conceptual Approach.* New York: Holt, Rinehart, Winston.

A non-technical introduction to a variety of problems in social science research. Contains a discussion of "interaction effects" of two or more variables on a dependent variable in Chapter 7. Illustrations help explain the concept.

Turner, Ralph H.
1957 "Role Taking, Role Standpoint, and Reference Group Behavior." in Lewis A. Coser and Bernard Rosenberg (eds.). *Sociological Theory: A Book of Readings.* New York: MacMillan.

A classic statement in reference group theory. Discusses the process of taking a role associated with a reference group and viewing an issue from the perspective of that role and group. Indicates how being a member of a group can influence how one views events in the world.

CHAPTER 6

Increasing Receptivity Through Contact

There is a small church in central Massachusetts where a woman has been serving as pastor for several years. Before she assumed her responsibilities there, the congregation had been "going downhill" steadily. They had been losing members. Those who remained had become increasingly apathetic, seldom going to church and contributing barely enough money to keep the church doors open. They had had a recent series of pastors who were fresh seminary graduates and who viewed the small church as but a necessary first charge to serve until they could find a position in a larger church. Some of them were also "absentee pastors" coming to the community on weekends but living elsewhere and spending most of the rest of their time in other pursuits.

The last time their pastor resigned, they faced a crisis. At an otherwise routine search committee meeting, the denominational executive serving that area recommended that they consider calling a *woman* as their next pastor. He pressed his case hard. After the search committee went home, the word spread through the community like a brush fire driven by the wind. Within twenty-four hours, virtually every member knew what was in the offing. Their next pastor might be a woman!

Every "horror story" on record circulated through the congregation. It looked like the end. The members quickly reached a firm consensus that several key families would leave the church, those who didn't pull out would stay home from worship services, and the budget would suffer so that it wouldn't be long before the building would be boarded up tightly forever—or at least until it burned to the ground from a lightning strike or something. "You know old man Jackson will never put up with this! He'll leave the church before he'll listen to some dame squawking in the pulpit every week! And it's been his money that has kept this place alive for the last five years!"

How the executive who advocated the clergywoman was able to prevail upon that committee in such a climate still remains a mystery, but he did. They called the woman—and she wasn't even from the same denomination as the bulk of the congregation! The stigma of failing so miserably really hit them. Had they "become so bad" that they couldn't even get a man to come and serve them? Had they "sunk so low" that they "had to take a woman?" Their days were numbered.

That was the late 1970's—and the church is still functioning! Did anyone leave the congregation? Yes, as they suspected, old man Jackson pulled out and took his money with him. Another family started going to church in the next village. But the rest remained "to tough it out" as they defined the situation. At first they came to church only out of curiosity, you know. "What would a lady preacher be like, anyway?" "What would she wear?" "I bet all we'll get is a lot of 'women's lib stuff'!"

Gradually, that "lady preacher" won them over. She knew what was coming at first, but she decided to simply accept them where they were—to love them, to understand them and to try to put into practice all the best things she had learned about how to minister to them as a pastor. Or was it really so "gradually"? By the end of only one year, the atmosphere in the congregation had so changed that one wouldn't think it was the same group of people! Instead of pessimism about the inevitable folding of the church, there was planning to find ways to meet the needs of a changing community. Instead of a sense of stigma, there was a profound feeling of pride in being sufficiently venturesome and open-minded as to try something new—"much more admirable than those tradition-bound folks who still do things the same way as they always did!"

Did the church rolls and budget also do a major turn-around? No, not really. There were no miracles. But there were no mass resignations as had been predicted either. A few new families moved into the community, and they were participating in church regularly. The budget was holding its own, based not on large contributions from one or two families but on small pledges from just about everyone. It was simply a functioning congregation, dependably meeting the needs of its members. *The actual experience of working with a woman as pastor had very different results from what the members expected at the outset.*

"Well," you might say, "anyone can find a story like that. It's just an isolated case. That's not what usually happens!" Well—let us respond—that is just the issue we want to address. The evidence from another segment of the study indicates that it *is* what usually happens. *Contact with clergywomen in the role of pastor usually results in increased receptivity to women in ministry.* Not only do the horror stories not come true, but the congregations continue to function under the pastoral leadership of a woman just as well as they do under the pastoral guidance of a man.

This chapter and the two which follow describe the results of a study of the effects of contact with clergywomen in the role of pastor. From the perspective of one who has wondered about the outcome of these kinds of contacts, the results were quite encouraging. The remainder of this chapter is devoted partially to an overview of the rationale behind using contacts like this to change people's attitudes. There has been considerable study of the effects of such interaction, especially involving minority and majority groups. This section also describes the outlines of the study itself. The next two chapters focus on the results of the analysis—evidence of changes in attitude toward women in ministry and the apparent reasons for those shifts.

Sources of Attitudes

One aspect of the nature of attitudes that can make contact important is the simple fact that many of our attitudes toward a wide variety of objects—other individuals, groups, values, rules for behavior, social situations, etc.—are formed *in the absence of any contact* (see Horowitz, 1965). Most of us have never met a "Russian politician," for example, but we still tend to have rather negative attitudes toward them. We have never experienced Antarctica, but we don't think we'd like to live there. We have never personally endured human slavery, but our attitudes toward that kind of status are also clear.

Many of our attitudes come from *sources other than contact* (see Allport, 1958). One important source is our family. We pick up ideas that it is appropriate to think and feel certain ways toward many different people, groups and objects from our parents and siblings. The process begins very early, before many parents are aware of the influence they are having. The family is an important reference group, i.e., a group with which we identify and whose perspective we tend to take as our own (see Turner, 1957). We obtain an image of the world and a set of assumptions about appropriate ways of reacting to it as those concepts have been translated and interpreted by our parents. (They too, of course, got much of their orientation from their own parents.)

Another important source of attitudes is our peers. We learn about the "kids on the other block" from playmates, the neighbors' kids and other friends. From the same sources come our early notions about school teachers, the other school's team, and sex. The older we become, the more some other sources come into play—others at work, the union, the professional organization, the fraternal group, and mass media. Our conceptualizations of reality are usually filtered through these sets of collective eyes. How we feel about particular objects is usually based on second-hand opinions validated by second-hand subcultures. A major source of most of our "of-course-assumptions" about reality and how to deal with it is "what everybody knows" in one or more groups to which we belong or aspire (see Newcomb, *et al*, 1965: pp. 109–110, 145–147).

A major problem should be obvious. Quite often the prevailing attitudes toward people, groups and objects shared in human communities have little or nothing to do with reality. The impressions upon which the attitudes are based have little resemblance to the actual people, groups and objects. The source and persistence of the attitudes resides in consensus mostly.

This is the stuff of prejudice. Over time a congeries of negative perceptions of members of group emerges based on hearsay. The negative images become amplified by mistrust. They crystalize into stereotypes which feed on themselves, generate more dislike and distrust, and become commonly accepted justifications for discrimination toward members of the group in question. Yet any resemblance of these images to those other people is likely to be absent at worst and accidental at best.

Changing Attitudes Through Personal Contact

For many years social scientists have assumed that social interaction—contact—with a flesh-and-blood member of the group toward whom prejudice exists will present the prejudiced person with information about such people that doesn't jibe with what he/she already knows. This inconsistency often forces prejudiced individuals to adjust their opinions and feelings about the group in question. As a result, stereotyping diminishes, antipathies fade and instances of discrimination become less frequent. In short, contact is supposed to bring about greater acceptance of people who were formerly objects of prejudice and discrimination. This expectation is called the "contact hypothesis" (see Allport, 1958; Amir, 1969; and Schofield, 1978).

Social contact has been used in efforts to improve intergroup relations in a variety of settings—housing developments, factories, military units, etc. (see Deutsch and Collins, 1951). Sometimes this experimentation has succeeded, but in other instances it has failed. The failures indicate that a series of conditions must be present if social contact is to result in decreased prejudice (Amir, 1969). One such condition is the relative status of the people involved. A major problem with some efforts at implementing the contact principle is that the two groups in question—usually members of a dominant group and a subordinate group—were not engaged in social interaction *as equals*. Status differences were present in the structure of the interaction. The minority group, be it blacks, Orientals, Hispanics, Catholics or Jews, were structurally placed in positions of having to interact as inferiors of members of the superordinate group. Structurally the deck was stacked against them. Under such circumstances, additional factors come into play which militate against attitude change. The action in such a situation would be such as not to challenge existing stereotypes but to reinforce them. For contact to alter preexisting attitudes, it must call negative images into question. If these encounters are to reduce prejudice, it is also helpful if they are characterized by mutual interdependency, are reinforced by favorable social norms, are more personal or intimate than casual, and include high-status members of the minority group. Where most or all of these conditions exist, contact among members of conflicting groups tends to result in reductions of inter-group hostility and to engender positive shifts in attitudes toward members of each group involved (see also Petty and Cacioppo, 1981). When administered correctly, contact is a form of social engineering that can work.

Applying the Contact
Hypothesis to Clergywomen

In 1977 the Vocation Agency of the United Presbyterian Church, U.S.A., kicked off a project which involved the contact hypothesis. Designed to run for a period of five years, the project's mandate was to facilitate the placement, acceptance and support of women employed by the church. It was called the Women-in-Ministry Project (WIM). It represented a more unified and centrally orchestrated approach to the promotion of church women's interests (especially those of clergywomen) than had been taken by that denomination at any time in the past.

WIM proceeded under the guidance of a number of explicit assumptions. One such principle was the necessity for "visiblity." It was assumed that in order for church members (and denominational officials) to learn to accept women in ministry as fully qualified professionals, they would have to experience clergywomen working routinely in a variety of ministerial roles. They needed to see women as pastors, chaplains, educators and denominational office holders. They needed to hear women preaching sermons, conducting funerals, performing weddings and counselling individuals with personal problems. They needed to experience women moderating the session, planning the budget and coordinating the church staff. The assumption was that having such experiences with clergywomen would transform resistance into receptivity and would move the denomination a step closer to the day when women in ministry will be an accepted presence in the life of the denomination. WIM applied the contact hypothesis to the problem of increasing receptivity to women in ministry.

One phase of WIM established structures within which church members and clergywomen could interact as incumbents of their roles as laity and clergy. The arrangements were developed under a variety of names, but for present purposes we shall refer to them as the "Minister-at-Large Program" (MAL).

The Minister-at-Large Program involved placing seminary students and recent seminary graduates in a variety of positions in ministry to give them experience and to give church members and denominational administrators opportunity to interact with them. The students typically were placed in positions associated with Synod or Presbytery structures for a short period of time such as a summer.

The seminary graduates were attached to a Synod or Presbytery (see Office of the General Assembly, 1967) and were assigned the responsibility of serving as interim pastor in area churches whose pastors had left either permanently or temporarily. The length of time the graduates served in these churches varied. Some tenures were as short as three months, and one was as long as a year. In each case the church knew that the clergywoman had been placed there under the auspices of the Minister-at-Large Program, and they knew that she would not be able to accept any permanent employment with their church when her interim service was completed.

The placement of the seminary graduates in interim pastorates represents a primary attempt to implement the contact hypothesis. The goal was to give church members opportunities to interact with a clergywoman in the role of pastor. If the contact hypothesis is successfully applicable to women in ministry, this interaction should provide people in those congregations with positive impressions of women in ministry and should bring about a change in their attitudes toward clergywomen. After such contact, church members should perceive female ministers in less stereotyped terms, should be more willing to allow women to function in pastoral roles and should be less prepared to discriminate against women who apply for positions in their church. Ultimately the MAL program should lead those churches to install women as pastors more readily than they would have prior to their experience with a woman interim pastor.

The assumption that church members need to have contact with women in ministry in order to improve clergywomen's chances of being accepted as ordained ministers is actually rather widespread throughout the denomination. In response to the Panel questionnaire, for example, many members recommended the idea. One person said, "Don't discuss the proposition (of women in ministry) hypothetically! Send women ministers around to fill pulpits during vacations, have congregations with women ministers exchange with those having men from time to time. The reality is more acceptable than the proposition." Said another, "Since most members such as I have seldom heard a woman preach or handle a regular service, it is difficult to make a decision on how well a woman could handle the work. I would be open minded if only I had the opportunity to observe." In the minds of many, this kind of contact should be so routinized that the issue can be settled in the minds of search committee members before they conduct their search. As one person put it, "Churches and their individual members need somehow to ex-perience a woman minister before the nominating committee has to do its thing. So many of us have never experienced a woman as minister that we can't imagine or picture God's helpmate in that role. The easiest thing to do (without that experience) is vote 'NO'."

Some members see contact with clergywomen as not only necessary for enhancing their acceptance but also as sufficient for getting the job done. One pastor wrote, "The need I feel most of all is for exposure to the congregations of women who are com-petent in pastoral roles, particularly preaching. One excellent ser-mon by a woman serving as pulpit supply does more than years of pastoral efforts to promote their acceptance in ministry."

The placement of the women as interim pastors in the MAL program put them into interactional situations having most of the characteristics previously identified as necessary for bringing about reductions in negative attitudes. The clergywomen were screened so as not to reinforce stereotypes. The experiment en-joyed the positive sanctions of the national and local denomina-tional offices and thus a supportive climate reinforcing the legitimacy of the arrangement. The women were in structural positions that let them interact not merely as equals but actually as superordinates in the congregations. In each placement, the woman interim occupied the position of senior minister. In all but one situation, the role was also that of solo pastor. The women were to act in all ways as though they were the spiritual and organizational leaders of their respective congregations, and the churches were to relate to them in that role just as they would to any other (male) interim pastor. The organization and functioning of the local churches was dependent on the joint efforts of interim pastor and congregation. Thus, in terms of the factors listed above, the contact was with a high-status member of the minority (the women), it was reinforced by favorable social norms, it involved mutual interdependency, it would not reinforce stereotypes, and the interaction would be more personal than casual. Virtually all of the conditions necessary for contact to result in attitude change were present.

The Danger of Tokenism

If there is any problem with the test of the contact hypothesis using the ministers-at-large and their churches, it may be that the situation involves a phenomenon under more recent scrutiny, and that is "tokenism" (see Kanter, 1975; 1977). Under current laws governing equal employment opportunity and/or affirmative action, large secular employers feel constrained to place members of minority groups (including women) in their organizations in order to comply with anti-discrimination guidelines. The same regulations enjoin them to treat minority staff fairly in matters of salary, promotions and other perquisites. Some firms establish formal or informal quotas in order to be sure that they are conforming to the law. Once the quotas are filled, the efforts to place and reward minority group members sometimes subside, with those few whom the organization has already accepted enjoying their positions as symbols of the firm's good will. These individuals are in danger of becoming "tokens" (see also Hennig and Jardim, 1977).

The token black or token woman in a formerly all-white-male structure can be recognized by several unique characteristics of his/her actual role in the organization. Some other research (Kanter, 1975) has pointed out, first of all, that token individuals are "highly visible." Their racial or sexual uniqueness makes them stand out as clearly "different" from other persons in their segment of the organization. As a consequence of this hyper-visibility, tokens are also "overobserved" in their work and other activities in the group. Performance norms that supposedly apply to all members of the organization actually become applied to the token more stringently than to others, and the classic "double standard" comes into effect. The token has to comply with performance standards more consistently than do the typical group members, and in many instances the standards themselves become inflated for the token. Tokens often try to protect themselves from the implications of this situation in opposite ways. They may overconform and overachieve to obtain the acceptance of their peers. But the danger involved in being willing to pay such a high price for acceptance is simply that they become burned out very quickly. The other mode of adaptation to the role of token is *not* to perform up to ability. By underachieving, the token reinforces the stereotype of not really being able to do the job anyway, and the pressure of the double standard is removed.

A second characteristic of "tokens" is that their presence polarizes others in the group. The token becomes a symbol of organizational change, and this symbol becomes a basis on which other participants feel they must take sides. This situation could become a general barrier to intragroup cooperation and to a collective realization of the goals for which the group was created. A typical mode of adaptation to these pressures by other group members is to isolate the token in his/her role. This insulation is especially useful during informal moments when more personal relationships normally are evident. By excluding the token, a potential source of conflict is eliminated, and everyone can relax more easily, assured that the token's presence will not rock the boat.

It has been suggested also that the personal characteristics of tokens tend to be distorted and otherwise misperceived in order to bring them in line with existing stereotypes. This issue is related to the problem of heightened visibility. Of all of the activities of the token within the organization, actions which reinforce stereotypes (of Blacks or women) become noticed selectively, and actions which are inconsistent with traditional images are glossed over. By perceiving the token in terms of stereotypes instead of his/her actual characteristics, other members of the group have to wrestle less with the necessity of changing their view of reality. The token becomes entrapped in a stereotyped image in spite of the fact that he/she does not really resemble it personally. One way in which tokens can adapt to these pressures is to select role activities that minimize the comparison of themselves with traditional stereotyped images. For example, the female physician can specialize in pediatrics or gynecology, and the clergywoman can become known for her excellent children's stories or her unique ability to comfort people when they are ill.

The relevance of this discussion of "tokens" to the contact hypothesis is that if indeed tokenism develops within churches in the MAL program, then the placement may do little to change attitudes. Tokenism may militate against the capacity of contact to generate attitude change. If the woman interim minister becomes a token woman in the congregation, then the experience may not have the effects predicted by the rationale of the contact hypothesis.

Some people expect women interims to be treated in precisely these ways. The ranks of clergywomen constitute scarcely five percent of United Presbyterian clergy. They are a distinct minority. Their pressures on the seminaries, their campaigning in national conventions and their support for other women's issues have been covered widely in the religious press and to some extent in the secular media, so they are relatively "visible" to some members. This media image of clergywomen has led some pastors and lay members to define them in terms of radical segments of the feminist movement, perceptions virtually guaranteed to polarize some people in relation to women in ministry. Where these conditions exist, they may undercut the intentions of the MAL program and the contact may result in no attitude change at all.

Are clergywomen placed as interims in the minister-at-large program also likely to take on the role of tokens? It is certainly possible. From the very beginning of negotiations with members of a church to place a woman among them as an interim minister, the clergywoman is highly visible. Typically at least a few members are sufficiently opposed to the arrangement at the outset to threaten to withdraw from church participation, so it is easy to envision some local polarization over the matter. Once the woman interim arrives on the scene, her high visibility hardly subsides. In all likelihood she will be scrutinized more than a man would be. In order to prove herself and be accepted as a competent pastor, she probably will enjoy less room for error than a man would have in similar circumstances.

On the other hand, it is likely that the minister-at-large will be viewed as a token more in the context of the local denominational organization than in the local church. The woman pastor ought not consider the congregation the only significant local group with which she will have to work. She will also (at least temporarily) be a part of a local group of pastors and perhaps other denominational officials. While she may enjoy a status advantage within the congregation, she has reverse status in relation to this set of her peers. In that circle, she is but one minister among others, and she is the newest, least experienced and perhaps youngest minister at that. In relation to appointments associated with the MAL program—and perhaps in other circumstances as well—her arrival is considered a significant event. Before she comes, there doubtless will have been cautious and protracted negotiations between denominational representatives and participants in the local scene. Virtually everyone there is watching carefully "to see how it will work out." She is "on stage" even before she arrives. The clergywoman could easily become the token woman in this local network of colleagues.

In the local congregation, on the other hand, where she is assigned as interim pastor, she at least potentially enjoys the status of "leader." Since there is but one senior minister in the church, she has a great deal of implicit status associated with simply occupying that role. This status can be used to avoid taking on the role (and potential stigma) of the token woman. By drawing on that status, something any minister has to learn to do in order to be effective in a variety of ways, the clergywoman can have the leverage needed to avoid being devalued and isolated. She is not likely to be a token in such circumstances. To the extent that she can exploit the status associated with her position in the local congregation, she will also be creating important impressions on those in her professional peer group and minimizing tendencies for them to treat her as a token.

The Problem of
Minimal Commitment

A third problem that needs to be considered derives from the fact that interim ministers and members of churches utilizing the services of interims typically have low levels of commitment to each other. The interim's appointment is known by all parties to be explicitly temporary. In some instances a termination date has been identified from the beginning of the interim's service. Unlike the situation in which a church installs a minister as their pastor for the foreseeable future, an "open-ended" arrangement, the interim pastorate is "closed-ended."

When almost any social interaction is known to be of short duration, most people make little commitment to the relationships involved. They make little effort to become well acquainted with each other. They place little importance on the relationships. They perceive few lasting negative consequences resulting from the relationships. They become neither very pleased if the relationship is a positive one nor terribly displeased if the interaction does not go as smoothly as they would like.

This approach is both rational and appropriate in many situations. Making heavy personal investments in all social relationships, no matter how fleeting they may be, could be emotionally draining. Most of us learn very early that it is critically important to invest a great deal in our family relationships, for example, for we are dependent on them for meeting so many of our daily needs, both physical and emotional. We also learn *not* to bother with doing the same thing with relationships to the clerk in the store or the gas station attendant, for they are replaced very easily. The person who does not make routine distinctions like this in his or her social life is, to most of us, a confused individual who at best is to be pitied and at worst derided.

It is quite likely that church members make similar distinctions in their relationships to ministers installed as their pastor versus those serving as their interim minister. Especially for persons to whom church life is very important, their relationship with their pastor is typically something they work on rather hard. Their pastor is likely to be an important source of support, guidance and inspiration for many years. Such a relationship should be entered into cautiously and nurtured continuously. It is common knowledge that often when this social interaction sours, both pastor and church member grieve over it.

But why should people make the same investment in their relationship to an interim minister? Like the postal delivery truck driver, interim ministers will be delivering their goods elsewhere very shortly, perhaps never to be seen again. "So what if this one doesn't work out well? Another one will be along soon, perhaps the one who really counts."

These distinctions have clear implications for implementation of the contact hypothesis using the interim pastorate as the context in which perceptual and attitudinal change is to take place. It has become almost axiomatic among social psychologists that attitudes change more in situations in which the individual has made some personal investment than where little commitment is involved (see Petty and Cacioppo, 1981). For example, individuals who have committed themselves to a course of overt action that is contrary to preexisting attitudes apparently find it necessary to bring those attitudes into line with their behavior. Conversely, where there is little commitment to a divergent form of behavior, there is little pressure for attitude change. The more committed they are to the action, the more their attitudes change to correspond with their overt activity (see Festinger, 1957). An illustration of this pattern is that of a person who is prejudiced against blacks accepting a job knowing that it requires that he/she work closely and cooperatively with blacks. More often than not, his/her prejudiced attitudes will subside after a few weeks on the job. The person whose actions toward blacks have not become discordant with his/her prejudices in this way experiences no such pressure to change.

The question becomes whether interaction with a clergywoman in the role of interim pastor over a short period of time involves "enough" commitment to bring about the anticipated attitude change. It is possible that simply having to relate to the clergywoman as pastor for even a short period is sufficient to dispel negative images of women in ministry, diminish preferences for a man in traditional clerical functions and eliminate willingness to discriminate against a clergywoman so that another clergywoman can realistically expect to be placed in a pastoral position there in the future. It is also possible that the opposite holds true, i.e., that the interim situation does not involve sufficient levels of church members' commitment to the relationship to make them any more willing to install a woman as their pastor after the minister-at-large experience than before.

An Evaluation Study

Does personal contact with a clergywoman serving in the role of interim pastor result in more positive attitudes toward women in ministry than those prior to such contact? To answer this question, we designed and implemented a study of attitude change among members of congregations who had participated in the MAL program. The basic design of the project called for obtaining measures of the appropriate variables from members of churches where ministers-at-large had served to determine whether this contact had had any impact on their levels of receptivity toward clergywomen. These data were obtained through a survey conducted over a one-year period, roughly from the spring of 1980 to the spring of 1981. By this time five minister-at-large appointments had been completed in which the clergywomen served full-time as interim pastor. One was in Texas, one in southern California, two in the state of Washington, and one in Delaware. They ranged in duration from three months to a year. All appointments were as senior minister. All but one of them were also solo pastorates.

Each of the five churches supplied lists of their resident members, and each list was sampled systematically so as to obtain a sample of about 30 persons per church. As can be seen in Table 6.1, these procedures yielded a total sample of 151 names. Where the lists supplied by the church were found to be in error, as in the case of persons selected into the sample but who had died or moved away since the list had been constructed, the problem was resolved by taking the name next on the list.

The data were collected from each church member in the sample by means of a telephone interview (Dillman, 1978). We wrote a letter to each individual describing the purpose of the study and indicating that the author would be calling him/her to conduct an interview either on a weekend or during a weekday evening. The level of cooperation of these church members was unusually high, for only 7 percent of those contacted in this way refused to complete an interview. In those few cases where the church member did not wish to participate in the study, that person was replaced by the person whose name was next on the list. There was also a high level of interest among most of those interviewed. The interviews averaged 30 minutes in length, and each was completed in one sitting. The author conducted all of the interviews himself.

TABLE 6.1   SAMPLE SIZES OF THE THREE POPULATIONS

Population	Ultimate Sample Size	Response Rate
members of minister-at-large churches	151	100%*
members of churches with female pastors	101	100%*
Panel participants:		
lay members and elders	1696 (out of 2263)	75%
clergy and special ministries	1143 (out of 1414)	81%
(total Panel)	(2839)	(77%)

*Persons in churches served by the clergywomen who refused to participate in the study when contacted by telephone were replaced in the sample by taking the next name on the church role. The rate of such replacement was 7% in the minister-at-large churches and 3% in the churches with women installed as pastor.

The Panel as a Control Group

In order to determine whether the level of receptivity toward clergywomen was due in fact to contact with the woman minister-at-large and not due to some other factor, the study incorporated two control groups. One control group consists of church members who had not experienced clergywomen as pastors, either interim or permanent. The group used as this control group consisted of those participating in the April, 1980, Presbyterian Panel. The Panel, it will be recalled, is the source of the data discussed in the preceeding four chapters. Only about 5 percent of the lay members on the Panel had had any significant contact with clergywomen, so the Panel members as a whole serve as an adequate control group in this regard as well. However, only the 1696 laypersons in the Panel comprised this control group. Since the data obtained from members of churches in the MAL program was restricted to the laity, there is no point in including the clergy segment of the panel in this analysis.

A Second Control Group

The design of the evaluation project also involved the use of a second control group in order to consider the impermanence of interim pastor appointments. As mentioned above, the transient nature of relationships between a congregation and an interim minister is usually known to both the clergy person and the members of the congregation. This knowledge is important in determining the closeness of the relationship that develops between pastor and lay people. Members of congregations typically make little commitment to a relationship with an interim pastor, because that person will be "here today and gone tomorrow." It is questionable whether such transitory relationships can be sufficient to bring about attitude change.

The second control group consists of a sample of church members in congregations that had autonomously called and installed a clergywoman as their pastor. Unlike the interim pastors, these female pastors were the accepted spiritual and organizational leaders of their respective congregations. Rather than being transient, they were "permanent" in the sense that any clergyperson would be considered the incumbent of a pastorate for the foreseeable future. The woman's installation in each pulpit was in no way contingent. The future of the relationships between these clergywomen and their congregations was "open-ended."

The overall commitment of members of these churches to the relationship with the clergywoman as their pastor is very different from that of members of churches served by women interims. If this deeper commitment makes any difference in the impact that clergywomen can have on laypersons' perceptions and attitudes toward clergywomen in general, then the members of these churches should be systematically different in these regards from members of churches served by the ministers-at-large. If, on the other hand, the impermanent relationship to the woman interim pastor is sufficient to bring about changes in perceptions and attitudes toward clergywomen in spite of the low levels of commitment lay persons have to make to that interaction, then the members of the churches served by the interim and permanent clergywomen should manifest similar orientations to the issue.

The members of churches where women have been installed as pastor were samples in two stages. The first stage involved taking a systematic sample of ten churches from the total of about seventy-five UPCUSA congregations being served by clergywomen either as sole pastor or as co-pastor. This procedure resulted in a list of churches located in Arkansas, California, Idaho, Illinois, Kansas (two), Maryland, Missouri and New York (two). One of these churches was served by a husband/wife team of co-pastors. The rest were solo charges. This geographic distribution corresponds roughly to that of all churches actually being served by clergywomen in this denomination.

Then, after obtaining a list of resident adult members from each church selected in the first stage, the second stage involved using a sampling interval on each church list that would yield ten members from each. As can be seen in Table 6.1, the ultimate sample contained 101 members of these churches. Data were collected from these people by telephone interview, following the same procedures used in contacting members of churches served by the ministers-at-large (see above). The characteristics of the interviews were also basically the same as with members of the churches served by the interims.

The data from these three samples enable us to make several strategic comparisons. The most general of these involve comparing responses of church members who had experienced clergywomen in any pastoral roles with those of members who had not, and contrasting responses of those who had had such experiences with an interim minister with those of members whose contact with a clergywoman had been as installed pastor. Comparisons such as these constitute the bulk of the analysis in the next chapter.

Measures of Receptivity

The interviews with members of the MAL churches and of those where women had been installed as pastor were highly structured. For the most part, they consisted of the same questions asked of the Panel—those discussed in chapters two and three. The same sets of items were used to obtain measures of differences in members' levels of receptivity to women in ministry. The only differences

TABLE 6.2 RESPONSES TO QUESTIONS INDICATING TENDENCY TO
STEREOTYPE WOMEN IN MINISTRY (percent)

Questions	Percentage responding "definitely" or "probably" correct		
	Members served by interims	Members with installed clergywomen	Laypersons on Panel
*1. A woman minister who is married can fulfill her responsibilities as wife and mother just as well as if she were not working full-time.	63	68	47
2. Women ministers are likely to have higher levels of absenteeism from work than men.	14	20	27
3. Women ministers are likely to change jobs more often than are men.	12	21	18
4. Women who try to be both full-time ministers and wives and mothers are likely to have emotional problems due to all the demands placed on them by both jobs.	47	45	53
5. The children of women who are full-time ministers are likely to have personal problems due to the lack of adequate care and attention.	25	24	30
6. Since most churches today are competing with each other for members, they need the strong leadership that mostly men can give.	20	33	37
*7. A woman's temperament is just as suited for the pastoral ministry as a man's.	91	89	82

Agreeing with this item indicates the *non*-stereotyped response. Assenting to the other items indicates the stereotyped response.

were in the instructions associated with each set of questions, i.e., in the case of the Panel, the respondents were dealing with a self-administered questionnaire; while in the churches served by interims or installed women pastors, the respondents were being interviewed. (There is no evidence that the mode of data-collection influenced the patterns of response to the questions.)

The responses to the stereotyping items are contained in Table 6.2, in the form of the percentage of each sample who basically agreed with each item. While the bulk of the analysis of attitude change is covered in the next chapter, this table does indicate some differences that are consistent with the idea that contact does produce increases in receptivity. That is, on most individual indicators, members of the panel gave the stereotyped response more frequently than did members of the churches served by the clergywomen. *Contact with a woman pastor is associated with lowered levels of stereotyping.* The magnitude of the differences varies from question to question, but the pattern is fairly consistent.

Table 6.3 contains the percentage of each sample indicating preference for a man in specific clergy roles. The basic pattern of responses on these questions is similar to that noted on the stereotyping items above. There is a basic tendency for more members of the Panel than members of churches served by women to indicate a preference for a man in specific parish positions and activities. The major exception to this pattern is in response to the question concerning working with a contractor to renovate the church building. More members of churches where women have served than members of the Panel preferred a man for that activity. Among members of congregations served by women, there was more preference for a man in relation to this question than in response to any other preference item. Perhaps women have been so thoroughly socialized away from such "masculine" activities that their actions reinforce the notion that dealing with contractors is indeed primarily "men's work." Nevertheless, on most of the other preference items, members who had experienced a woman's leadership were less prone to prefer a man in clergy roles than those who had not. This, too, supports the contact hypothesis.

Finally, Table 6.4 indicates the relative willingness of persons in each sample to discriminate against female candidates. The patterns of response to this question are different from those observed

TABLE 6.3   RESPONSES TO QUESTIONS INDICATING PREFERENCE FOR MEN IN MINISTERIAL POSITIONS AND ACTIVITIES (percent)

Questions	Percentage indicating preference for a man		
	Members served by interims	Members with installed clergywomen	Laypersons on Panel
PARISH POSITIONS			
1. senior or sole pastor	32	21	60
2. associate or assistant pastor	9	10	21
3. Minister of Education	2	9	7
4. Minister of Music	2	4	7
5. Youth Minister	18	13	21
PASTORAL ACTIVITIES			
6. performing baptism	16	19	27
7. administering the Lord's supper	8	13	27
8. preaching a sermon	9	11	33
9. leading a pastoral prayer	6	9	14
10. conducting a funeral	17	15	33
11. advising you about a personal problem	22	25	25
12. moderating the session meeting	9	11	21
13. coordinating church staff as senior minister	20	20	39
14. working with a contractor to renovate the church	53	58	45
15. planning your congregation's annual budget	11	20	17

above in relation to the other two major dimensions of receptivity. In the case of the behavioral dimension, the members of churches served by women tended to respond in proportionately similar ways, i.e., *very* few are willing to discriminate against a woman outright, but less than one-third are willing to support her candidacy unequivocally. About two-thirds take the safe ground of deferring to the congregation and being willing to discriminate in the name of majority rule.

The members who have *not* been served by clergywomen indicated *both* more willingness to discriminate unilaterally *and* more readiness to stand by the woman in the face of conflict. It is the middle ground that is less popular among the panel, for only about one-half of them indicated a desire to defer to the congregation. This set of differences is *not* consistent with what one would expect to find if the contact hypothesis holds true for clergywomen. It would suggest that there are no linear differences in willingness to discriminate between those who have experienced a woman's pastoral leadership and those who have not. We shall put off further consideration of this issue until the more elaborate analysis contained in the next chapter.

TABLE 6.4   WILLINGNESS TO DISCRIMINATE AGAINST FEMALE
CANDIDATES, BY STUDY POPULATION (percent)*

	Support the candidate	Defer to church	Withdraw her name
members of churches served by interims (n = 148)	30	66	4
members of churches with female pastors (n = 99)	23	69	4
Panel members (n = 1673)	37	52	11

*Percentages may not total 100% due to the possibility of rounding error.

Summary

Most of us initially develop the majority of our attitudes toward other people and objects in something of an experiential vacuum. Instead of learning about actual persons or objects and then responding with appropriate attitudes out of direct experience, we learn those ideas and feelings from other people. Those others probably also did not develop their attitudes from direct experience, but instead picked them up from the attitudes of yet others. An advantage of this pattern is that we have modes of responding to entities and situations before we confront them. However, a disadvantage of picking up our attitudes from others is that what we learn from them may have little correspondence with reality. The attitudes may be totally inappropriate.

The "contact hypothesis" argues that erroneous attitudes may be corrected by personal experience with the person, group or object in question. Prejudice especially can be reduced and intergroup relations made more positive by means of direct contact among members of the groups in question. However, not all such contact works in this way. For contact to generate positive attitudes, the interaction must be between equals, must not reinforce existing stereotypes, must be more personal than casual, must involve a degree of mutual interdependency and must enjoy normative support in the community.

A program was developed involving an application of the contact hypothesis to the situation of clergywomen. Women seminary graduates were placed as interim pastors in several churches in an effort to alter the level of acceptance of women in ministry in the denomination. Contact with the women in the position of pastor involved most of the conditions necessary for positive attitude change. The question is, "Did it work?" Is this kind of contact with its dangers of tokenism and its impermanence sufficient to bring about more positive attitudes toward women in ministry?

We constructed a project to evaluate the effectiveness of this contact for increasing receptivity to clergywomen. It involved obtaining measures of receptivity among members of churches where women interim pastors had been placed. The design of the undertaking incorporated data from the Panel as a control group (no contact with clergywomen). It also used a second control group of members of churches where clergywomen had actually been installed as pastor (more permanent relationships). Comparisons of data from these samples allow us to evaluate the effects of contact in general, as well as specific types of contact, on levels of receptivity to women in ministry.

The study employed the same measures of receptivity as those discussed in Chapter 2. Initial review of the responses to these questions suggests that contact increases receptivity on the cognitive and affective levels. There is a question about its effectiveness in reducing willingness to discriminate against female candidates. We will look at these patterns in detail in Chapter 7.

Suggestions for Additional Reading

Allport, Gordon W.
  1958 *The Nature of Prejudice*. Garden City, New York: Doubleday.

    A classic study of the characteristics of prejudice. Discusses the cultural sources of prejudice and its frequent basis in group norms rather than direct experience. Introduces the contact hypothesis as a means of reducing prejudice.

Amir, Yehuda.
1969 "Contact Hypothesis in Ethnic Relations." *Psychological Bulletin*. 71:5 (May), 319–342.

A thorough review of the research dealing with the contact hypothesis as applied to relations between ethnic groups. Discusses the conditions under which the thesis seems to hold.

Kanter, Rosabeth Moss
1977 *Men and Women of the Corporation*. New York: Basic Books.

A classic discussion of the role of "token" in organizations. Applies the concept to both men and women. Concludes that tokenism operates for members of both sexes (and all races) and that it explains a wide variety of actions of people toward each other when working in the context of large organizations.

Petty, Richard and John T. Cacioppo
1981 *Attitudes and Persuasion: Classic and Contemporary Approaches*. Dubuque, Iowa: William C. Brown.

A study of attitude change especially by means of persuasive communication. A thorough review of the theoretical and research literature. Includes discussions of events such as contact and the possible mechanisms by which they can bring about attitude change.

CHAPTER 7

Effects of Contact on Receptivity

Is the contact hypothesis applicable to the case of women in ministry? Is this set of assumptions about reducing inter-group prejudice and tensions as applicable to misogyny as it appears to have been to racial and ethnic hostility? Once church members have seen a woman functioning in the role of pastor, do they still think of clergywomen the same as before that experience? Do they prefer men in pastoral roles as much? Are they as prone to discriminate against female candidates? These are the central questions the evaluation study addressed.

The basic thrust of the evidence described in this chapter and the next is that *contact with a woman in the role of pastor does alter misogynous attitudes.* Whatever dynamics were operating in successful desegregation programs of the past also seem to be occurring at least in part in these efforts to alter basic sex roles within the church. *The analysis indicates that contact with a woman as pastor increases members' levels of receptivity, breaks down the pervasiveness of institutionalized sexism in the church, and overrides the effects of other factors influencing levels of receptivity.* Predictions of organizational decline do not materialize, and the clergywoman's congregation exhibits normal functioning and growth. These are dramatic claims, so let's look at the evidence.

The Effect of Contact on Level of Receptivity

One basic strategy for analyzing the data from the evaluation study is to compare the measures of receptivity in each sample. If the contact hypothesis is correct, measures of receptivity among members of congregations where women have served as pastor should be systematically different from those measures among people who have not had such contact. For purposes of making such comparisons, we structured the measures of receptivity along the same lines as those used in Chapter 2. The stereotyping items were combined to form an index of tendency to stereotype women in ministry—the cognitive dimension. The gender-preference questions were divided into three sub-dimensions to create indexes of feelings about the "sacramental," "organizational" and "subordinate" components. The behavioral dimension was measured by the question dealing with willingness to discriminate against female candidates for pastoral positions.

Before we make these comparisons, let us note that data from the Panel members alone supports the idea that contact with a woman as pastor reduces resistance to women in ministry. The Panel survey asked people whether they had ever personally experienced a woman in the positions of either pastor, associate pastor or assistant pastor. About five percent of the lay members indicated that they had had this kind of contact.

We compared the receptivity scores of those who had experienced women in these positions and those who had not, and the results indicate that contact does explain some of the differences in receptivity scores. As can be seen in Table 7.1, differences in the levels of every dimension of receptivity were correlated with whether or not the members had had some form of "pastoral" contact with a clergywoman. There was less tendency to stereotype, less preference for men in clergy roles, and less willingness to discriminate against female candidates among Panel members who had interacted with a woman in a pastoral role than among those who had not. All of the coefficients were statistically significant.

Comments volunteered by Panel members reinforce these statistical data. One elder wrote of what could be considered some "ideal" reactions to this type of contact, "Four years ago our church was part of a three-church cooperative ministry. It was decided to call a woman as assistant pastor. This meant that we had this woman in our pulpit every other service. Attendance and offering was greater at her service than (that of) the senior male pastor. One-and-one-half years ago one church decided to go on its own. For a year this woman was our only pastor. Attendance in our church increased over 20 percent. Offering over 28 percent. If we can have our own pastor in the future, a woman will certainly be considered."

There were also comments indicating that women serving in roles other than that of "senior minister" can bring about similar responses. A lay member said, "My ideas changed within the year from a most traditional viewpoint to one of understanding better the role of women in the ministry. We have had female interim pastors and female lay assistants, and they've been a joy to be around. (They also) performed other jobs extremely well. It is possible for women after all!"

TABLE 7.1 CORRELATIONS OF
RECEPTIVITY SCORES WITH CONTACT,
PANEL MEMBERS ONLY

DIMENSION	Correlation
stereotyping score	.17
sacramental score	.30
organizational score	.19
subordinate score	.29
willingness to discriminate	.26

Does "Type" of Contact Make a Difference?

We raised a question in Chapter 6 concerning whether or not the type of contact church members have with a female pastor make any difference in their receptivity to women in ministry. Specifically, do the very transient relationships an interim minister has with a congregation have the same potential for altering attitudes as do the deeper and more permanent relationships an installed pastor has? (Indeed, does relating to a woman even as installed pastor influence attitudes?) This issue was the reason for incorporating the second control group in the design of the research—the members of churches where women had been installed as pastor.

To determine whether type of contact—as interim minister or installed pastor—makes a difference in receptivity scores, we correlated the scores of the members of the two groups. If type of contact makes a difference, there should be systematic differences in the scores of members in the two types of placement. The correlations that resulted indicate that *there tends to be little or no difference in the levels of receptivity found in each type of church.* Most coefficients were both weak and systematically non-significant.

The exception to this pattern involved the relationship between type of contact and differences in subordinate score. The correlation involving those variables was .53 and was statistically significant. It indicates that members of churches where clergymen were installed as pastor were more resistant to the idea of having women in subordinate roles than were members of the churches served by the interim ministers. This result is the opposite of what one would expect on the basis of the discussion of degrees of commitment to the two types of relationships. The pattern may be a consequence of the fact that all of the churches with installed clergywomen were solo pastorates in small to medium-sized churches and actually had no subordinate professional positions, whereas some of the interim situations were large enough at least to consider seriously the idea of having persons in those forms of ministry, if not to have had some experience with women in such positions already.

In any case, all of the other and more salient correlations between the measures of receptivity and the distinction betwen having clergywomen either as interims or as installed pastors indicate that *it makes no difference which type of situation exists.* This answers one of the questions we started out with, i.e., are church members more or less likely to be receptive to clergywomen if their experience with a woman in the pastoral role has been as one of the ministers-at-large (interims) or as one of the installed pastors.

This result means that for most purposes it is no longer necessary to analyze the data from the two types of churches separately. We can now combine data from the members of the interim and installed situations into one category and compare them with data from the panel members. Such a step makes certain phases of the analysis both simpler and clearer. For the sake of simplicity, we shall refer to members of churches that have been served by clergywomen (as *either* minister-at-large [Interim] or installed pastor) as the "contact members." We shall continue to refer to the others simply as "the Panel." (In any instances in which we look at the two types of contact members separately in subsequent analyses, the reactions for doing so will be apparent.)

Contact Members versus the Panel

Does the contact with a clergywoman in the role of pastor affect levels of receptivity to clergywomen in general? If the contact hypothesis is applicable to the situations we are studying, then the levels of receptivity to clergywomen among "contact members" should be higher than among "the Panel." We can test this hypothesis by comparing the various receptivity scores of the two sets of members.

The results of correlating the receptivity scores of contact members and the Panel are portrayed in Table 7.2. They indicate a general pattern that is consistent with the contact hypothesis. On every dimension but the behavioral one, contact members have lower resistance scores than do Panel members. Contact members manifest less stereotyping of clergywomen than do Panel members, and contact members prefer men less frequently than do the Panel for sacramental, organizational and subordinate roles.

TABLE 7.2   CORRELATIONS OF
RECEPTIVITY SCORES WITH CONTACT

DIMENSION	Correlation
stereotyping score	.21
sacramental score	.34
organizational score	.18
subordinate score	.22
willingness to discriminate	—*

*indicates a statistically non-significant coefficient.

The comments made by members of the churches where women had served as pastor reveal a few details about what seems to have been basically positive experiences. The things that impressed these members the most were very "pastoral" in nature. As much as anything else, the clergywoman's visits to the sick and elderly turned out to be positive influences. By helping people deal with crises of disease, surgery and bereavement, the clergywomen fulfilled their ministries and gained strong advocates. Working with members undergoing marital separations and divorce was another plus, especially for those clergywomen who had been divorced themselves.

Another theme in these comments was a desire to give personal testimonies about having been converted to the ranks of supporters of women in ministry. A typical statement reflecting this impulse by members of a church served by an interim pastor (MAL) was, "She really did a great job with us! A lot of people changed their minds. At first they were afraid that she would stay beyond the interim period, *but then after she came they were afraid she would leave!*" (italics added) Another of the interims got the following characteristic response, "She was excellent! Oh, there were many reactions at first. The older men especially didn't take her seriously at the outset. They were very condescending! They did not accept her as a 'minister.' But she broke through that very quickly. She was good at what she did. She changed a lot of attitudes. The reaction was good. The very last Sunday she was here was very beautiful—a very different reaction from the way it started. If they're all like Michelle, the churches they serve will be successful." (The woman's name here and in other quotes is a pseudonym.)

Most of the clergywomen who were installed pastors had similar experiences. A typical comment of a member of one of those churches said, "It was really a new experience for us! I had doubts at first. In fact I voted *against* it when it came up! But she surely opened my eyes and turned me on! She is very good. I'm glad we've got Margo with us. It's a good experience. She's bringing the congregation back slowly but surely. Getting members back. She's having some successes with some pretty zany people. She's done well."

Contact seems to be more strongly correlated with differences in preference for men in *sacramental* roles than with other dimensions. Whether the member has experienced a woman in the role of pastor appears to make more difference in whether or not that person prefers a man for liturgical or "Sunday morning" roles than for other things. We might speculate about this difference.

One reason could be that the sacramental roles are more "visible" than the organizational ones. Most members see the clergywoman functioning before the congregation every Sunday morning. She is in the public eye in other ritual situations too— weddings, funerals and other church gatherings. Other pastoral functions, such as those measured on the organizational dimension, are considerably less visible. Few members, for example, see the clergywoman directing church staff, advising committees or pondering the budget. Relatively few also have direct access to her actions in balancing the roles of pastor with wife and mother, managing stress on the job or keeping her monthly periods from interfering with her daily routines. This pattern would be consistent with the smaller differences in the stereotyping scores also. Actual "contact" for most members is probably largely restricted to those roles subsumed under the sacramental dimension, and this may be why the fact of contact is more strongly related to differences in receptivity along those lines.

There are no linear differences between contact members and the Panel in willingness to discriminate against clergywomen. While contact is associated with few tendencies to define clergywomen in stereotypical terms and to have few preferences for men in clergy roles, it is not clearly predictive of variations in tendency to act these orientations out. A fairly obvious direction to go for an explanation of this result is the distinction between attitudes and behavior. It may be that contact influences attitudes—perceptions and feelings—more effectively than it alters overt actions. However, this approach would be helpful primarily in explaining the absence of a *linear* relationship between contact and willingness to discriminate. Data in Chapter 6, it will be recalled, shows a *curvilinear* association between this dimension and contact, i.e., contact members tended more than did the Panel to defer to the vote of the congregation rather than to take an unequivocal stand pro or con. This curvilinear pattern may be another indication of the operation of the organizational concerns of congregations. That is, the members of churches that have had to work through the idea of having a woman as pastor may be more sensitized to the need to maintain congregational solidarity in the face of such a change than do those who have not experienced the situation directly. Such heightened sensitivity would tend to make them want to consider the wishes of others in the congregation more than to take a unilateral stand. Unfortunately, at this point while such an explanation is plausible, it remains speculative.

Contacts With Women in Other Occupations and Positions

Another question to be pursued in conjunction with the contact hypothesis is whether contact with women functioning in *other* kinds of positions or occupations is similarly related to receptivity to clergywomen. Does contact with women in *lay* leadership positions in a church also result in high levels of receptivity to women in ministry? Does contact with women in *secular* life have similar effects? Does it make any difference whether the contact is with a woman in a high or low *status* position? In other words, in order for contact to influence receptivity to women in ministry, must that contact be with a clergywoman *per se,* or will contacts in other milieus have the same kinds of effects?

The interview schedule used with the contact members and the questionnaire used with the Panel contanied questions to ascertain whether the members had had contacts with women in several other positions. Each person was asked the following:

"These days people are experiencing women in a variety of occupations. I'm going to read you a list of them. After I read each one, would you please tell me whether *you* have *personally* experienced a *woman* in that position?

The list of other positions members responded to is shown in Table 7.2. These other occupations and positions differed widely in terms of the proportions of the members who had encountered women as incumbents. Very few members had personally experienced women in the positions of pastor as counselor, union leader, tax auditor or lawyer. This could be a consequence of the small number of women functioning in these positions. However, most members had encountered women as directors of Christian education, elders and deacons. Outside the church, a majority of members had known women in roles of business proprietor, bus driver and gas station attendant. In general these differences are consistent with what one would expect on the basis of impressions of trends in society as a whole.

TABLE 7.3   PERCENTAGE OF ALL LAY MEMBERS AND
CLERGY WHO HAD PERSONAL EXPERIENCE WITH A
WOMAN IN SELECTED POSITIONS

	Lay members	Clergy
your pastor, associate or assistant pastor	26	21
minister other than your pastor	33	72
director of Christian education	70	88
clerk of the session	50	75
member of the session (elder)	94	95
member of the board of deacons	79	89
your pastor as your counselor	7	5
your elected political official	44	47
your employee	45	72
police officer	42	53
gas station attendant	56	69
bus driver	63	65
union leader	9	8
business proprietor	63	72
your doctor	29	32
your lawyer	9	12
income tax auditor	16	17
church custodian	32	51
your employer	31	23

These patterns are replicated in the responses of the clergy. The general ordering of occupations by clergy who had known women working within them is similar to that of the laity. However, the clergy report having encountered more women in each occupation than did the lay members, with the exception of women as pastor, pastor as counselor and employer. The clergy's occupation tends to explain these exceptions, i.e., they are less likely than lay persons to interact with women as either pastor or as employer.

The first thing we wanted to determine about these other contacts was whether the responses to these questions indicated that the members themselves grouped them in any way. Did the

respondents answer in ways that indicate that they viewed the occupations as belonging together in clusters? To find this out, we
did a factor analysis (see Kerlinger, 1979; Ch. 12) on them in the
same manner as with other sets of items discussed in previous
chapters. Before subjecting them to a factor analysis, however,
we eliminated the questions dealing with the pastor herself—the
first and second items in the list and the one about pastor "as
counselor." We did so because in this section we are primarily
interested in contacts between women in positions *other* than
pastor.

Table 7.4 shows the results of that factor analysis. It indicates
clearly that the questions do cluster in sub-groupings. It also
shows that the groupings in fact are based on some clearly identifiable criteria. They factor according to whether they are church
or non-church positions and whether they are high or low-status
positions. The first grouping in the lay members' responses consists of secular occupations that are mostly low status jobs—bus
driver, police officer, gas station attendant—or jobs that could be
of moderate status, i.e., employer or business proprietor. They are
all positions that are relatively low in power and authority.

These attributes of positions in factor #1 are especially clear
when contrasted with the occupations listed in the third factor. Factor #3 contains four positions characterized by considerably more
power and authority than those in the first factor. These roles are
physician, lawyer, income tax auditor and employer. Most people
would relate to incumbents of these four positions as to persons
with high status. They are defined that way by the society as a
whole. They either require a great deal of training (doctor, lawyer),
or we are required to relate "up" to such people simply due to the
nature of the relationship involving them.

The remaining factor included most of the church-related positions, clerk of the session, elder, deacon and education director.
These are all positions in which lay people assume leadership roles.
A possible exception to this is the post of director of Christian
education, but in fact most members appeared to respond to that
item with the "church school superintendent" in mind—a lay post.

Two items did not load on any of the three factors. These are
elected political official and church custodian. Thus they will not
be included in the analys.ɔ to follow.

TABLE 7.4   FACTOR ANALYSIS OF CONTACT ITEMS OTHER THAN MINISTER

LAY MEMBERS	Factor 1 "low secular"	Factor 2 "low religious"	Factor 3 "high secular"
your employee	.23	.13	.13
police officer	.51	.05	.14
gas station attendant	.62	.03	.04
bus driver	.54	.09	.15
business proprietor	.46	.21	.18
director of Christian education	.18	.31	.05
clerk of the session	.01	.32	.01
member of the session (elder)	.05	.61	−.01
member of the board of deacons	.08	.47	.05
your doctor	.07	.04	.40
your lawyer	.04	−.01	.43
income tax auditor	.12	.01	.23
your employer	.12	.04	.34

CLERGY	Factor 1 "low religious"	Factor 2 "low secular"	Factor 3 "high secular"
director of Christian education	.40	.20	.07
clerk of the session	.35	.09	.02
member of the session (elder)	.82	.07	.03
member of the board of deacons	.60	.14	.04
employee	.31	.28	.16
police officer	.11	.46	−.29
gas station attendant	.16	.53	.10
bus driver	.12	.58	.16
business proprietor	.27	.48	.10
employer	.07	.19	.28
union leader	.01	.10	.41
your doctor	.03	.20	.28
your lawyer	.02	.03	.50

The factor analysis of the responses of the clergy produced almost identical results. Low status religious positions factored together as they did among the laity. The clergy added the position of "employee" to this factor, an understandable shift in light of the fact that most employees of clergy would be working in a religious setting. Minus the "employee" position, the low-status secular factor is also the same as for the laity. The high-status secular factor is also mostly the same, except that "union leader" for the clergy takes the place of "income tax auditor" for the clergy. Finally, the low-status religious factor is the major one among the clergy responses, whereas the first factor was low-status secular in the lay answers, an outcome determined by the number of items involved in each case.

The most general point to be made about the factor analyses of the lay and clergy responses to the other contact items is that *they sort themselves into the same set of three factors—"low-status secular" positions, "low-status religious" positions, and "high-status secular" occupations.* For the most part, these factors are composed of the same items among all of the respondents.

The question now is whether or not contacts with women in each of these types of other positions has any effect on receptivity to women in ministry. To pursue this issue, we first constructed an index of the concept reflected in each factor. As in creating indexes discussed earlier, each member received one point for each position in a given cluster in which he/she had had contact with a female incumbent. Thus each person received a score on each type of other contact based on the total number of positions in that factor in which he/she had encountered a woman. The more the female contacts of a given type, the higher the score.

Next we compared scores on these three indexes with receptivity scores to determine whether such contacts have anything to do with attitudes toward women in ministry. The results of those correlations are portrayed in Table 7.5. The most striking pattern in the table is that *contact with women in positions other than the pastorate is related to receptivity to women in ministry among the Panel but not among the contact members.* In the absence of having interacted with clergymen in the role of pastor, the more members have interacted with women in either low or high status secular positions or in low status church-related positions, the less resistant they are to women in ministry. Persons with many such contacts tend to stereotype clergywomen less and to prefer a man for pastoral functions less than do persons who have had few contacts. There is also a slight tendency for high-status secular contact to be more predictive of receptivity than is either low-status secular or low-status religious contact, so the "authority" component of the contact situation may be operative to create such differences.

BY STUDY POPULATION

	Prior experience** with clergywomen	High status# religion	Low status religion	High status secular	Low status secular
A. CONTACT MEMBERS					
stereotyping score	—	—	-.14	-.13	-.17
sacramental score	—	—	-.20	—	—
organizational score	—	—	—	—	—
subordinate score	-.38	—	-.49	—	-.26
willingness to discriminate	—	—	—	—	—
B. PANEL MEMBERS					
stereotyping score	—	-.17	-.07	-.16	-.10
sacramental score	—	-.30	-.13	-.14	-.12
organizational score	—	-.19	-.08	-.21	-.12
subordinate score	—	-.29	-.32	-.26	-.21
willingness to discriminate	—	-.26	-.12	-.12	-.12
C. CLERGY					
family stereotyping	—	-.18	—	-.13	-.09
job rule stereotyping	—	—	-.13	-.12	-.14
temperament stereotyping	—	-.21	-.14	-.18	-.13
general preference score	—	-.12	-.12	-.21	-.14
subordinate score	—	—	-.15	-.10	-.10
willingness to discriminate	—	-.22	-.23	-.18	-.15

*All correlations listed in this table are statistically significant at the five percent level if a coefficient is shown. Coefficients not shown are statistically non-significant.

**The question about "prior experience with clergywomen" was not asked of the Panel members.

#"High status religious" refers to contact with a woman as pastor, associate pastor or assistant pastor. It is not applicable to the contact members as a *variable*, since *all* of them had had such contact.

The major exception to the absence of relationships between other contacts and receptivity to clergywomen among the contact members has to do with the stereotyping score. The more members of churches where female pastors have served have had these other contacts, the less likely they are to stereotype women in ministry. The only gender preference score influenced by other contacts is the "subordinate" score. Both low-status secular and low-status religious contacts are related to preferences for men in subordinate positions, a pattern that may be associated with the fact that both variables are dealing with the basically subordinate positions in the leadership structure of the local church. Finally, among contact members low-status religious contact score is associated with receptivity score on more dimensions of receptivity than is either low or high secular contact score, a pattern that could be due to the great salience of religious contacts for attitudes toward clergywomen.

We also asked the contact members whether they had any experiences with a clergywoman prior to their contact with the woman who served as their pastor. Slightly more than one-fifth of them responded affirmatively. We wanted to see whether such contact with clergywomen *other* than in the role of pastor had any influence on receptivity. A previous study of receptivity among American Baptists (Lehman, 1979) had indicated that this kind of contact "out of role" had little or nothing to do with subsequent attitudes toward women in ministry. The data in Table 7.5 indicate that the result was the same among United Presbyterians. That is, while contact with a female minister in the role of pastor is related to high levels of receptivity to women in ministry, just having met, seen or heard a clergywoman in *any* role is *not* predictive of receptivity. Only in relation to "subordinate" score is such unspecified contact related to receptivity, and that pattern may be due to the fact that often such other experiences are with women in those subordinate positions.

We may conclude, then, that contact with women in positions other than pastorate is related to attitudes toward clergywomen. However, *such contact appears to make a difference in receptivity primarily in the absence of contact with clergywomen in the pastoral role.* The relationships between other contacts and receptivity are weaker than those between pastoral contact and receptivity, and the effects of other contacts seem to disappear in the face of contact with the clergywoman as pastor. Accordingly, this implies that to have an impact on levels of receptivity to women in ministry, contact in role appears to make more difference than any other kind.

Contact and Changes in Receptivity

The analysis above deals with relationships between *levels* of receptivity to clergywomen and contact with women occupying pastoral roles. It indicates that resistance to clergywomen tends to be lower among members of churches where women have served as pastor than among members where there has been no such contact. These patterns are consistent with what one would expect if the contact hypothesis is applicable to women in ministry.

However, the contact hypothesis implies an even more rigorous test. That is, if the contact hypothesis holds for attitudes toward clergywomen, contact should be associated not only with differences in levels of receptivity but also with *changes* in receptivity. There should be greater *change* in those attitudes among church members who experienced women in pastoral roles from before contact to after than among members who have not had such experiences during the same time period. Ideally, if it is the contact *per se* that makes church members change their minds and not something else, there should be no attitudinal differences among members either prior to contact or in the absence of contact. Any changes that do appear should be only among members of churches served by the female pastors. Is this the case?

Measuring Change in Receptivity

The study incorporated questions through which the issue of "change" could be addressed. The interviews of contact members included a series of items designed to ascertain how they had viewed clergywomen *prior to* their experience with their female pastor, along with their gender preferences and willingness to discriminate prior to contact. In the context of being asked questions to measure each dimension, the respondents were informed that we were also interested in "whether they had changed their minds." Then the members were instructed to answer the same sets of questions in the way they would have responded *prior to contact* with the clergywoman who had served (was serving) them as pastor.

The procedure was slightly different in collecting data from the Panel, for the instrument used with them was a self-administered questionnaire. They also had had no contact with a clergywoman as pastor. Yet we needed to obtain parallel data in order to make comparisons necessary to assess the extent to which changes in receptivity were associated with contact. Since we could not ask questions about how they felt about clergywomen "prior to contact" with a woman pastor, we asked them instead to indicate how they would have answered the questions measuring each dimension of receptivity "a year ago." We selected the one-year time period primarily because most of the ministers-at-large completed their work as interim pastor in each particular church within a year or less, thus making the time periods roughly comparable.

If such instructions had been asked "in a vacuum," i.e., in the absence of any plausible reason for inquiring about how they had felt a year earlier, the level of respondent cooperation in answering those particular questions among the Panel might have been low. The directions would not have made much sense to them. However, a series of fortuitous events did occur which gave the Panel members an answer to "why they were being asked such a question," and the level of their cooperation on those questions was just about as high as it was on the rest of the questionnaire.

In the spring of 1980, the General Assembly of the denomination was confronted with a proposition that all UPC churches be required to seat women on their governing boards as full-fledged lay leaders, a proposal filled with both symbolic and organizational meanings. This was "Overture-L," and it became the focus of a great deal of controversy. It received nation-wide media attention, and even some members of non-UPC churches became involved in the issues vicariously. In the end the overture did pass with minor modifications, and a few local churches withdrew from the denomination in response. The debate brought the issue of the role of women as church leaders to the consciousness of many church members for the first time. The simple acts of following the discussion and thinking through the issues could have been the impetus for some attitude change on the related matter of clergywomen. Accordingly, asking about earlier attitudes toward women in ministry would make sense to the Panel members who had not had contact with a clergywoman in the role of pastor but who had heard about the controversial overture.

Patterns of Past Receptivity

Using questions that require respondents to recall something about the past, as was done in this study, constitutes an approximation of an "experimental study design." It makes possible comparisons of variables "before" and "after" an event, and it allows one to determine empirically whether that event had any effect on those variables, effects that would be in accordance with some theory. In the case of this evaluation project, the event is contact with a clergywoman in the role of pastor, and the expected outcomes are changes in receptivity to women in ministry.

Since memory can be somewhat unreliable as a measure of past attitudes, it is important to determine empirically whether the results of asking respondents to recall the past did result in valid measures of previous levels of receptivity. Did all church members in fact have similar levels of receptivity to clergywomen before some of them experienced a woman in the role of pastor?

Table 7.6 contains the results of comparing past levels of receptivity (as measured by memory): (a) among contact members only and (b) between contact members and the Panel. The results of comparing the past receptivity scores of members of minister-at-large churches with clergywomen installed as pastor indicate that there were no meaningful differences between them on nearly every dimension. The correlations are generally very small and statistically non-significant. Members of the churches with the two types of contact reported very similar amounts of past stereotyping, past gender preferences and past willingness to discriminate against clergywomen. The only exception to this pattern is on the subordinate dimension, where members of churches with females installed as pastors tended to be smaller than those where ministers-at-large had worked, so that the former congregations may have had less opportunity to see women performing in the education and music leadership positions than did the latter. If this is the case, it could explain some of their greater tendency to prefer men in those roles even in the past. In any case, the more general tendency for persons from these two types of churches to report *similar* levels of past receptivity appears to be the most noteworty pattern, and the basic picture is one of no difference.

TABLE 7.6   CORRELATIONS BETWEEN PAST RECEPTIVITY SCORES AND
STUDY POPULATION

	Contact members only	Contact vs. Panel
past stereotyping score	—	—
past sacramental score	—	– .26
past organizational score	—	– .27
past subordinate score	.35	– .22
past willingness to discriminate	—	—

The more critical comparison in Table 7.6 is between the members combined (both types of contact situations) and the Panel. Did the members of churches served by clergywomen report the same levels of receptivity prior to contact as did the Panel members who, of course, had had no contact? The answer depends on the dimension of receptivity in question. There appear to have been no differences between contact members and the Panel in tendency to stereotype clergywomen at the outside. The correlation is both small and statistically non-significant. The same applies to willingness to discriminate, for which the correlation is almost zero. On these two dimensions, the two populations appear to have been the same prior to contact.

However, there are differences in past gender preference scores. Contact members report *more* past preferences for males in clerical roles than do members of the Panel. If these differences had been such as to indicate that the contact members reported *less* past resistance to clergywomen than did the Panel, then one would wonder whether the contact with the female pastor had had a "halo effect" on reports of past attitudes. The feelings of the present could have been projected into the past. But that is not the pattern shown in the table. The difference is in the *opposite* direction. The contact members report themselves as having had *more preferences for men as clergy* in the past than did the Panel.

One can only speculate about the reason for more contact members than Panel members to indicate past preferences for male ministers over clergywomen. One possibility is that the recollections are accurate, but that is not likely. There is no plausible reason why members of churches served by ministers-at-large or by females installed as pastor should have been *less* receptive to clergywomen before such contact than were members of the Panel (where no contact followed).

Two other possibilities are more likely correct. One interpretation is that the contact members simply exaggerated the extent to which they had changed their minds from previous levels of receptivity. In an effort to say, "Yes, I did change my mind about my preferences for men in clerical roles after contact with this clergywoman," the contact members may have shown themselves to have been more prejudiced against clergywomen in the past than they actually had been. Another possibility is that the contact members reports are accurate, but that the *Panel* members portrayed themselves as less prejudiced than they actually are, a common occurrence when people answer questions that may not portray them in a very desirable light. In either case, since the direction of the differences in reports of past gender preferences portrays the contact members as more resistant than the panel prior to contact, rather than vice versa, we need not be overly concerned about the appearance of such "initial" differences because of their direction. An assumption of "no difference" before contact is still the most plausible position to take.

Changes in Receptivity

We turn now to the more central question of changes in receptivity to clergywomen. Regardless of the initial level of resistance to women in ministry, to what extent does contact with a woman in the role of pastor result in a *change* in that resistance.

The measure of change in members' receptivity was simply the difference between their present and past receptivity score on each dimension. Since past resistance is likely to be higher than the present, we subtracted present score from past score. The result was used as an indication of the direction and amount of change that had taken place as a result of contact. If a given individual had a stereotyping score of "6" in the past and "4" in the present, for example, that person's change score would be "2," an indication of the extent to which the person became less inclined to stereotype after contact. (A negative number resulting from the subtraction, e.g., "-2," would be an indication that the person had become more prone to stereotype due to contact.) "Zero" would indicate no change. This procedure was followed for every dimension of receptivity, and it allowed us to repeat the type of analysis done with "level" of receptivity to determine the extent to which contact results in "change" in receptivity.

Table 7.7 shows the proportion of respondents in each sub-population who became *more receptive* to clergywomen according to this measure of change. Several patterns are apparent in the table. Regarding the various dimensions, the greatest amount of change took place on the sacramental and organizational indexes. There was almost as much change on the stereotyping index. Thus it would appear as though contact with a clergywoman in pastoral roles has its greatest effect on the extent to which church members prefer men performing priestly and liturgical functions and running the organizational machinery of the church. Such changes can be very important.

The smallest amount of change seems to have occurred on the subordinate index. Less than twenty percent of either set of members manifested any change in preference for men in those roles. Willingness to discriminate shows a few more people changing positively after contact, but the amount of change on that dimension is small also.

TABLE 7.7   CHANGES IN RECEPTIVITY TO CLERGYWOMEN BY STUDY
POPULATION (percent)

	Percent becoming more receptive		
DIMENSION	panel	interim members	installed pastor members
stereotyping change	21	45	42
sacramental change	19	55	55
organizational change	23	64	66
subordinate change	4	12	19
discriminating change	14	25	15

Comparisons across the sub-population also reveal important differences. First, the differences between the two types of contact situation are neither great nor consistent. The amount of change that took place upon contact with the interim minister is almost identical to that which occurred upon contact with a woman as installed pastor. This observation is particularly important, because it reinforces the earlier observation that there were few differences in *levels* of receptivity among members of churches having the two types of contact. This indication that there are also few differences in the amount of *change* that takes place upon contact supports the earlier conclusion that contact with the interim had as much impact as contact with the installed pastor and that differences in the structure of the relationship between pastor and congregation in the two situations is not as important as suspected initially.

The second pattern observable in comparing sub-populations is the difference between contact members and panel members concerning the number of people whose receptivity increased. On almost every dimension, between two and three times as many contact members as panel members became more receptive to clergywomen. The major exception to that pattern is the amount of change in each sub-population's willingness to discriminate against female candidates, where the differences are less clear. Overall, however, there is clearly more change in attitudes associated with contact than in the absence of such interaction.

Barring any other intervening events, there should have been no change in the Panel's receptivity scores at all. Yet an average of about one-fourth of them (across dimensions) became more receptive over the period in question. This slight change is probably due to two realities. First, some people indicate change in response to questionnaire items like this simply because they think they are "supposed to." It is usually a small minority who manifest such tendencies, but it is rare for no one to do so. Most likely some Panel members did so. Second, there *were* other intevening events that could account for some shifts, i.e., the controversial overture concerning women in leadership positions in local churches that sparked so much controversy in the spring of 1980. Accordingly, it is not surprising to observe some change in the control group even without the effect of contact with the woman pastor experienced by members in the experimental group. We can be satisfied that the approximation of experimental design was successful, because the contact members did manifest *greater* changes than did the Panel. Contact with the minister-at-large or the installed pastor did have the effect one would predict on the basis of the contact hypothesis.

We also calculated correlation between receptivity scores of members of the minister-at-large churches and the churches with installed female pastors. The results appear in Table 7.8. The table indicates what the percentages in Table 7.7 showed, i.e., that there are no significant differences in the amount of change that occured on the indexes of nearly every dimension of receptivity. The exception to this pattern is the indicator of willingness to discriminate, according to which there was greater liberalization of attitudes in response to the ministers-at-large than to the installed pastors.

TABLE 7.8 CORRELATIONS BETWEEN
CHANGES IN RECEPTIVITY BY MEMBERS
OF CHURCHES SERVED BY
MINISTERS-AT-LARGE AND BY
INSTALLED PASTORS

DIMENSION	Correlation
stereotyping change	—
sacramental change	—
organizational change	—
subordinate change	—
discriminating change	− .30

While this is opposite from what one would expect, at this point the reasons for this difference are not known.

We then combined the responses of contact members as was done in the analysis of levels of receptivity above, and we ran correlations between the amounts of change manifested by the contact members and the Panel. Those coefficients are contained in Table 7.9. As appeared in the examination of percentages in Table 7.7, there were meaningful and significant differences between contact and Panel members in the amount of change that took place on every dimension of receptivity but one. The greatest differences in amount of change occurred on the gender preference indexes, and almost as much change took place on the stereotyping index. There were no significant differences in change in willingness to discriminate.

A third approach to this issue is to examine the "amount" of change in score that took place on each dimension, comparing

TABLE 7.9 CORRELATIONS BETWEEN
CHANGES IN RECEPTIVITY AND
CONTACT WITH CLERGYWOMEN IN
PASTORAL ROLES

DIMENSION	Correlation
stereotyping change	.51
sacramental change	.69
organizational change	.65
subordinate change	.53
discriminating change	—

responses of contact members to those of the Panel. It will be recalled that Table 7.7 demonstrates differences in the percentage of *members* who became more positive in attitudes toward women in ministry. There were differences both by population and by dimension of receptivity. Now we ask a different question, i.e., about the *average amount of change in receptivity score* on each dimension, again comparing responses of members who experienced a woman in the role of pastor with those of respondents who did not.

Table 7.10 indicates the average (mean) amounts of change on each dimension of receptivity among contact members and Panel members. The pattern in the Table is consistent with much of what has been observed in the preceding three tables. Each cell of the table indicates two kinds of information: (1) the mean change on a particular dimension—e.g., contact members' average degree of change on the gender preference index was 3.86 out of a total range of scores of 15; and (2) the percentage that this mean change represents of the total amount of change possible on that dimension (shown in parentheses)—e.g., the mean change of 3.86 is 26% of the total possible change on the gender preference index.

The most obvious pattern in Table 7.10 concerns the differences between responses of the contact members and the Panel. The mean changes in receptivity scores are much smaller among

TABLE 7.10   MEAN CHANGES (AND PERCENT OF POSSIBLE CHANGE) IN RECEPTIVITY SCORES BEFORE AND AFTER CONTACT WITH CLERGYWOMEN, BY CONTACT

	Contact members	Panel members
stereotyping change	1.07 out of 7 (15)	.19 out of 7 (3)
sacramental change	1.62 out of 5 (32)	.18 out of 5 (4)
organizational change	1.71 out of 6 (29)	.24 out of 6 (4)
subordinate change	.18 out of 2 (9)	.02 out of 2 (1)
discriminating change*	.19 out of 2 (10)	.17 out of 2 (9)

*Differences between these mean scores are statistically non-significant.

the Panel than among contact members. Much of the change among the Panel could be accounted for quite easily either by the controversy in the spring of 1980 or by the typical "guinea-pig effect." The mean changes among the contact members, however, cannot be explained away in terms of these factors. Instead, they appear to be due to the effects of the contact experience itself. The one exception to these differences concerns the mean changes in willingness to discriminate. As noted in Table 7.9 also, the mean changes in willingness to discriminate against clergywomen tend to be the same among both contact and Panel members. Table 7.10 simply indicates what the level of those average changes are. They are slight, only about 10 percent of the total possible change on that dimension.

The second pattern in Table 7.10 that is worthy of note concerns the differences in mean changes on each dimension among contact members. The greatest average degree of change occurred on the sacramental dimension. The mean change of 1.62 represents 32 percent of the total possible change. In translation this means that contact members changed their minds about women in public liturgical and sacramental roles more than in other kinds of functions. Almost as much change took place on the organizational dimension (29 percent). Taken together these figures indicate that more changes take place in members' "preferences" for a man (or willingness to work with a woman) especially in liturgical roles and in running the organizational machinery of the church than with their tendencies to stereotype clergywomen or to discriminate against them.

As one might expect, the least overall change took place on the subordinate dimension. Members changed their minds the least on the issue of whether to accept a woman working in the typically subordinate ministries of education and music. Nevertheless, the difference between contact and Panel members' changes even on this dimension were sufficiently great as to be not attributable to change, i.e., the differences are probably real. Finally, the amount of change in tendency to stereotype lies between these extremes. Contact brings about changes in members' inclinations to perceive clergywomen in traditional stereotypical terms, but not as much as the changes in gender preferences associated with most clerical functions. Overall, while the average amount of change is not great, it does appear to be conceptually meaningful and statistically significant.

The patterns in the preceding four tables support the findings from the earlier analysis of receptivity levels. Basically there was the same amount of change in receptivity among members of churches served by ministers-at-large and those served by installed female pastors. Differences in degree of commitment to the two types of pastors have no observable effect on changes in receptivity. But *contact with a clergywoman either as interim minister or as installed pastor does bring about meaningful change in levels of receptivity in terms of tendency to stereotype and preferences for men in various pastoral roles.* The absolute amount of change is a bit limited, but it is real and more than can be accounted for by chance alone. The contact hypothesis does appear to be applicable to the situation of women in ministry.

Do the "Horror Stories" Come True?

A second approach to the task of documenting the effect that contact with a woman as pastor has on church members is to examine the level of church involvements those members manifest once the woman assumes her pastoral duties among them. We looked at these reactions in terms of members' church participation, financial contributions and their decision to remain members.

It will be recalled that the panel data examined in Chapter 5 indicated that most church members believed that introducing a clergywoman's candidacy for the position of pastor of their congregation would create serious problems. They typically felt that such an event would be tension-producing and would result in declines in church attendance and financial contributions. Members who had these perceptions also tended to be opposed to women in ministry on virtually all dimensions of receptivity/resistance. Expectations of these threatening reactions by others appeared to be important bases for resistance to clergywomen in pastoral positions.

Accordingly, it is important to ask whether predictions such as these actually materialize. Do the horror stories actually come true? This issue is another facet of the general question concerning the responses of church members to direct experiences with clergywomen as pastors. We asked the contact members a series of questions about such reactions, and summaries of their responses are shown in Table 7.11.

Analysis of data from the members of churches where clergy-women actually served as pastor indicate that the predictions of doom for the congregation as a result of the clergywoman's presence did not materialize. Instead, just as usually happens with a new male pastor, once the clergywoman was on the scene there was typically neither miraculous growth nor precipitous decline. The arrival of the new woman pastor signalled an initial renewal of stability, and then once she was settled in the congregation also resumed its normal activity associated with simply being the church.

The top portion of Table 7.11 repeats some of the figures previously shown in Chapter 5. In the absence of any direct experience with women in ordained ministries, approximately two-thirds of the members anticipated problems, i.e., the woman's candidacy was expected to create tension and to lead members to stay home from church and reduce their giving. While the proportions of the congregations expected to be involved in these reactions were relatively low—median expectations of 3 percent to stay home and 1.5 percent to reduce their contributions—the predictions of dire consequences of calling a woman were relatively widespread.

However, the record of what actually happened is quite different. In churches where women had served as pastor, only one-third of the members reported *anyone* staying home from church, and where this happened it tended to involve less than 2 percent of the congregation. Similarly, only about one-in-ten members of churches served by clergywomen reported that anyone actually withheld funds from the church, and where this was reported it involved an average of no more than one percent of the congregation. We also asked whether any members had simply left the congregation for another church in response to the woman pastor's arrival. In this case only about 15 percent reported that anyone had moved for this reason, and it typically averaged little more than one percent of the membership. *In short, the horror stories simply did not come true.* The churches adapted quickly and successfully.

We also asked about members' expectations for the future. Now that their church had had direct experience with a woman as pastor, how would the members react to a future recommendation that another qualified woman be called as pastor? Table 7.11 indicates that after having interacted with a woman as pastor,

TABLE 7.11   INDICATIONS OF EXPECTED AND ACTUAL RESPONSES
TO A WOMAN PASTOR

No prior contact: expected responses to clergywoman	Percentage reporting	Median expected proportion
tension and conflict	65	—*
stay home from church	71	3.0
reduce financial giving	63	1.5

Actual reductions after woman pastor arrived:	Percentage reporting	Median expected proportion
attendance	32	1.5
contributions	11	1.0
membership	15	1.2

Having experienced woman pastor, expected responses to nomination of another clergywoman:	Percentage reporting	Median expected proportion
still have reservations	49	—*
stay home from church	25	4.8
reduce financial giving	13	4.9
change congregations	18	3.2

Positive responses after woman pastor arrived:	Percentage reporting
members increased participation	58
members increased contributions	28
attracted new members	58

*data not available

few members expected any negative response to the idea in the future. On the one hand, fully 49 percent said that they thought others in their congregation *would still have reservations* about calling a woman as pastor. From the perspective of those promoting the interests of clergywomen, this figure is high. Nevertheless, the figure is also consistent with other figures (above) that indicate that the actual amount of attitude change resulting from contact was relatively small. On the other hand, the proportions of members of these churches who also expect some sort of drastic response to another nomination of a clergywoman remains small—an average of about one-in-five members—and the proportion of members expected to be involved in any such action remains less than five percent.

Positive Reactions to Women Pastors

Information obtained from members of churches where women had served as pastor indicate some clearly positive outcomes too. In addition to asking them about conflict and declines in membership and contributions, we asked whether the clergywoman was instrumental in promoting aspects of the congregation's life that signalled church growth. The answers indicate the kind of response one would want to see in relation to any new pastor. As portrayed in the bottom of Table 7.11, about 58 percent of the contact members reported that people in their congregation *increased* their participation once the clergywoman arrived. This figure is nearly twice that associated with reports of people withdrawing from church involvements. Similarly, nearly three times as many contact members reported that people increased their financial contributions once the woman assumed the pastorate as reported that some had decreased their giving.

Another question about positive trends in church membership once the woman arrived was phrased explicitly to take the woman into account. It read, "As far as you know, did (the woman pastor's) presence attract any new members to the church? Nearly three-fifths of the members indicated that new members had joined their congregation directly in response to the clergywoman's presence, a figure nearly four times that linked to reports of people leaving the church.

These patterns suggest that *not only is the members' response to a woman pastor not negative, but the impact on the church also tends to be quite positive.* Not only do the "horror stories" fail to materialize, but also "success stories" tend to proliferate.

Summary

In this chapter we examined evidence from the evaluation study to determine the effect of contact with a woman in the role of pastor on levels of receptivity to women in ministry. We focused on the question of whether the contact hypothesis is applicable to changing attitudes toward clergywomen. What happens in a congregation when a woman assumes the role of pastor? The analysis provided evidence in support of the following generalizations:

1. Differences in level of receptivity to women in ministry can be explained partly in terms of whether members had had contact with a clergywoman in the role of pastor. Members who had personally experienced a woman in the role of pastor tended to have higher levels of receptivity to women in ministry than those who had not. Contact is especially useful for explaining differences in members' preferences for men or women in sacramental roles, and it is least useful in relation to differences in willingness to discriminate against female candidates for pastoral positions.

2. These differences in receptivity to clergywomen are due to changes that occur during the process of interaction with a woman pastor. Levels of receptivity increase as a result of contact. The greatest amount of change takes place in preferences for men or women in clergy roles. Change is negligible in members' willingness to discriminate against female candidates.

3. The changes in receptivity occur regardless of whether the woman is serving in the role of interim pastor or is installed as pastor. There are no significant differences in level of receptivity or the amount that it changes associated with these two placement situations.

4. Differences in level of receptivity are also partly explained in terms of contact with women in other positions and occupations both in the church and in secular life. However, the influence of these other types of contact on level of receptivity is found primarily among members who have not personally experienced a womas as pastor. Direct contact with a female pastor tends to suppress the influence of other contacts on level of receptivity.

5. Predictions of large-scale withdrawal of church members in response to a woman pastor did not materialize in the congregations involved in this study. Very few members reported any such problems in response to a woman's assuming the pastorate of their church, and where such problems were perceived they involved less than 2 percent of the congregation. Moreover, members of churches served

by women pastors tended instead to report significant gains in membership, budget and participation in their congregations in relation to the clergywoman's assuming the role of pastor there.

Having demonstrated these ways in which church members respond to having women as their pastor, we next want to ask why these changes occur. What happens in the contact situation that results in increased receptivity in the members participating in it? What other changes take place in members' orientations to women ministry? We shall discuss those issues in the next chapter.

Suggestions for
Additional Reading

Colwill, Nina L.
   1982 *The New Partnership: Women and Men in Organizations.* Palo Alto, California: Mayfield Publishing Co.

   A study of the behavior of women and men in large organizations. Reviews the literature on patterns of interaction involving attitudes, roles, power, communication, stereotyping, etc. Points out the common problems men and women have in entering new forms of relationships in work organizations and suggests new approaches to dealing with those issues.

Lehman, Edward C., Jr.
   1980 *Project S.W.I.M.: A Study of Women in Ministry.* Valley Forge, Pennsylvania: The Ministers Council, American Baptist Churches.

   A study of placement of women in ministry in the American Baptist Churches. Includes a section dealing with the reactions of church members and people in the surrounding community to the introduction of a clergywoman as an ordained minister in a church.

Weidman, Judith L. (ed.)
   1981 *Women Ministers: How Women Are Redefining Traditional Roles.* New York: Harper and Row.

   A collection of essays by clergywomen describing and reflecting on their experiences as women in ministry. Most of the selections are written by women who are pastors, and most of them are members of "mainline" Protestant denominations. Especially insightful are the selections dealing with their affective reactions to problems of assuming the role of pastor, church administration, preaching and supportive ministries. Many selections also deal with how church members reacted to the clergywomen as perceived by those women themselves.

CHAPTER 8

Explaining Contact Effects Upon Receptivity

The evidence reviewed in Chapter 7 demonstrates that contact with a clergywoman in the role of pastor produces changes in the levels of church members' receptivity to women in ministry. Out of this interaction come reductions in both stereotyping of clergywomen and preference for a man in clergy roles. The experience of having a woman as pastor seems to produce these outcomes in some members regardless of whether the woman's position with the congregation is as installed pastor or interim minister. The data also indicates that instead of the widespread withdrawals of members from church involvement which most members expect to take place when a woman becomes pastor, the congregations tend to stabilize or to realize some modest gains. Church members respond well to what they initially consider a potentially threatening situation.

Why do these reactions take place? How does contact with a woman as pastor bring about changes in receptivity? These are the questions on which most of this chapter is focused. The evidence reviewed here supports a theory of attitude change which argues that contact involves more than a process of simply correcting bad information. Interacting with a woman as pastor places members in a situation in which it is easier for them to change their attitudes than to retain previous feelings, given their commitments to their church. They virtually force attitude change upon themselves! The contact situation also challenges previously shared assumptions about sex roles in the church, with the effect that contact seriously erodes what is commonly referred to as institutional sexism. Finally, we shall also demonstrate that the contact experience suppresses the impact of several background variables which influence levels of receptivity where no contact has occurred.

Attitude Change as Response to Information

Several theories purport to explain the effects of contact (Cook, 1969). This study includes data that allow us to address two of them. The first of these is probably the classical argument for the contact hypothesis. The main thrust of the theory rests on the assumption that persons in contact situations react to each other in relatively rational or logical ways. The theory argues that in the course of contact with members of groups which are the object of prejudice, new and accurate information is obtained. Existing stereotypes find little support in the person of the flesh-and-blood individual with whom interaction is taking place. The participants recognize this inconsistency, and they change their attitudes toward the group in general. The outcome of contact, then, becomes a matter of reorganization of beliefs and restoration of a cognitive balance (Cook, 1969: pp. 223–224).

Another argument emphasizes the concept of "individuation" (Zimbardo, 1969: p. 234). According to this approach, contact leads to improvement in inter-group attitudes because the situation provides an "individuated" perception of the minority group member, which means that he is now perceived as something other than a mere manifestation of a class of objects. Direct contact forces the perceiver to respond to the other's unique individuality. In the process the other (object) person is transformed "from ground to figure." As the focal figure, the person's unique individual attributes are perceived. To the extent that these characteristics do not support existing stereotypes brought into the contact situation and assumptions associated with the class of objects, this individuation makes the person question those stereotypes and eventually change his attitudes. This is another argument that assumes a basically rational actor. Both of these arguments view attitude change as largely a matter of processing information.

Is this rational mode of reaction the process whereby contact with clergywomen in the role of pastor results in positive changes in receptivity toward women in ministry? The argument certainly seems consistent with oft-heard calls for "visibility" and for "role models." Data obtained during the interviews with contact members include their perceptions of the clergywomen's role performance. Comparisons of differing performance evaluations with various degrees of change in receptivity can show whether such perceptions play any role in attitude change. If the positive effects of contact are the results of rational processing of information, then positive evaluations of the clergywoman's performance should be associated with greater attitude change in a positive direction than would negative assessments. Any other pattern would be inconsistent with the assumption that attitudes change in contact situations if the participants are primarily reacting to and processing new and positive information.

The indicator of members' evaluation of their female pastor is as follows:

> "Ministers, like people in any occupation, differ in what they do well. I'm going to read a list of activities that most pastors engage in. After I read each one, would you please tell me how effective you think ____(name)____ was in that activity in comparison to other ministers you know? Please tell me whether you think her effectiveness was either "AVERAGE" (which would be "like other ministers"), "ABOVE AVERAGE" (better than most others), or "BELOW AVERAGE" (not as good as most others).

The list of activities to be evaluated were those contained in Table 8.1, which also indicates the result of performing a factor analysis (see Kerlinger, 1979: Ch. 12) on the total set. The respondents did differ in their answers. The most common distinction was that between "average" and "above average." Few members wanted to cast their pastor in too much of a negative light. Nevertheless, the full range of responses was used in the analysis.

As seen in Table 8.1, the members' evaluations factor into three groupings, i.e., a "general leadership factor" indicated by the first and major set of loadings, a "teaching" factor as the second, and a "woman's advocacy" factor as the third. We combined the items in the "general leadership factor" into a performance evaluation index. A performance evaluation score was calculated for each person by awarding one point for each item in factor #1 on which the pastor was seen as performing at a level of average or below. The higher the score, the *lower* the performance.

TABLE 8.1 FACTOR ANALYSIS OF ITEMS EVALUATING CLERGYWOMAN'S EFFECTIVENESS

ITEMS	Factor #1	Factor #2	Factor #3
leading small groups	.40	.23	.15
managing the church budget	.45	.16	−.11
counselling people with problems	.55	.16	−.22
pleading the cause of the disadvantaged	.50	.20	.12
presiding over a meeting of a large group	.46	.18	.10
presenting an argument in favor of a position	.63	−.01	−.02
preaching sermons	.67	.17	.06
leading public worship in general	.63	.21	.02
teaching small children	.17	.89	−.10
teaching teen-agers	.32	.78	.05
advocating women's issues	.03	−.03	.97

We then correlated these evaluation scores with the indexes of change on the five dimensions of receptivity. The resulting coefficients are shown in Table 8.2, where the pattern is relatively clear. With the exception of stereotyping, there is no significant relationship between members' evaluations of the woman pastor's performance and the extent to which their levels of receptivity changed from the time she started working with them. Whether the woman's work was evaluated positively or negatively tends to be unrelated to any change in members' preferences for men in clergy roles or their willingness to discriminate against female candidates.

TABLE 8.2 CORRELATIONS OF CHANGE IN RECEPTIVITY SCORES
WITH SCORES ON EVALUATION OF CLERGYWOMAN'S
EFFECTIVENESS AND ESTABLISHING PRIMARY RELATIONS

	Evaluation score	Establishing primary relations
stereotyping change	−.12	.19
sacramental change	—*	.18
organizational change	—	.26
subordinate change	—	—
discriminating change	—	.17

*statistically non-significant coefficient

Evaluations of performance are related to changes in stereotyping, however. As one would predict, positive assessments of the woman's role performance were associated with a decrease in the extent to which members perceived clergywomen in stereotypical terms. The more roles on which they evaluated the pastor's effectiveness as only average or below, however, the less likely the contact situation was to reduce stereotyping. The correlation is quite weak, indicating that there isn't much effect here, but it is statistically significant.

Accordingly, church members in contact situations changed their minds about women in ministry somewhat independently of their evaluations of the work of the particular woman serving as their pastor. These evaluations made little difference in their perceptions of women in ministry, but apparently the members did not translate those ideas into their feelings about having a woman pastor. While preferences for men in clergy roles did change as a result of contact, this shift was not due to the members' assessments of how the woman did her job. This pattern is not consistent with the assumption that attitude change is a rational response to the information obtained about specific clergywomen serving as pastor. The result does not adequately support theories which view such attitude change as primarily a matter of processing accurate information.

Attitude Change as Resolution of Cognitive Dissonance

A most recent theory of attitude change views it as a matter of finding a way to reduce "cognitive dissonance" (Cook, 1969: p.

266; Petty and Cacioppo, 1981: pp. 146–152). Cognitive dissonance is a state of mind in which two clusters of information—"cognitions"—more or less clash with each other. The thought that I am a law-abiding citizen does not square with the realization that I have just been stopped by a policeman because I was exceeding the speed limit on the highway, for example. Another illustration is the logical conflict aroused by the two ideas that I consider my spouse a loving parent, but I have just witnessed him/her strike my child so hard as to inflict physical injury. In these situations, one thought would lead to the *obverse* of the other. The two pieces of information do not fit together. They are "dissonant" (see Festinger, 1957).

Cognitive dissonance appears to be a potent source of attitude change. The key is the actor's having to take responsibility for actions which are not consonant with preexisting attitudes. Dissonance is engendered in individuals when they are forced to conclude that they are the willing causal agent of some incongruous and personally meaningful decision that leads predictably to some type of negative consequences (Petty and Cacioppo, 1981: p. 146). In the classical studies of the concept, naive subjects were paid different amounts of money for participating in very distasteful activities. The subjects who were paid *little* money manifested more attitude change than those who were paid much. In the absence of substantial payment for unpleasant action, the subjects had to take more responsibility for their decision to engage in the activity, and the tension (dissonance) which derived from that situation led them to change their attitudes toward the unpleasant actions. "It wasn't so bad after all" was the result of dissonance reduction. This resolution of dissonance is not what most people would consider "logical," but it is quite "psycho-logical."

The presence of cognitive dissonance as a factor in members' attitude change is reflected in the closeness of the relationships they voluntarily established with the woman pastor. Many sociologists have found it useful to distinguish between two broad types of social relationships—"primary" versus "secondary" relationships (Cooley, 1962: pp. 23–30). Primary relationships refer to the kinds of interpersonal relations that classically exist in nuclear families and groups of close friends. These relationships involve the total person rather than a segmented role alone. They tend to be centered in the person *per se* rather than the position he or she occupies. Primary relations are usually desired as ends in themselves and not merely as means to other ends. They are intrinsic rather than extrinsic. We invest our emotions in them. They "matter" to us.

Secondary relations, on the other hand, are the opposites of primary relations. They refer to the fleeting and impersonal interaction between the clerk and customer in the store and between the job applicant and the employment interviewer. Secondary relations are highly segmented, instrumental, devoid of emotion— very impersonal. They matter little to us intrinsically. They are important only as they give us something else they were intended to produce.

Contact between church member and clergywoman can be either of these types. Certainly at the outset the interaction tends to be secondary. At first the two parties are total strangers to each other, except for the mutual "reviews" each has done of the other, and even that process is highly impersonal. In fact, prior to the initial contact, the relationship is about as instrumental as one could hope to find. The church is seeking "someone" to assume the pastoral leadership of the congregation, and the kind of person they are seeking is typically defined in highly extrinsic performance-oriented terms. "Can she (or, usually, "he") preach?" "Can she attract more young people to the church?" "Is she married?" The clergywoman is doing qualitatively very similar things. Especially if she has been seeking a position for a long time (which is typical), she simply is seeking "someplace" where church members will take her pastoral skills seriously and give her an opportunity to serve them—and sometimes it matters little where.

After a pastor is on the scene, many members establish relationships with him/her that are primary in nature. Some members learn to trust the new pastor more deeply than do others. As the parties to the relationship become better acquainted with each other, they become more than co-members of an organization. They start to become "friends." The relationships become ends in themselves, and the people involved learn to enjoy being with each other not only as pastor and member but also as friend to friend. Other members never make this transition. They remain aloof from the new pastor, perhaps because they simply choose to remain marginally involved in the church as a whole. They never really "get to know" the minister. The relationship remains "secondary."

Some observers would argue that contact with a particular clergywoman as pastor is likely to be associated with improved receptivity to women in ministry in general to the extent that the interaction becomes primary rather than secondary. Establishing a primary relationship with the woman pastor promotes attitude change because it engenders cognitive dissonance. It is counter-attitudinal. For persons who have reservations about women in ministry to voluntarily establish a close personal relationship with a particular clergywoman as pastor is to make a commitment to patterns of action that are contrary to preexisting attitudes. One way of reducing those conflicts is to bring the negative attitudes into line with the relationship established with the woman pastor.

The study of the contact members includes a question which can be used as an indicator of differing amounts of cognitive dissonance engendered in the contact situation. The item is a question which seeks to determine differences in the extent to which members developed close relationships with their woman pastor. The question stated:

"While _____(name)_____ was working with your church, would you say that you got to know her:

```
as a close personal friend . . . . . . . . . . . . . . . . . . . . .31%
fairly well. . . . . . . . . . . . . . . . . . . . . . . . . . . . . . . . . . .45%
a little  . . . . . . . . . . . . . . . . . . . . . . . . . . . . . . . . . . . .15%
not very well . . . . . . . . . . . . . . . . . . . . . . . . . . . . . . .10%
```

The results of comparing amount of change in receptivity to the extent to which members established primary relationships with their woman pastor were mostly in line with what one would predict. We correlated closeness of relationship with amount of change on each dimension of receptivity to pursue the question, and the results of that analysis are shown in Table 8.2. Establishing primary relations with the woman pastor is related to amount of change in receptivity to clergywomen on every dimension except that of preferences for men in subordinate roles. The more personally members get to know the female minister, the more they change their minds about clergywomen, the more they alter their preferences for men in most clergy roles and the more they depart from previous willingness to discriminate against female candidates. The correlations involving change in preference for men in organizational roles is slightly stronger than the others, suggesting that changes in this type of gender preference is more susceptible to the influence of establishing close relationships than are changes in stereotyping, sacramental preferences and willingness to discriminate. But the differences in coefficients are so small as to be easily overemphasized. Suffice it to say that all three dimensions of receptivity change more if the respondent develops a close relationship with the clergywoman serving as pastor than if the relationship remains distant.

At first glance, this pattern would lead one to conclude that the quality of the relationship is what induces the change in level of receptivity. Indeed, this is the point we wish to make. However, it must be acknowledged that the opposite could be true; i.e., it is possible that different *preexisting* levels of receptivity caused people to be willing to establish varying degrees of primary relationships with the pastor once she arrived. There is abundant evidence in other research that such preexisting attitudes influence the kind of social interaction in which one is willing to engage with another person (e.g., Bogardus, 1951). Accordingly, it is possible that the same pattern exists concerning the willingness of church members to establish close relationships with the clergywoman who is their pastor. Negative attitudes are not likely to encourage members to get to know the woman minister well. They are a barrier to close relationships.

We were able to check out this possibility by correlating the degree to which members established primary relationships with the clergywoman and the level of their receptivity to clergywomen *prior* to their experience with her. The results indicate that the variables were unrelated. *There was no statistically significant correlation between quality of relationship and any dimension of prior receptivity to clergywomen.* This pattern suggests that it was *not* prior attitudes that led to either close or distant relationships with the woman pastor. Instead, it was more likely the quality of the relationship with the pastor that influenced the members' levels of receptivity *during and after* contact. Having the close relationship led to positive attitudes toward women in ministry, and not vice versa.

Explaining the Effects of Contact

The patterns in the observations about attitude change in the preceding section provide us with some important information for developing insights into why and how contact with clergywomen in pastoral roles can bring about reductions in resistance to women in ministry. What appears on the surface as anomaly is often the critical juncture for distinguishing the applicability of divergent theoretical perspectives. Such appears to be the case in the sets of correlations between amounts of attitude change and evaluations of effectiveness and closeness of relationships.

The patterns of relationships between changes in receptivity and evaluations of clergywomen's effectiveness and closeness of relationship of clergywomen suggest that *it is primarily reduction of cognitive dissonance that is producing the attitude change*. The simple version of the contact hypothesis argues that persons change their attitudes toward objects of prejudice simply on the basis of the information received in the context of social interaction with particular concrete instances of those attitude objects. In the case of women in ministry, that would mean that attitudes toward clergywomen would change from resistance to receptivity primarily on the basis of the information about female pastors obtained in the context of interaction with them. Accurate information about their characteristics would replace inaccurate prejudices and stereotypes. Conceptualizing attitude change in this fashion portrays it as a very *logical* process. Real perceptions replace unrealistic images. Accurate information displaces heresay. Truth replaces falsity.

It may be true that abstract logic is one of humanity's crowning attributes, but attitude change is more subtle and less rational than such a logical characterization depicts. In fact, to the extent that attitudes involve positive and negative feelings, matters of "affect" which do not conform to rules of logic (in fact they are often seen as a-logical), rationality may not be an appropriate focal point for dealing with attitude change at all.

Attitudes changing regardless of the logic involved is precisely the image portrayed in the relationships between changes in receptivity and evaluations of the clergywoman's effectiveness. Church members where women served as pastors changed their perceptions of clergywomen partly on the basis of positive perceptions of their minister. But they changed their minds about preferring men for clergy roles and altered their readiness to discriminate against women in ministry *independently* of the "real" information they obtained through observations of the particular clergywoman who served them as pastor. If attitude change were primarily a matter of logic, then all components of attitude should have become more positive in the presence of positive perceptions of the female pastor, and they should have remained negative (or become more negative) in the face of negative evaluations of the woman pastor. But they did not. Other forces must have been at work producing the attitude change.

Instead of logic being responsible for church members' altered attitudes, it seems that "psycho-logic" was at work. In this instance the particular aspect of individual psychology operating seems to have involved cognitive dissonance, an interpretation consistent with the relationships between amount of attitude change and the closeness of the relationship the members established with the woman pastor.

Establishing a close relationship with the clergywoman is a manifestation of the kind of actions that can lead to attitude change. Members have varying degrees of choice in the extent to which they develop a close relationship with their pastor. The situation is not totally devoid of coercive elements—with board members and other incumbents of lay positions in the church being forced structurally to interact with the clergywoman, whereas others may not be—but such structured relations need not necessarily lead to close personal relationships with the pastor. They can be kept "secondary" if the member wants. But whether by choice or by role compliance, some members did develop close relations with the pastor and others did not. Establishing those close relationships are the behaviors that are dissonant with previous resistance to women in ministry—dissonant with former stereotypes, but more importantly dissonant with former preferences for men in ministerial roles. The member who develops primary relationships with the woman pastor thus becomes committed to overt actions that are contrary to preexisting attitudes. This overt commitment creates cognitive dissonance. Since the member has already committed him/herself to the interaction, it is more difficult to change the behavior than the attitude, and the result tends to be attitude change. As a result of committing oneself to developing good relations with the clergywoman, the cognitive dissonance is resolved by changing receptivity toward women in ministry. Stereotyping diminishes, preference for men in pastoral roles subsides, and there is less willingness to discriminate against the female ministerial candidate. These changes take place because of the overt commitment to the pastoral relationships, and they occur to the extent that such a commitment is present—regardless of the member's assessment of the effectiveness of the particular clergywoman's work. The process may seem "illogical," but that is not always important when dealing with attitudes. It is the "psychological" dynamics that are important, and in the case of dissonance reduction those processes appear to be a-logical.

Applying cognitive dissonance theory to changes in receptivity to clergywomen does not invalidate the contact hypothesis. In fact the concept reinforces contact theory. It offers an explanation of *how* resistance turns to receptivity in the pastor/member interactional situation. Given the fact of contact, what is the nature of the process by which contact can result in reduction of prejudice toward clergywomen? One aspect of that process appears to involve reduction of cognitive dissonance, especially on the part of those members who try to establish good relationships with the woman pastor. The idea that "we've got to make a go of it" becomes transformed into the perception that "we really had nothing to be concerned about in the first place." The contact simply structures a situation which gives church members an opportunity to act overtly in such a way that they in effect force attitude change upon themselves!

Changes in the Structure of Preferences

To this point we have demonstrated that degree of receptivity to women in ministry is related to contact with clergywomen in a pastoral role. The level of resistance to women in ministry is lower among church members who have experienced a woman pastor than among those who have not. Resistance diminishes and receptivity increases as people interact with a woman in the role of pastor. The more personal that interaction is, the more it will result in change.

The question to which we turn now concerns not changes in the *level* of receptivity to clergywomen but rather shifts in the *structure* of receptivity. By "structure" we mean the pattern of distinctions which church members make in their preferences for men or women in specific clergy roles as discussed in Chapter 2. Those patterns are reproduced in the bottom of Table 8.3. The structure of those preferences was based on at least three criteria. Their preferences tended to cluster so as to comprise a liturgical or sacramental dimension, a second dimension focusing on organizational leadership, and a third dimension involving subordinate clergy roles. Preferences for men or women specifically in the role of pastor tended to cluster with preferences associated with organizational leadership rather than the other two dimensions.

Does this structure of attitudes change in the contact situation? We approached this question by comparing the results of two factor analyses of the gender-preference items, one prior to contact and one following the interaction. Any differences between the results of those two factor analyses would constitute "changes" in the structure of those attitudes and should be attributable to the contact experience itself.

Some of the results of this analysis are contained in Table 8.3. At this point we analyzed the combined data from members of churches served by both interim and installed pastors as was done in much of the preceding analysis. A number of interesting patterns are apparent in the outcome. These concern the number of factors, the nature of the items within them, the order of importance of the factors and the location of particular items. The table shows that *prior* to contact there were basically three dimensions to the gender-preference answers. The first factor is the sacramental one. It contains primarily questions dealing with public worship, nurturance and the sacraments. This factor accounted for approximately 79% of the variance. The second factor is organizational, containing the dominant leadership positions and matters of running the church as an organization. The third factor contains the typically subordinate staff positions.

The fact that the "pastor" items ("pastor" and "lead staff as senior minister") loaded on the organizational factor more than on the sacramental one is probably meaningful. Remembering that the items specifically ask whether the respondents prefer a man, a woman, or have no preference for each position or function, the dimension on which the pastor items load implies the criteria members had in mind when indicating their preference for men or women in the pastor position *per se*. Since the pastorate loaded with the "organizational" items, the pattern suggests that members' gender-preferences specifically for the pastor are associated primarily with their concerns about the identity of the person responsible for keeping the church's organizational

TABLE 8.3 RESULTS OF FACTOR ANALYSIS OF GENDER PREFERENCE QUESTIONS BEFORE AND AFTER CONTACT WITH A CLERGY WOMAN AS INTERIM OR INSTALLED PASTOR, AND AMONG PANEL MEMBERS WITH NO CONTACT

	Factor #1	Factor #2	Factor #3
BEFORE CONTACT			
administer Lord's Supper	.79	.29	.11
conduct a funeral	.72	.44	.13
administer baptism	.71	.31	.06
preach a sermon	.66	.49	.15
lead pastoral prayer	.64	.24	.23
associate pastor	.40	.27	.29
	(79%)		
lead staff as senior minister	.34	.72	.11
work with a contractor	.19	.64	−.02
pastor	.39	.62	.06
lead the session	.36	.61	.17
		(13%)	
Minister of Music	.01	−.07	.65
Minister of Education	.15	.09	.59
Minister for Youth	.18	.30	.44
			(8%)

	Factor #1	Factor #2	Factor #3
AFTER CONTACT			
preach a sermon	.77	−.05	.06
conduct a funeral	.75	.09	−.17
administer Lord's Supper	.69	.09	−.10
lead pastoral prayer	.69	.04	.20
administer baptism	.61	.28	.01
pastor	.55	.33	−.11
lead staff as senior minister	.52	.36	−.09
counsel person with problems	.47	.17	.06
lead the session	.40	.32	.12
	(74%)		
work with a contractor	.01	.47	−.13
work on the budget	.14	.45	.03
		(15%)	
Minister of Education	.07	.06	.69
Minister of Music	−.04	−.09	.32
			(11%)

TABLE 8.3   (CONT.)

	Factor #1	Factor #2	Factor #3
CONTROL PANEL			
administer baptism	.84	.27	.19
administer Lord's Supper	.77	.32	.19
conduct a funeral	.65	.44	.10
preach a sermon	.55	.47	.18
	(82%)		
lead staff as senior minister	.32	.70	.08
pastor	.33	.61	− .01
work with a contractor	.15	.58	.01
work on the budget	.21	.50	.27
lead the session	.39	.50	.34
counsel person with a pro-blem	.22	.46	.21
		(11%)	
Minister of Education	.17	− .02	.55
Minister of Music	.03	.09	.40
			(8%)

machinery running. These activities are at the heart of sexual stereotyping not only in the church but secular organizations as well, i.e., leadership in finance, architecture and construction, and organizational administration in general. Corporate leaders tend to be men. Before contact, preference for a man or a woman specifically as pastor appears to be mostly a matter of *organizational* leadership.

Conversely, since gender-preference associated with "pastor" did *not* load as strongly on the sacramental dimension, members' concerns about the pastor's sex evidently is not associated as much with the more explicitly theological component reflected in the first factor. Preferences for liturgical and sacramental functions before contact are not the main criteria that influence pastoral preferences. The same applies to preferences for men or women in subordinate staff positions.

Since these patterns are based on answers to questions calling upon members to *remember* their preferences before they met the pastor, it is important to be cautious in interpreting them. Memory is not always a trustworthy source of data. It is also possible that members felt led to give socially acceptable answers to questions dealing with whether they had changed their minds after contact with a woman pastor. However, we can be more confident in these patterns than we might otherwise expect when dealing with most memory-based data, because they parallel those observed in the control group as well. *The similarity constitutes an important validation of the memory questions*. If the request that members recall their past preferences yields responses that actually represent past reality, i.e., preferences they had *before* contact with the clergywoman, then the patterns of factors or dimensions based on memory among the contact members should correspond to the *present* preferences of the Panel. The Panel, as a control group, did not have contact with a woman pastor, and their present preferences are just that, i.e., "present"— not based on memory. *A comparison* of past preferences of the contact members with the present preferences of the Panel in Table 8.3 shows that they are very similar. The two factor analyses result in the same number of dimensions, virtually identical contents of the first, second, and third dimensions, and the pastor items loaded on the same dimension—the organizational. These patterns reinforce the validity of similar comparisons between contact members' memory and Panel members' preference concerning the *level* of receptivity to clergywomen. The present comparison also indicates a basic similarity in terms of *structure* of preferences. These patterns give us even more confidence in the comparability of the two subpopulations, and it lends credence to the assertion that the memory-based responses of contact members are sufficiently accurate to be analytically useful.

We may now turn to the question of whether the structure of gender-preferences changed after contact with the woman pastor. These shifts may be seen by comparing the results of the factor analyses in the top and middle portions of Table 8.3, those corresponding to measures before and after contact. There are some ways in which the structure of attitudes toward clergywomen remained stable. First, the number of factors is the same. Second, the main factor remains the same, i.e., the sacramental one. The first factor also accounts for roughly the same amount of the variance. The identities of the second and third factors are basically the same, i.e., the organizational dimension and the subordinate dimension, respectively.

However, the comparison of attitude structures before and after contact also reveals an important change. Whereas prior to contact the "pastoral" items load on the organizational dimension, after contact they load primarily on the liturgical or sacramental dimension. This indicates that after the contact experience, lay church members no longer conceptualize their preferences for men or women explicitly as "pastor" in organizational terms, but instead view the matter as primarily liturgical in nature.

Without additional data it is not possible to explain these patterns of stability and change in gender preferences with absolute certainty. However, at least one explanation seems plausible. The stability of the sacramental dimension as the first factor is probably associated with the fact that it is the most public and most widely scrutinized dimension. It reflects the major arena in which most members see the pastor. It is also the most popular criterion used when people think of searching for a new pastor. It contains the activities or functions most uniquely associated with the church when it is an interacting social entity—during the ritual experiences. This high visibility of the woman in those roles probably also explains movement of the "pastoral" items primarily into the liturgical dimension. After contact gender-preferences associated with the position of pastor are less exclusively concerns about organizational leadership. Instead, gender-preferences for the pastor are conceptualized more in terms of the total life of the church, particularly the liturgical sphere.

The subordinate dimension appears to be quite stable, with the exception of the fact that after contact the position of "Minister for Youth" did not load on any dimension. The remaining items, formerly associated with organizational concerns, appear after contact as matters of technical competence with which males are popularly identified. These functions involve technical matters associated with constructing buildings and organizational financing. In the minds of most people, handling these issues is usually left up to men.

These patterns emerged from a comparison of the structure of attitudes toward clergywomen using data from *all* of the contact members. The contact members are comprised of lay members in congregations served by a woman as *either* interim pastor or installed pastor. It is important to ask again whether this combination of the two groups is legitimate analytically, because the appointment of the clergywomen in each type of situation differs. The characteristics of the congregations themselves also differed markedly in each situation. Congregations where interim clergy-women served tended to be large churches enjoying ample economic and social resources. The congregations which had installed women as pastor, on the other hand, tended to be small bodies with few economic and social assets. The role of pastor in each type of situation is likely to be quite different. Accordingly, we need to examine changes in the structure of attitudes before and after contact in each of the two leadership situations alone.

Table 8.4 contains the results of the factor analyses of gender-preference items before and after contact in *the MAL churches—* those served by interims. The structure of attitudes to women in ministry before contact closely resembles that of the attitudes of members in the control group (Table 8.3 above). That is, in each case there are three factors, the main factor is the liturgical/sacra-mental one, the second is the organizational one, and the third involves the subordinate roles. In both cases the items specifically pertaining to the position of "pastor" load primarily on the orga-nizational dimension. This comparison validates again the measure of attitudes prior to contact, procedures relying on the respon-dents' memory.

Among the members served by clergywomen as interim pastor, comparisons of the structure of attitudes before and after contact are instructive. Once again a few points of similarity re-main. The main dimension is still the sacramental one, the position of pastor does not appear to be identified with that dimension, and the subordinate positions also load elsewhere.

Nevertheless, the contact experience among members served by women as interim pastor appears to result in some noteworthy changes in the structure of their attitudes toward women in ministry. First, the number of factors after contact increases from three to four. Second, the preferences pertaining explicitly to the "pastor" items constitute a dimension unto itself, clearly loading with none of the other three. Finally, the clarity of the organiza-tional and subordinate dimensions diminishes. Each of the third and fourth factors contains items previously associated with both dimensions.

The comparisons of attitude structures before and after con-tact with a clergywoman as an *installed* pastor are contained in Table 8.5. The structure of attitudes prior to contact in this situa-tion shows both similarities to and differences from those noted previously. The initial attitude structure among these members is similar to that of others in that the liturgical dimension is still the dominant one, with the subordinate dimension as a secondary

TABLE 8.4   RESULTS OF FACTOR ANALYSIS OF GENDER PREFERENCE
QUESTIONS BEFORE AND AFTER CONTACT WITH A WOMAN AS
INTERIM PASTOR

	Factor #1	Factor #2	Factor #3	
BEFORE CONTACT				
conduct a funeral	.82	.23	.11	
preach a sermon	.77	.32	.06	
administer Lord's Supper	.74	.21	.03	
administer baptism	.66	.21	.07	
lead pastoral prayer	.65	.15	.05	
associate pastor	.44	.33	.16	
counsel person with problems	.40	.26	.01	
	(71%)			
lead staff as senior minister	.21	.85	.02	
pastor	.44	.63	.04	
lead the session	.36	.58	.04	
work with a contractor	.14	.52	− .01	
		(16%)		
Minister of Education	− .01	.10	.80	
Minister for Music	.15	− .06	.62	
			(13%)	

	Factor #1	Factor #2	Factor #3	Factor #4
AFTER CONTACT				
preach a sermon	.80	.10	.05	.10
administer Lord's Supper	.65	.15	− .03	− .07
lead pastoral prayer	.65	.22	.26	.18
administer baptism	.65	.29	− .06	.01
conduct a funeral	.57	.28	− .09	.15
associate pastor	.54	.03	.06	.05
	(55%)			
lead staff as senior minister	.24	.78	− .03	.12
pastor	.23	.57	.03	− .02
		(22%)		
Minister of Education	.01	.01	.95	.08
Minister of Music	− .06	− .15	.44	.31
work with a contractor	− .05	− .03	− .33	.05
			(14%)	
lead the session	.16	?2	− .01	.60
Minister of Youth	.05	− . ?	.04	.48
				(10%)

matter. The structure of these attitudes is different from that observed in the other situation in several respects. First, the number of factors is smaller, there being but two dimensions in this situation and three dimensions among members served by interim pastors. Second, the main factor among members of congregations which had installed women as pastor contains the items previously identified with two separate dimensions, i.e., the sacramental and the organizational components. Before contact with a clergywoman members of these churches conceptualize gender-preferences involving these functions in more definite terms.

It is interesting to speculate about reasons for these differences between the two types of congregations prior to their contact with a clergywoman. The answer probably resides in congregational differences noted previously, divergences having nothing to do with whether they experience the clergywoman as either interim minister or installed pastor. Another stage of the analysis (Chapter 9) indicates that the churches differed markedly in their economic and social resources. Churches where *interims* served tended to be above-average in these areas, i.e., they were larger, had more young people, had members with higher incomes, and were located in stable communities. Churches that had *installed* women as pastor were characterized by traits which were the opposite of each of these factors. In short, churches served by interim ministers, being able to depend on adequate resources, could afford to make relatively fine distinctions in the roles they wanted their pastor to play and the things they wanted her to emphasize. In smaller churches with fewer resources, the members do not have that luxury. Their pastor must be the "jack of all trades." Unless pastors of these marginal situations possess leadership skills of all types, leadership is simply less likely to take place. These variations in the structure of attitudes between members served by women in the two types of roles probably have more to do with those differences in basic congregational resources than with the kind of leadership situations.

Even though these differences existed prior to contact with the clergywomen, the experience itself seems to have brought about very similar changes in attitude structures in both types of contact situations. First, the number of attitudinal dimensions increased after contact from two to four. Second, the primary factor became less inclusive than it was prior to contact. Next, the

TABLE 8.5 RESULTS OF FACTOR ANALYSIS OF GENDER PREFERENCE QUESTIONS BEFORE AND AFTER CONTACT WITH A WOMAN AS INSTALLED PASTOR

	Factor #1	Factor #2		
BEFORE CONTACT				
conduct a funeral	.86	.13		
preach a sermon	.84	.21		
lead staff as senior minister	.83	.16		
administer baptism	.81	.05		
pastor	.70	.14		
lead the session	.70	.18		
work on the budget	.70	.15		
lead pastoral prayer	.68	.23		
work with a contractor	.66	.06		
counsel person with problems	.47	.33		
	(88%)			
Minister for Youth	.27	.67		
Minister of Music	− .10	.51		
Minister of Education	.30	.47		
		(12%)		

	Factor #1	Factor #2	Factor #3	Factor #4
AFTER CONTACT				
conduct a funeral	.84	− .10	.12	.13
preach a sermon	.78	.31	− .13	.01
administer Lord's Supper	.71	.07	.26	.05
lead pastoral prayer	.68	.24	.01	− .12
pastor	.63	.28	.32	− .10
administer baptism	.57	.22	.38	− .11
lead staff as senior minister	.55	.36	.21	− .30
counsel person with problems	.47	.32	.25	.11
	(66%)			
Minister for Youth	.24	.70	− .07	.20
associate pastor	.08	.49	.21	− .04
		(12%)		
work with a contractor	.03	.15	.61	− .14
work on the budget	.32	− .04	.50	.23
			(11%)	
Minister of Music	− .03	.10	− .03	.72
				(10%)

technical competency items concerned with constructing buildings and working on budgets became a distinct dimension. Fourth, the subordinate dimension became divided into two factors. Finally, the items specifically concerned with the "pastor" remained associated more with the sacramental dimension than the organizational one.

By way of summary, then, what generalizations can we make from these patterns of change in the structure of attitudes before and after contact with a clergywoman as pastor? *Among the individuals involved, the major change that results from contact with a woman as pastor seems to be one of increased cognitive complexity.* Prior to contact, attitudes toward women in ministry tend to be relatively undifferentiated. The dimensions are few in number. They tend to involve some stereotyping, as illustrated in members' conceptualizing female leadership in terms of the quality of organizational leadership. After contact, however, having observed a woman functioning in pastoral roles perhaps for the first time, early perceptions tend to break down into more complex distinctions. "Reality" doesn't seem as simple and clear-cut as it did in the absence of the contact experience. The members find that there is more to a clergywoman than initially meets the eye.

Among the congregation as a whole, much of the consensus that existed prior to contact concerning the desirability of a woman functioning in various areas begins to break down after direct experience with a clergywoman. While the sacramental factor remains clear, the remaining dimensions tend to become "unglued." With the possible exception of the organizational dimension, given its retention of organizational items in most cases, the loadings on the factors beyond the first one contain few items and involve increasing amounts of ambiguity. This pattern makes it difficult to consider them distinct "dimensions" of gender-preferences at all. Once members who have had contact with the woman pastor get beyond the sacramental functions in which her work is so public, there appear to be few clear distinctions left. The previous clarity with which members segregated their preferences for men—for tasks of running the church versus for specific subareas of church programs such as music, education, and youth work—gives way to uncertainty.

It would probably be a mistake to try to interpret each specific shift in loadings separately. Instead, it is best to view them together as indicating increased uncertainty about preferences beyond the sacramental ones. This reflects a change not just in the individuals but most likely also in the amount of consensus that exists among them. The shared meanings and norms that governed these distinctions prior to contact seem to break down, leaving individuals to structure their gender-preferences more idiosyncratically. Prior to contact, "everyone knew" what the rules of the game were. Having a female as minister of education or youth was "one thing," but having one as senior minister was "something else." Hearing a woman preach sermons or perform other liturgical roles "had its place," but a woman's playing a major role in leading the session or constructing the church budget was "a different matter." The common understandings in these various arenas were "known" well enough before contact so as to produce the patterns in the factor analysis that involved the three dimensions and the relatively clear loadings on each. After interacting with a woman pastor, however, the consensus on these issues broke down. What "everyone knew" became matters of individual experience and choice. The subculture of rather clear male/female distinctions began to disappear.

This kind of change probably amounts to a decline in institutionalized sexism—male/female distinctions in gender-preferences are no longer shared on as much of an "of course" basis, precisely the kind of change anyone positively concerned about the interests of clergywomen would want to observe resulting from the contact situation.

The shift of the two specifically "pastoral" items, typically from the organizational dimension to the sacramental one, is worthy of one final note. It indicates that after contact with the clergywoman, members articulate gender-preferences for pastor mainly on the basis of sacramental concerns. These choices are grouped with choices about men or women for preaching and worship, funerals, and personal counselling. This shift is most likely to be associated with the other patterns already noted. It is also consistent with the previous discussion about the role played by cognitive dissonance in the changes noted in receptivity levels. It is in the context of these public liturgical situations that most members make the commitment to interact with the clergy-women. For them "getting to know her well" takes place almost exclusively in the context of public activities such as worship and other services. For a subset of the members, these highly structured and formal interactional settings are but a starting point and a catalyst for developing more personal relationships, interaction peripheral to the public forums themselves but necessary to them—occasions such as planning meetings, committee and board meetings, programmatic consultations, etc. An even smaller segment of members moves in even closer, coming to know the clergywoman as a personal friend. They go to entertainment events together, share rides, borrow tools and other goods, and pass leisure time over coffee. Clearly and objectively, the latter persons develop relationships with the clergywomen which carry more personal investment and commitment. But whether in the public or the very private sphere, it is the members themselves who "decide" whether they have made commitments to member/pastor relationship that are either consonant or dissonant with prior attitudes. If there is such dissonance, whether based on sacramental or personal interaction, it is likely to be productive of attitude change.

Contact and the Effect of Background Characteristics

In Chapter 4 we observed sets of relationships between the measures of receptivity and a wide variety of predictor variables. These relationships indicated that some difference in receptivity to women in ministry can be explained in terms of at least three perspectives. Resistance to women clergy was found to be partly a feature of sexism in general, partly a reflection of religious traditionalism and partly a derivative of the type of congregation in which the members participate. These differences in church members' personal and social characteristics render many variations in receptivity to women in ministry both understandable and predictable.

We are now in a position to ask whether these factors continue to influence levels of receptivity after the members have personally experienced a woman in the role of pastor. Since such contact alters the extent to which lay members stereotype clergy-women and prefer men in clergy roles, it is possible that the interaction also affects the impact of various background variables upon receptivity. After contact do men still manifest more resistance to women in ministry than do women? Are people in large churches still more opposed to female pastors than are those in small congregations? Does church attendance still make a difference? We can answer questions such as these by correlating the relevant variables with the receptivity scores among the contact members only and then comparing the results to those obtained in Chapter 4.

Individual Traits

The results of this analysis indicate that *contact does dampen the effect of some of these background characteristics, but that others of them still retain their impact when the effects of contact are held constant.* These patterns are shown in Table 8.4. The variables that continue to be correlates of receptivity are mostly in the category of personal traits. Sex is still predictive after contact, but with a noteworthy modification. More males than females still tend to stereotype clergywomen and to prefer a man in a variety of organizational roles. Preference for men in sacramental functions after contact becomes the same for men and women. However, there is a reversal on the behavioral dimension. Whereas prior to contact sex made no difference in willingness to discriminate against women candidates, after having interacted with a woman as pastor it is the *women* who are the more prone to discriminate against clergywomen.

A similar shift occurs regarding race. Prior to contact, race differences were unrelated to variations in receptivity. After the contact experience, however, race turned out to be associated with differences in sacramental score and subordinate score. In churches served by clergywomen, more non-whites than whites prefer a man performing sacramental functions and in subordinate clergy positions. Several of the churches in the evaluation study were located in neighborhoods where the racial composition of the population was in transition. A number of respondents in those situations made comments that may shed some light on

TABLE 8.6 CORRELATIONS BETWEEN RECEPTIVITY SCORES AND SELECTED BACKGROUND CHARACTERISTICS: CONTACT MEMBERS ONLY

INDIVIDUAL CHARACTERISTICS	Sex	Age	Race	Marital Status	Education	Income	Occupation
stereotyping score	-.14	.17	—*	—	-.09	—	.14
sacramental score	—*	—	.35	—	-.12	-.18	.17
organizational score	-.28	.10	—	—	—	-.08	—
subordinate score	—	—	.40	—	-.38	-.41	—
willingness to discriminate	.27	—	—	—	-.17	-.12	.18

RELIGIOSITY	Church attendance	Church contributions	Ideology	Say grace	Church officer
stereotyping score	—	—	—	—	—
sacramental score	-.16	—	—	—	—
organizational score	—	—	-.20	—	—
subordinate score	—	—	—	.41	—
willingness to discriminate	—	—	—	-.17	—

CHURCH CHARACTERISTICS	Church size	Community size	Member trend	Budget trend	Dual alignment	Multiple staff
stereotyping score	—	—	.12	-.11	.28	—
sacramental score	—	—	.16	—	—	—
organizational score	.10	—	—	—	.37	.32
subordinate score	—	—	—	—	—	.34
willingness to discriminate	—	—	—	—	—	—

Indicates statistically non-significant correlation.

this pattern. The general thrust of their remarks is that they liked the clergywoman serving as their pastor. They thought she related to them well, was not prejudiced toward other non-whites and did a good job leading the congregation. Nevertheless, their reservations about their white-female pastor centered on their young people, especially the young men. The young people were in a process of drifting away from church. To bring them back would require the presence of a Black male in the pulpit, in their opinion, someone to whom the young people could relate more easily than to a white female. The non-white members who indicated such preferences were quick to point out that this was not any reflection on the competence of the woman pastor. Instead it reflected a simple fact of life in the black community, one which they thought should be taken into consideration.

Another shift in the patterns after contact is more perplexing. Members' income and occupation became *more* predictive of some components of receptivity after contact than before. Members with low income were more resistant to clergywomen than were those with high income, and those in low status occupations (clerk, laborer) were slightly more resistant than were those in high status jobs (manager, engineer). If these changes are meaningful, the explanations for their having taken place are not known at the present time.

The major reduction in capacity for predicting receptivity among these variables occurs in relation to age. Prior to contact, age predicted level of receptivity on every dimension. The older a person was the more he/she tended to resist the idea of having a woman as minister. After contact these correlations were restricted to stereotyping and organizational preferences, and age was no longer associated with gender preferences in sacramental or subordinate roles or with willingness to discriminate against female candidates. The clergywomen tended to win the older people over.

Individual Religiosity

In contrast to the individual traits discussed above, contact made a great deal of difference in the effects of religious involvement on receptivity. Whereas in the absence of direct experience with a woman pastor every dimension of individual religiosity was related to variations in receptivity, the opportunity to have such a relationship eliminated nearly all of those correlations. After contact members' attitudes toward women in ministry tended to be independent of their religious ideology and their public and private ritual behavior. These figures are also shown in Table 8.6.

Only two relationships remained consistent with the Panel data. Members with a conservative religious ideology still preferred a man in the organizational roles. Those who are high in devotional behavior still preferred a man in subordinate roles.

However, there are also two reversals in the direction of relationships between religiosity and receptivity. Whereas prior to contact members who attended church frequently tended to oppose the idea of women in liturgical roles, after experiencing the woman first-hand those who are high in attendance not only no longer show such an inclination but also manifest the opposite tendency. That is, after contact the preference for men in sacramental roles shows up mainly among members who did *not* attend church very often. Similarly, the association between devotionalism and willingness to discriminate reverses direction. After contact members who say grace at meals often are less willing to discriminate against female candidates than are those who seldom say grace at meals.

By far the most general tendency involving the religiosity variables is for their impact on receptivity to be cancelled out by contact with a woman pastor. The experience of interacting with a clergywoman in the pastoral role appears to overshadow the former effects of any differences in religious commitment.

These differences between members with and without contact with women in the role of pastor also support the earlier discussion of the role of cognitive dissonance in producing attitude change. Cognitive dissonance refers to the inconsistency experienced internally upon realization that one is committed to a line of action that is contrary to preexisting attitudes. The two bits of information do not go together—they are "dissonant."

Dissonance affects the patterns associated with personal religiosity in that it is the more traditionally religious persons who are the more likely to experience cognitive dissonance in relation to working with a clergywoman, because they tend to be both opposed to female pastoral leadership and committed to working within the church where they encounter the clergywoman. The personal commitment to the church locks them into situations in which they must develop working relationships with the female pastor to whom they were opposed initially. Breaking the relationship with the church to avoid having to work with the clergywoman is probably too difficult or painful socially and religiously. Thus the conflict is resolved by changing one's mind about women in ministry. *The people who most need to be convinced— the most resistant—are the ones who change their minds. From the standpoint of trying to implement the contact hypothesis, this represents success.*

Church Characteristics

Contact with a woman as pastor also muted the effects of differences in congregational characteristics upon receptivity to clergywomen, but not as much as did differences in religiosity. Church size made less difference among the contact members than among the Panel. After contact, members of large churches were less accepting of clergywomen only in relation to organizational functions—running the church. Whatever predictiveness community size had prior to contact also disappeared among the contact members. Budget trend also lost most of its impact where members had a woman pastor.

There were also a few reversals in the directions of the relationships between some church characteristics and receptivity. Among contact members, members of UPD-only churches were *less* resistant than were those in dually aligned churches, and persons in churches with multiple staff were also *less* resistant than were those in solo pastorates. Overall, however, the general pattern involving church characteristics tends to resemble that of religiosity—*contact tends to mute the impact of differences in congregational characteristics on receptivity to women in ministry.*

Which Members Are More Likely to Change?

Before we leave our examination of the effects of background factors on receptivity, it will be helpful to turn the analytical kaleidoscope one more time, this time to look at the relationships between *amount of change in receptivity* and the set of variables discussed above. To this point the study of effects of background factors has concentrated on their associations with *levels* of receptivity/resistance. A number of seemingly important patterns emerged from

that analysis. Now we ask whether there may be important relationships between background factors and not "level" but *change*
in receptivity. Do members with only certain characteristics
change their receptivity to clergywomen after experiencing a
woman in the pastoral role? If so, what are those unique traits—
demographics, religiosity or type of church?

The results of correlating amount of change in receptivity
scores with the background variables are contained in Table 8.7.
A few patterns in the table are noteworthy. First, it is clear that
whereas "level" of receptivity was found related to quite a few
background factors, "amount of change" in receptivity is related
to far fewer of them. The basic implication of this pattern is that,
according to most considerations, *one church member is as likely
to change in level of receptivity after experiencing a clergywoman
in the pastoral role as is another*. For example, men are as likely to
change as women, even though men tend to be more resistant at
the outset. Married persons are as likely to change as are the unmarried, rich as likely as poor, leaders as likely as rank-and-file
members, persons in dually aligned churches as likely as those in
UPC-only churches. The same applies on almost every dimension
in relation to nearly every other factor—age, occupation, piety,
community and size of church staff.

This relative lack of specificity in type of persons likely to
change in receptivity due to contact appears to have an important
programmatic implication. That is, one need not be unduly concerned about where ministers-at-large are placed. They appear to
have similar impact in small towns and cities, in small congregations and large ones, etc. The amount of cognitive dissonance
engendered in all such contact situations evidently is sufficient to
reduce the prevalence of resistance to women in ministry.

The patterns of relationships that do exist between amount of
change in receptivity and several background factors are also important. The most noteworthy set of correlations is between race
and receptivity change. *White* church members' levels of receptivity clearly change more as a result of contact than do the receptivity levels of *black* members. Two minister-at-large churches
and three churches where clergywomen had been installed as
pastors involved racially transitional neighborhoods. In those
situations, the white members' preferences for a man tended to

TABLE 8.7 CORRELATIONS BETWEEN CHANGES IN RECEPTIVITY SCORE AND SELECTED BACKGROUND VARIABLES

INDIVIDUAL TRAITS	Sex	Age	Race	Marital status	Education	Income	Occupation
stereotyping change	—*	—	—	—	—	—	—
sacramental change	—	—	-.55	—	-.12	—	—
organizational change	—	—	-.51	—	—	—	—
subordinate change	—	.16	-.38	—	-.18	—	.45
discriminating change	—	—	—	—	—	—	—

RELIGIOSITY	Church attend	Monthly contribution	Ideology	Say grace	Church officer
stereotyping change	—	—	—	—	—
sacramental change	—	—	-.22	—	—
organizational change	—	—	-.15	—	—
subordinate change	-.22	—	-.37	—	—
discriminating change	—	—	-.55	-.32	—

CHURCH CHARACTERISTICS	Church size	Community size	Member trend	Budget trend	Dual alignment	Multiple staff
stereotyping change	.16	—	-.17	-.18	—	—
sacramental change	—	—	-.11	-.20	—	—
organizational change	—	—	—	—	—	—
subordinate change	-.23	.27	—	—	—	—
discriminating change	—	—	—	—	—	.42

*Indicates a statistically non-significant correlation.

223

change more than did those of blacks. These differences are probably understandable in terms of the black members' concerns for the religious involvement of the young people as suggested above.

The other set of patterns in the table that may be noteworthy are those involving religious ideology, church attendance, membership trend, budget trend and education. In each case, they deal with factors associated with differing levels of receptivity (above), and the correlation shows that *members with characteristics associated with resistance to clergywomen before contact are the ones who change the most.* Both those who were theologically liberal and theologically conservative tended to manifest greater receptivity after contact. However, the religiously conservative members showed greater change in this direction than did their liberal counterparts. The same pattern appears when comparing members according to frequency of church attendance. Both high and low attendees had predominantly increased receptivity after contact, but the greatest amount of overall change in that direction was among those who participated in church activities frequently. In terms of membership and budget trends, we have a similar pattern, i.e., predominantly positive attitude shifts in all categories, but greater shifts among members of growing congregations. These differences are noteworthy primarily in relation to the stated goals of the M.A.L. program, i.e., to allow church members to experience women in ministry directly, and through that experience to realize that negative attitudes toward female clergy are inappropriate. The fact that members with the most negative attitudes manifested the greatest amount of change in the contact situation should be encouraging to persons wishing to promote the interests of women in ministry in this way. The program was effective in cracking even the "toughest nuts."

Other relationships in the table are scattered and isolated, and it would be easy to overinterpret them. Thus at this point we shall regard them as basically indeterminate.

Summary

We considered two theories of attitude change that could be applicable to shifts in receptivity to women in ministry associated with having experienced direct contact with a woman as pastor. One is a basically "rational" theory depicting attitude change as mainly a result of processing correct information to displace incorrect cognitions. The second theory focuses on more affective responses associated with having to reduce cognitive dissonance engendered in the contact situation.

The theory focusing on cognitive dissonance is supported more than is the one dealing with rational processing of information. Attitude change as correction of information somewhat applies to the changes in tendency to view clergywomen in stereotypical terms, but it does not explain changes in preferences for men in clergy roles or willingness to discriminate against women candidates. Attitude change as a consequence of having to reduce cognitive dissonance generated by relationships established with the woman pastor, on the other hand, appears to account for shifts on all three major dimensions of receptivity. Apparently the decision to remain involved in the congregation and to develop positive relationships with the clergywoman as pastor is sufficient to bring previous, negative attitudes toward women in ministry into line with the counter-attitudinal behavior. Thus traditional religious commitments, which initially tend to be bases for resistance to women in ministry, become part of the mechanism for transforming resistance to acceptance.

Contact with a woman as pastor also produces changes in the "structure" of attitudes toward clergywomen. Preferences for men or women in clergy roles manifest relatively clear dimensions in the absence of contact. The criteria for these preferences enjoy considerable consensus among the lay members. However, the clarity of the structure of those preferences diminished greatly upon members' interaction with a woman as pastor. Members were still clear about their preferences for men or women in sacramental roles, but their feelings about the organizational and subordinate components became fractionated. These aspects of the subculture deteriorated; the basis for making such choices appears less to be matters of shared consensus than idiosyncratic considerations. In other words, after contact lay members depended less for their reactions to women in ministry on "what everybody knows," because they weren't so sure about it collectively any more. Instead, they were left to their own perceptions and reactions. This pattern represents a decline in the extent to which sexism was institutionalized in the congregational subcultures and an increase in the extent to which individual members were left to their own devices.

Just as the attitudinal changes associated with the contact situation muted the influence of contacts with women in other occupations, these shifts in receptivity as a result of contact also suppressed the effects of most background characteristics. This outcome is especially true in relation to differences in religious commitment and type of church. After direct experience with a woman pastor, far fewer differences in receptivity to women in ministry can be explained by these variables than was the case prior to contact. Evidently the impact of the contact experience rendered inert most predictive background factors.

Finally, background characteristics of church members are not predictive of which members are more likely to increase their receptivity to women in ministry as a result of contact. One type of person is generally as likely to change as another. Members of one type of church are as likely to shift as another. The major exception to this pattern is race. White church members are more likely than non-whites to increase their receptivity to clergy-women due to contact. This pattern apparently is based on perceptions of those blacks that a white female pastor could not meet specific felt needs as well as a black man could satisfy them. Contact with the white woman as pastor did little to alter those perceptions.

Suggestions for Additional Reading

Deutsch, Morton and M. E. Collins
   1951 *Interracial Housing: A Psychological Evaluation of a Social Experiment.* Minneapolis: University of Minnesota Press.

   A classic study of the contact hypothesis. An evaluation of the effects of interracial contact in a non-segregated housing project. Shows early thinking about the contact hypothesis, illustrating the need to pay attention to other dimensions of the contact situation.

Festinger, Leon A.
   1957 *A Theory of Cognitive Dissonance.* New York: Harper & Row.

   Leon Festinger is the social psychologist who coined the term "cognitive dissonance." This book is the classic initial systemization of his thinking on the idea. Contains numerous references to experimental studies in support of his theory, as well as the study of the apocalyptic religious group around which much of the initial formulation took place.

Liska, Allen E.
   1975 *The Consistency Controversy: Readings on the Impact of Attitude on Behavior.* New York: John Wiley & Sons.

   A collection of essays dealing with the problem of the relationships between people's attitudes and their overt behavior. Traces the historical development of interest in the problem. Indicates ways in which the relationship may be said to exist in the light of recent research.

CHAPTER 9

Getting into the System: What Makes a Difference?

Whenever individuals or groups try to move into a social arena that traditionally has been closed to them, they face an identifiable series of problems which must be solved if they are to succeed. They must be recognized as persons seriously interested in participating, they must establish the legitimacy of their participation, and they must get individuals already in the system to respond to them as practicing members. A generation ago, for example, black Americans began their big drive to be included in the mainstream of American society. Enroute to this goal, blacks had to destroy the myth that they really didn't want to move out of their own separate communities and be integrated into white institutions; they had to establish their right to do so at the most inclusive level, i.e., legal interpretation of the Constitution; and they had to obtain concrete legislation and other enabling policies from all three branches of the Federal government to get members of the white community to allow blacks to enter into their life-space.

Women seeking to enter occupations and professions in which men have enjoyed monopolies must deal with the same kinds of problems (see, for example, Stromberg and Harkess, 1978). Women moving into medical practice, for example, had to get functionaries in colleges and universities to take them seriously; they had to establish legal precedent for their aspirations; and they needed enforceable affirmative action and equal employment opportunity (AA-EEO) guidelines to get into and through medical schools. Similar events occurred in relation to other professions, jobs in commerical enterprises and many blue-collar vocations. Women had to get male gatekeepers to take them seriously, to accept the legitimacy of their presence and to act in ways that make it possible for women to function in new roles.

Getting Into the Ministry

The same kinds of hurdles stand before women seeking to enter the ministry. Women clergy need to be recognized, legitimated and accepted. Most mainline Protestant bodies have recognized the concept that women can be called to religious vocations involving ordination. During the decades spanning the middle of the twentieth century, several of them formally sanctioned the ordination of women to the ministry. With those acts, the theological legitimacy of women's claim to be called to minister as ordained clergy was established. Unfortunately, the formulation of such ordination policies apparently was not sufficient to get church members to actually act toward clergywomen as ministers in ways that parallel their responses to male clergy. They still held back.

A recent radio interview with one of the first Episcopalian clergywomen to challenge that denomination's stance on the ordination and installation of women as priests illustrates the situation. At one point in the dialogue, she commented on her own prospects for ultimate success. "It is an honor to be among the pioneers," she said, "to be among the first women to be ordained as ministers of the Gospel in our denomination. However, don't let these actions lull you into thinking that the battle is over! I may be 'ordained' now, but I'm not experiencing hoards of people beating on my door to get me to come and serve as their pastor!"

The basic point she was making is simple (and perhaps commonplace). The symbolic act of changing church policy dealing with the ministry is important, as is the act of conferring ordination upon her as a woman. Such events are causally necessary if women in fact are to enter the ranks of professional clergy. However, in her denomination being ordained is one thing, and finding placement in a parish is something else. The process of occupational attainment cannot be considered complete until an individual is actually functioning in the position in question and until other persons in the system are acting toward that person according to the roles involved in the structure. Socially the woman is not a minister until she is in position to act as a minister. For most clergy this means that they simply have to have a job in the ministry, usually as pastor of a church (see Carroll and Wilson, 1978). Actually getting a job is still the final hurdle (Lehman, 1980).

Moreover, women entering the ministry have at least two additional obstacles to deal with, barriers that women moving into most other fields do not have to confront (see also Bock, 1967; Jones and Taylor, 1971). First, other fields are not bolstered by centuries of religious tradition as the major criterion determining who may practice within them. There is no set of religious doctrines defining the nature of a dentist or an electrician, for example. One need not claim to be called by God to enter the fields of accounting or carpentry. The concept of ministry, however, is cloaked in layer upon layer of Scripture, interpretation, tradition and church law. Even denominational resolutions have a difficult time unravelling such trappings.

The second obstacle clergywomen face may be even more critical. AA-EEO legislation does not seem to apply to religious pursuits. Medical schools stand to lose research programs and training grants if they do not satisfy at least the letter of the law. Construction companies forfeit lucrative government contracts if they are shown to discriminate against minorities. But churches can thumb their noses at such regulations with impunity, usually on the simple basis of doctrine. The threat of "blowing the whistle" on an employer is effective in reducing discrimination in secular occupations, but it does not work in the churches, which are effectively insulated from such strategies by the doctrine of church/state separation.

It is true that some religious organizations have codified their own AA-EEO regulations, but in comparison to state and federal statutes the church-based rules appear benign. In theory individuals and groups may be sanctioned for not complying with those guidelines. Denominational officials can be fired for not supporting the interests of minorities, but with the pervasive declines in membership and budget that most religious bodies face today, their leaders are loathe to alienate congregations for refusing to incorporate AA-EEO practices into their procedures for calling new pastoral leadership. The non-discriminatory guidelines may have some symbolic effects, but it is highly unlikely that their impact parallel that of law. They simply are not enforceable.

So—"what's a woman to do?" What can women seeking to enter the ministry depend on to facilitate their movement toward the time when they will be called to serve as ordained clergy? How can clergywomen get beyond simple recognition and legitimation to bona fide acceptance in the ranks of religious leaders?

Perceptions of the Process of Getting a Job

One's answer to that question will be based largely on one's understanding of what the basic process of getting a job is all about. If moving into an occupation is perceived as a routine matter of completing a series of preparatory steps and then demonstrating one's competence to perform the occupation's duties, then the answer to the question of "what to do" is not problematic at all. You get the training and take the test. The only "problem" is whether abilities and self-discipline match for demands placed on one.

On the surface it appears as though these conventions have applied for a long time in most men's careers. To enter medicine, for example, men have long assumed that they simply must perform well in secondary school, college and medical school in order to be admitted to each stage of the process and eventually pass the necessary examinations. The same pattern applies to most other professions (see Otto and Haller, 1979; Sewell and Havser, 1475).

The assumption is valid, for the most part, but not for all men. The history of minority groups in the United States, with its evidence of racism and anti-Semitism, demonstrates clearly that programs preparing men for medicine and other fields have turned blind eyes to applications from members of minority groups. It doesn't take a great deal of perspicacity to realize that the definition of "getting a job" or of "entering a profession" are very different matters for men in dominant and minority groups. It may be routine for "WASP" men, but it is hardly routine for men in minority communities.

The vexing experiences women have had in the process of entering previously male-dominated fields have shown that their attainments can be taken no more for granted than can those of minority men (see McClendon, 1976; Wolf and Rosenfeld, 1978; and Wolf and Fligstein, 1979). The same applies, of course, to women moving into the ordained ministry (Lehman, 1980). They have encountered obstacles at every step in the process. Since the seminary experience is central to their efforts, much of their time and energy devoted to overcoming impediments is concentrated in the seminary years (see Charlton, 1978). This is evident in the numerous "support groups" of clergywomen that have emerged on campuses of theological seminaries where women have been admitted to previously male-dominated educational programs (such as the Master of Divinity curricula). These women have encountered fundamentally sexist concepts of a religious tradition as frequently taught by sexist faculty meeting the needs of sexist churches. Providing psychological support in the face of the frustrations engendered by such experiences has been a major *raison d'etre* of these clergywomen's groups.

The concept of "coping" is an important theme in these circles. The view of the "system" shared in many of these support groups is that of an enemy. The sub-culture assumes that women still do not have the same kind of access to many positions in the church as do men. Differential access to sex-typed occupations is simply regarded as a fact of life. Denominational officials and search committees are viewed as guardians of the status quo. Formal placement systems (e.g., "the computer") carry an image in many of these groups as "make-work" operations that really won't make any difference in one's efforts to get a job. The denominational placement system itself viewed as fundamentally conservative, coupled with parallel perceptions of denominational staff whose responsibility it is to facilitate ministerial placement, causes the process of seeking a position in ministry to be viewed as a series of encounters with obstacles. *Actions in seeking placement are defined in terms of recognizing these obstacles and finding ways to cope with them. "Getting a job" is a matter of "coping."*

Coping with barriers to job placement may take a number of forms. The seminary "support groups" themselves tend to reinforce a "personal adjustment" approach. Meetings of these groups sometimes constitute arenas within which the women's frustrations can be aired in a climate of empathy and social support. The resulting catharsis and consensus provide important reinforcement to enable the women seminarians to continue in the struggle for acceptance and change.

Another approach to coping associated with some seminary women's groups is the development of strategy for bringing about cultural and social changes in the religious system. This orientation is reflected in a different label often assigned to the groups, i.e., "strategy groups." Offensiveness aimed at altering the sexist characteristics of seminary life is a direct assault on the sources of clergywomen's frustrations—at least those in the seminary itself.

To the extent that women seminarians become involved in support groups, especially those which emphasize ways of adjusting to the rigors of the male-dominated religious system, they may also adopt modes of viewing their life in the ministry that determine their approach to problems of job placement. The group constitutes the frame of reference within which participating clergywomen describe and explain their situation and what to do about it. It is the basis from which they understand why some people succeed and others fail, and thus it is the basis for deciding what to do in relation to their goals. It is the criteria by which both the nature of the problem is defined and the appropriate course of action is identified. If the problem is placement—women getting a job in the ministry—it is the source of clergywomen's approach to getting the job. The next question, of course, is whether it works. Does defining the situation in these terms help them get a position in ministry?

A Study of Job Placement

Data with which to answer questions such as these are available in a recent study of clergywomen completed for the Vocation Agency of the United Presbyterian Church, U.S.A. In 1978 the

Research Division of that denomination mailed questionnaires to all 393 UPCUSA clergywomen known to be affiliated with the denomination at that time. A total of 283 persons returned usable questionnaires, giving an effective response rate of 72 percent.

Normally when this proportion of a sample responds with acceptable data, the response rate is considered higher than usual in survey research, and the analysis proceeds under assumptions of representativeness. In this case, however, there may be reason to suspect some non-response bias that is relevant to the questions on which the research is focused. That is, officials of the sponsoring agency report that the roughly one-fourth of the clergywomen who did not respond probably contain a much larger percentage of persons either unemployed or not working in some form of ministry than are found in the returns. One would expect that to be the case. Unfortunately there is no way to determine the extent to which such a bias does exist. The reader simply should bear in mind the possibility of some bias when interpreting the results of the analysis.

We performed secondary analysis on several items from this study. These items include indications of results at several stages of the placement process concerning the number of contacts each clergywomen received, the number of job interviews completed, the number of times church members came to hear the woman preach pursuant to a possible offer, and the number of actual calls (job offers) received. We also include data on the nature of the position each clergywoman accepted, the level of her salary and whether or not she had been ordained. We can compare these "placement outcomes" with the clergywomen's modes of coping with the situation to see if they made any difference.

Patterns of Placement Outcomes

The women's "placement outcomes" are shown in Table 9.1. The distribution indicates a great deal of variability in the levels of success the clergywomen experienced. The number of contacts they received about jobs is widely distributed. At one extreme, 9 percent were contacted by no one, while at the other end 10 percent were contacted 10 times or more. The median number of contacts is 2. This pattern suggests that actually a great deal of communication goes on between clergywomen and churches concerning possible recruitment.

TABLE 9.1   OUTCOMES OF CLERGYWOMEN'S SEARCH FOR PLACEMENT IN MINISTRY

"In the process of seeking your present church or church-related employment, how many congregations:

A. contacted you about your interest in a call?	# contacts	0	1	2	3	4–9	10–19	20+
	n	20	54	37	34	54	20	3
	(percent)	(9)	(25)	(17)	(15)	(25)	(9)	(1)
B. sent representatives to hear you preach?	# sending	0	1	2	3	4+		
	n	177	48	15	7	4		
	(percent)	(71)	(19)	(6)	(3)	(2)		
C. invited you for an interview?	# invitations	0	1	2	3	4+		
	n	37	54	42	28	42		
	(percent)	(18)	(27)	(21)	(14)	(21)		
D. extended a call or job offer to you?"	# offers	0	1	2	3	4+		
	n	37	119	37	8	6		
	(percent)	(18)	(57)	(18)	(4)	(3)		

"What is your present position?"	n	percent
head of staff, solo pastor, co-pastor	70	25
associate/assistant pastor	78	28
interim pastor/stated supply/other church	48	17
non-church/unemployed	87	31

"What is your present salary range?"	n	percent
less that $10,000	110	39
$10,000–$14,999	88	31
$15,000–$19,999	57	20
$20,000–$29,999	23	8
$30,000 or more	1	1

The distribution of the number of churches sending delegates to hear the clergywoman preach implies the opposite tendency. Nearly three-fourths of the women reported that no churches responded to their candidacy in that way. Only 19 percent said that even one church sent people to hear them perform—not a great deal of contact. This pattern could indicate one of at least two underlying situations. One possibility is that the practice of churches' sending delegates to hear a potential candidate preach is waning in general. The procedure is still a part of the way recruitment of a new pastor ''is supposed to happen,'' but it may exist more in the ideal than in the real. The second possibility is that the practice of going to hear a person preach is still adhered to in relation to male ministers but not for females. In the absence of comparable data from the men, it is not possible to ascertain whether the latter interpretation holds.

The distribution of the number of actual job interviews in which the clergywomen participated parallels the pattern found in relation to the number of contacts they received, except that the highest total is much smaller in the case of the interviews. Again the median case falls on a number of 2. About 18 percent had no interviews at all. More than one-fifth took part in four interviews or more. Again, with more than half of the women having had 2 interviews or more, there appears to be a great deal of face-to-face contact between these candidates and the churches.

Most candidates ultimately look for the church to extend a call and make them an offer. The distribution of the number of actual offers the clergywomen received shows that as many of them received at least one offer as had at least one interview—82 percent in each case. More than half of them received one offer only, and 18 percent received two calls. Comparison between the distribution of interviews and job offers suggest that the interview stage is critical. It appears that if the clergywoman can get an interview, chances become much better that she will also get a job. From the perspective of the congregation's decisions, perhaps getting an interview as a serious candidate is the critical step. If the congregation agrees to do this, they have probably turned a major corner.

In general these patterns indicate that the placement process has been working for some of these women, all the way through to getting them placed in jobs. In interpreting the patterns, however, one must bear two caveats in mind: (1) we do not know the characteristics of the non-respondents, and it is plausible that their placement experiences were less favorable, and (2) we have no parallel data from men to enable us to say whether the placement patterns of males and females either diverge or are parallel. (In an earlier study in the American Baptist Churches, male candidates had more favorable placement outcomes than did females on every criterion.)

Table 9.1 also contains indications of the *type* of position the clergywomen obtained. Nearly seventy percent had accepted a position in a church. More than one-half had positions traditionally occupied by men; they enjoyed the titles of "pastor" or "associate/assistant pastor." Of the women in these positions, nearly half were either head of staff, solo pastor or co-pastor. Taken by itself, this pattern indicates considerable receptivity to clergywomen on the part of a large number of churches. Some women are placed in positions traditionally occupied by men. No doubt a greater percentage of the men than the women among seminary cohorts are in such pastoral posts, but the data indicate that just as the door is not completely open, it is also not completely closed, polemicists on either side not withstanding.

The final indication of placement outcomes concerns the issue of salary. Table 9.1 indicates considerable variation in the salary levels the clergywomen enjoyed. Nearly 40 percent earned less that $10,000, while only about 9 percent received $20,000 or more per year. One individual reported over $30,000. The median case falls in the salary range of $10,000 to $14,999. Some of this distribution is due to the effect of the salaries of part-time women. About 89 percent of them earn less than $10,000. However, even among the full-time clergywomen, the category below $15,000 still contains about 67 percent, so the distribution of the women's salaries cannot be attributed to the full/part-time dichotomy. While we have no data with which to make direct comparisons to male ministers' salaries, general perceptions are that these figures for the women are slightly lower than for the men. This type of pattern is hardly surprising, for it parallels data from other denominations and from similar male/female comparisons made in the context of other occupations. Women's salaries are typically 60–70 percent of those of men.

In general, then, these indicators of placement outcomes demonstrate that some clergywomen are more successful in job hunting than others. The next question concerns ways of explain-

ing these differences. What factors account for the different placement outcomes?

Characteristics of Churches
Where Clergywomen Are Placed

Before we examine the correlates of job placement in the 1978
clergywomen survey, however, it will be useful to return to some
data from the evaluation project described in the preceding
chapter to get a picture of the churches in which clergywomen
were placed as pastor. These congregational characteristics constitute another type of "placement outcome" to consider in addition to those described above. While the number of placements
involved in the evaluation study was small, they do represent a
probability sample of clergywomen serving as pastor at the time of
the study. By identifying distinctive characteristics of churches
where women have been installed as pastor, we may be able to
detect patterns that illuminate the ways in which clergywomen
are (or are not) being integrated into the ministerial leadership of
the denomination.

In this process we use the data from the Panel as the basis for
comparison. Since the Panel represents a sample of the
characteristics of churches and church members in the
denomination as a whole, by comparing the minister-at-large
churches and the churches with women installed as pastors to
those included in the Panel, points of departure from denominational norms can be identified.

The distribution of characteristics of the three types of churches
in the study are shown in Table 9.2. There do appear to be several
ways in which the churches in which female ministers-at-large have
been placed are atypical. As a group they tend to be in large communities, the sizes of the congregations are declining and they are
disproportionately solo pastorates. The congregations include
more members of minority groups than the average. There are
fewer married persons. There tend to be more older people than
usual. The level of educational attainment is below average, and
high status occupations are underrepresented in the congregation.

*The distinctive characteristics of the churches in which clergy-
women have been installed as pastor are even more dramatic.* In

TABLE 9.2 PERCENTAGE OF MEMBERS WITH SPECIFIC ATTRIBUTES, BY SUB-POPULATION

CHURCH CHARACTERISTICS	Members with interim ministers	Panel	Members with installed pastors
located in small city or smaller place	22	49	60
church has 301 members or more	44	56	5
church membership not growing	46	29	87
church budget declining re: inflation*	38	44	46
church aligned with UPCUSA only*	95	92	93
church has multiple clerical staff	10	41	10

INDIVIDUAL CHARACTERISTICS	Members with interim ministers	Members with Panel	Installed pastors
percent female*	61	54	59
percent aged 56 and above	46	39	48
percent non-white	13	2	2
percent currently married	74	82	73
percent widowed	9	—**	16
percent college graduates	41	51	30
percent with income of $25,000 or more	47	50	17
percent in high status occupations	64	66	47
percent spouse in hi-status occupation	55	62	38

*a statistically non-significant difference. All other differences were statistically significant at the .01 level or better.

**figure not available for Panel members.

239

general they appear to be small, struggling churches in economically sluggish communities, with members who are suffering from a relative lack of personal and financial resources and who are finding it difficult to replace themselves in the congregation. Specifically, these churches include almost no medium-to-large congregations, they are located primarily in small towns and rural areas (and those which are in larger places tend to be in racially transitional neighborhoods), and very few of them have growing congregations. They are predominantly solo pastorates. Their members tend to lack important resources for carrying on basic programs. Elderly people are overrepresented in them, particularly the widowed. The socio-economic composition of the congregations tends to be lower than average. Members with high levels of education, income and occupational status are underrepresented.

It is important to point out that most of these patterns were antecedent to the arrival of the clergywoman on the scene. Remarks made by both the members and the clergywomen themselves clearly indicate that the organizational decline of these churches had set in long before the clergywomen were installed. It is not a result of their ministries there. It is not "their fault." (In fact a few of these churches have "turned around" most recently.) Nor is it the "fault" of the members themselves. The concept of "blame" is probably inappropriate for most of the situations. Instead they are predictable consequences of broad changes that are sweeping such communities all around the nation. These small communities typically face a steady drain of young people who move to metropolitan areas in search of occupational opportunities. The older, the less well educated and the less occupationally skilled members are usually "left behind." The days of a church thriving numerically and programmatically are also left behind. The same applies to old neighborhoods in the cities. The young, the mobile, and the affluent move to the growing suburbs. The congregation left behind suffers. It is an old story, and current reversals of these trends are likely to be but temporary, because the tendencies spring not from what is being done (or not done) by the local church leadership. Rather the fate of the church is virtually determined by what is going on in the community around the church. It is the rare clergyman or clergywoman who can find ways to redeem it.

A more fruitful approach to these patterns is to ask what they portend for the eventual integration of clergywomen into the traditional career patterns of pastors. Not that clergywomen are any more or less potential organizational "climbers" than men, but they simply are asking for equal access to the range of opportunities for service open to other pastors. In terms of the total range of personal aspirations, female ministers as a group are probably no different from males.

The ministers-at-large were placed in churches that depart slightly from the mainstream, especially churches that were not really growing, did not involve multiple staff and were possibly in the early stages of becoming older congregations with reduced resources. The more general picture, however, is that the churches where women served as interims were fairly representative of those of the rest of the denomination.

The churches where women have been installed as pastors, however, depart radically from denomination-wide norms. In caricature they depict the kinds of situations to which most clergy do not want to be called and from which they usually choose to depart at the earliest opportunity. Since such other opportunities are in fact open to most *male* clergy, placement in a marginal church poses but a temporary stage in career development. The very concentration of women in these situations reinforces the broadly held perception that in fact there may be *few* other opportunities for them. Having gone to churches where few men would be willing to go, are they now "stuck"? Reports of the clergywomen indicate that they probably are *not* at "dead ends" personally. However, this does not mean that pastoral opportunities in churches that are more representative of the denomination are actually open to them. Instead, when most of the clergywomen we studied leave their work in these churches, *they tend to leave the pastorate*. As of this writing only one of the ministers-at-large has been installed as a permanent pastor. The others either are still searching for such a position or have returned to college and seminary to prepare for alternate careers. Among the women installed in the churches in the study, the tendency is to report either feeling "locked in" to their present charges or resigning and seeking more education or to enter another form of ministry. The door to a "normal" career as a pastor really doesn't seem to be open as yet.

Nevertheless, it is important to ask in what way this may be true. Reviewing these data suggests that women who find placement as pastors are in positions that are qualitatively different from those in which men are placed. Were that the case, we would be confronting a clear pattern of discrimination. Other surveys of clergywomen have suggested similar interpretations. However, before we jump to premature conclusions, two caveats are in order. First, in this study we have no comparable data concerning men. This means, of course, that *we do not know* whether the characteristics of the churches in which the women were placed were consequences of the fact that they are women or because they were first or second placements and that men at the same career point may have been placed in similar charges.

Second, recent data from a study conducted from Hartford Seminary (Carroll, *et al*, 1983) indicate that the latter interpretation may be the more accurate one. That is, in a study of male and female placements, no significant systematic differences were found between men and women pastors concerning the *type of church* in which they were placed initially. Men were typically in parishes with the same range of characteristics as those in which the women were working. *However*, the study also produced some evidence that the men and women differed markedly in their career mobility after initial placements. The farther down the career path they looked—second, third and fourth positions—the more differences emerged in the positions held by the men and the women. In later placements, the men had largely moved out of marginal parish situations, while the women tended to remain serving the struggling congregations (Carroll *et al*, 1983, pp. 125–135). If this pattern is representative, it indicates that while initial positions tend to be similar for men and women, the men can subsequently move into more attractive situations, but the women are more "locked in"—another form of discrimination.

Do Perceived Barriers Predict Placement Outcomes?

Returning to the data from the UPCUSA clergywomen, let's look now at the question of what makes a difference in placement outcome. Specifically, let's deal with the question of whether viewing the placement process as a matter of identifying various kinds of barriers and successfully coping with them is predictive of differences in the characteristics of the positions the clergywomen obtained.

The questionnaire contained several items that can be used as indicators of ways in which the respondents viewed placement as a process of coping. Chief among these questions are two that dealt directly with the coping ethos. One item asked, "What, if anything, do you think has been the major obstacle to achieving your present position?" The respondents were asked to write in their answers. We did a content analysis (see Babbie, 1983, pp. 273–290) on the nature of the obstacles they listed. The process of content analysis performed here involved reviewing the ministers' answers repeatedly until a set of common themes could be identified in them.

Four motifs emerged from this procedure which served as the basis for categorizing the data. These four criteria are shown in the top of Table 9.3. About one in six clergywomen saw their problems as being with "themselves"—poor attitudes, not enough Christian devotion, laziness, etc. Of the 83 percent who saw the problem as *other* than themselves, nearly one-third viewed it in relatively pragmatic terms, i.e., either as not having a variety of resources they needed for job-hunting or as constraints imposed by their families. More than one-half of the women, however, thought neither in terms of self nor of situational complications, but instead placed the blame on one or more segments of *the placement system itself*. They viewed the placement structures as basically sexist and the people working in them as reticent to respond to a woman's candidacy.

The second question associated with the adaptation approach is, "Please list the specific coping strategies you employed in overcoming this obstacle." We also performed a content analysis on the answers to this question, and the results are shown in the middle of Table 9.3. About two-thirds of the women acted in such a way as to attempt to remove the pragmatic constraints or to make it harder for the system not to respond to them. The category basically refers to doing something concrete either to change the situation or to get people to work with them. The remaining one-third in effect either did nothing or tried to find ways to adjust personally. It is likely that at least some of these clergywomen objectively *could not* do anything to change the situation, in which case the ritualistic or adjustment responses would be appropriate. Unfortunately, however, there is but a weak relationship between the type of barrier they perceived and the type of action on which

TABLE 9.3   TYPES OF BARRIERS AND COPING ACTIONS IN THE PROCESS OF PLACEMENT REPORTED BY PRESBYTERIAN CLERGYWOMEN

Types of barriers:	Percent
"Myself" (attitude, work, love, devotion, etc.)	17
"Resources" (money, time, experience, education, etc.)	12
"Family" (spouse occupation, children, etc.)	18
"Sexism in the system" (bias, PNC, laity, denomination, etc.)	53
"other"	0.5

Types of coping strategies:	Percent
"Goal Action" (get experience, make contacts, become known, get education, move, negotiate, etc.)	67
"Adjust" (psychotherapy, counselling, be better, etc.)	13
"Ritualism" (wait, keep trying, be patient, pray, understand, etc.)	21

"Do you have any of the following special needs that restrict the location or nature of your job? (Check ALL that apply.)	Percent
occupational needs—spouse	46
educational needs—spouse	10
special health needs—spouse	2
educational needs—self	20
special health needs—self	3
children's needs	26
opportunity to share job with spouse	19
other (specify) _____	12

distribution of "needs" scores:

score	0	1	2	3	4	5
n	79	94	56	36	14	4
(percent)	(28)	(33)	(20)	(13)	(5)	(1)

they embarked, so the type of coping response is not satisfactorily explained in terms of their identification of the problem.

One more question from the instrument relates to the issues associated with the adaptation perspective, and that has to do with specific circumstances that restrict one's movement in the job market. This item is shown in the bottom of Table 9.3. The most prevalent restriction concerns the husband's occupational needs, with nearly half of the women indicating this as a problem. Second in order of prevalence was the needs of children. The only items to portray few women concerned about them were those associated with health needs.

We incorporated this set of items in the analysis below in the form of a "needs score." That is, we added the number of special needs checked, and we assigned each respondent a score based on that total. The distribution of these scores is at the bottom of Table 9.3. Nearly one-third had at least one such special need. Significant numbers had as many as three. Only 28 percent indicated no such problems at all.

We now have measures of variables that allow us to pursue the issue of whether conceptualizing the placement process in terms of adaptation or coping is associated with actual placement outcomes. Does one type of placement problem or another actually inhibit one's finding a job? Does one kind of coping strategy predict successful placement outcomes better than another? Do special needs actually restrict access to the job market?

The results of comparing indicators of these coping orientations with placement outcomes are contained in Table 9.4. *The most striking pattern is the general absence of relationships between various types of barriers encountered and placement, as well as between coping strategies and placement.* Viewing the problem of getting a job as primarily a matter of deficiencies in one's self is *unrelated* to actual placement outcomes. The same pattern applies to perceiving the barriers as one's resources or one's family. The sole exception to this concerns salary, wherein persons whose family situation is perceived as problematic also tend to have lower salaries.

Most interesting in this regard are the relationships between placement outcomes and perceiving the problem as the placement system and the people in it. Clergywomen who identified a sexist system or unresponsive individuals and groups as barriers to getting a job had systematically different placement outcomes that did those whose perceptions were different. However, the correlations are the *opposite* of what one would expect if the system itself were actually the barrier. If systemic barriers were in fact inhibiting the placement process, then those problems would be associated with smaller number of contacts, interviews and calls. Instead the table indicates that the women with *more successful outcomes also perceived the system as the problem.* The

TABLE 9.4 CORRELATIONS* BETWEEN PLACEMENT OUTCOMES AND BARRIERS TO PLACEMENT ENCOUNTERED BY CLERGYWOMEN

	Self as barrier	Resources as barrier	Family as barrier	System as barrier	Adjust	Goal action	Ritual	Needs score
Number of contacts	—**	—	—	.14	.06	—	—	—
Number heard preach	—	—	—	—	—	—	—	—
Number of interviews	—	—	—	.16	—	—	—	-.11
Number of calls	—	—	—	.14	—	—	—	-.09
Obtained "male" position	—	—	—	.11	—	—	—	—
Salary	—	—	-.10	—	—	—	—	-.20

*The coefficients used in analyzing these data are called "tau-c." The differences in sign and magnitude of tau-c should be interpreted in the same way as the "gammas" employed in preceding chapters, i.e., as indicating differences in direction and strength of relationship respectively.

**Indicates a statistically non-significant correlation. Coefficients in this category averaged ± .03. All other coefficients listed in this table are statistically significant at the .05 level or beyond.

most obvious answer to the question that follows is that the causal sequence is just the opposite. That is, the women who reported a large number of contacts, interviews and calls experienced system responses that they perceived as barriers *after* they became involved in the recruitment process. Those who had fewer experiences with each stage of the process also had fewer opportunities to encounter sexist actions. Thus system character-istics may in fact act as impediments to placement, but they are not "barriers" in an absolute sense. Perceiving them occurs primarily *after* the clergywomen become involved in the place-ment process and in direct relation to the duration of that involve-ment. They are not barriers in the sense of preventing the process from going forward.

It is equally interesting to note that *placement outcomes were unrelated to the candidates' coping strategies.* Whether the women dealt with barriers they perceived by seeking to change "them-selves," to alter "the system" around them or "did nothing" appears to have made no difference in the number of contacts, in-terviews and calls they received, the kind of position they obtained and the level of their salary. (The one statistically significant coeffi-cient is so small that it is probably attributable to sampling or measurement error.)

The major implication of these patterns is that, from the stand-point of identifying what can be done to enhance one's chances of getting a job, identifying barriers and finding ways to cope with them are probably not the most important things to focus on. Bar-riers exist—true. One cannot ignore them—also true. But equally true is the observation that *identifying and coping with barriers is not what predicts success or failure at breaking into the supply of jobs.*

Finally, the number of special needs the clergywomen in-dicated they had, factors which would impede their flexibility and mobility, were related to some placement outcomes but not to others. These pragmatic variables had no effect on churches' con-tacting the candidates or coming to hear them preach. However, as one would expect, the more situational impediments the can-didates had, the fewer *interviews* they participated in and the fewer *calls* they received. These differences in personal circum-stances were also related to salary levels. The more problems the women had, the lower their salary tended to be, probably due to

their reduced bargaining power associated with diminished flexibility in the market place.

Placement in Ministry as "Status Attainment"

Another way of conceptualizing job placement is as a final step in
a process of "status attainment." Status attainment is a term
sociologists use to refer to being successful in entering a desired
level of the social stratification (class) system of a society (see
Sewell and Hauser, 1975). It is a matter of "making it." In our
society status attainment is usually defined in terms of occupational attainment, since our position in the broad societal pecking
order is so closely linked to the type of work we do. Most of us
work in occupations whose status roughly parallels that of our
parents. In this situation the parents are said to "transmit" their
status to their offspring by means of inculcating perspectives,
values and work habits needed to function at that level of society.
Where offspring attain in vocations at a higher status level than
that of their parents, they are said to be "upwardly mobile." Conversely, if the children's work puts them in a lower stratum than
their parents, they are considered "downwardly mobile."

The view of occupational attainment most frequently
associated with these ideas places a great deal of emphasis on the
socialization of the offspring to give them the traits which allow
them to earn the credentials they need to succeed (see Otto and
Haller, 1974). It attributes success or failure in occupational attainment to social psychological factors such as individual ability,
academic performance, credentials, values, expectations and am-
bitions—all outcomes of socialization processes. The model
typically asserts that mental ability and the milieu associated with
parents' socioeconomic status promote particular levels of educational and occupational aspirations and of academic performance, along with selective peer influences. Differences in these
attributes lead to divergent levels of educational attainment
which, in turn, lead to involvements in occupations that differ in
their prestige, power, and income. Children of a specific social
class background develop attitudes, work habits and friendships
appropriate to occupations in that social status.

According to this perspective, successful entry into a
desirable occupation is very much an individual matter. *The*

secret resides in one's personal abilities, aspirations and work habits and the credentials and skills these traits lead to.

Some other sociologists, however, argue that the socialization model and the research associated with it are characterized by "anti-structural biases" (Kerckhoff, 1976). The model is criticized as too individualistic. It ignores external societal factors having little or nothing to do with individual characteristics, but which influence individuals' chances for status attainment. Being identified with certain segments of society can lead to *selective* education, advocacy, receptivity, and recruitment; and when they do, the result is discrimination. The addition of these dynamics to the occupational attainment processes of minorities, for example, may be a major reason why the above socialization model is less predictive for them than for dominant whites. Abilities, aspirations and credentials make less difference for blacks than for whites. The influence of structural factors that differentially allocate positions of authority to men and women regardless of their qualifications also has been documented, as has the differential effect on vertical occupational mobility of working in gender-typed jobs. Being white or male gives one an edge in the competition *regardless* of abilities and credentials.

Considerations such as these lead some observers to postulate an "allocation" model of status attainment which attributes some success and failure in status attainment to social structural *barriers* such as segmented labor markets and differentiated educational systems, social arrangements *that allow some persons to achieve and keep other persons from achieving regardless of their individual levels of aspiration, performance, and credentials* (Kerckhoff, 1976).

These distinctions are useful for identifying possible explanations of differential placement outcomes not because they involve the broad process of occupational attainment per se. They do not. A sample of ministers is too homogeneous and the level of educational attainment they have achieved is too similar to allow study of the process as a whole. Most of the occupational attainment process has run its course. The ministers are all professionals already differentiated from their childhood and adolescent peers.

Instead, the distinction between the socialization model and the allocation model is useful because it embodies and symbolizes *two distinct frames of reference from which to view placement outcomes,* a step near the end of the occupational attainment process. One perspective assumes that the results of efforts to achieve reflect the effects of individual values, aspirations, and performance. The other view assumes that outcomes indicate what the rules of the game will allow. As one person put it, the significance of the distinction lies in the fact that "a socialization model. . .tends to view the individual as relatively free to move within the social system, his attainments being determined by what he chooses to do and how well he does it. In contrast, an allocation model views the individual as relatively constrained by the social structure, his attainments being determined by what he is permitted to do" (Kerckhoff, 1976: p. 369).

In a previous study I have argued that differential placement of men and women in the ministry is explained more by the allocation model than the socialization perspective (Lehman, 1980). *The distinction between being free to choose and being prohibited from entering certain fields is precisely at the heart of clergywomen's complaints.* The data indicates that the greater success of men than women in finding placement in ministry jobs is basically *unrelated* to their SES backgrounds, levels of academic performance, theological orientations and academic credentials, all of which are variables associated with the socialization model. On the other hand, variables associated with the allocation model are consistently predictive of male-female differences in placement outcome, i.e., the women were *not allowed* fluid access to positions in ministry. The response of placement structures to women is positive primarily if they conform to basic denominational placement policy and practice, while the placement mechanisms work for men regardless of their conformity or strategy. *Occupational attainment at the point of job placement is largely automatic for the men, while such allocation is highly contingent for the women.* As has happened so often to members of minority groups, the "price of the ticket" is higher for the women than the men. The situation reflects the classic double standard. On the average the women came from higher SES backgrounds than the men, and the women's grades in seminary were higher than those of the men, but these credentials could not be translated into an advantage in the competition for jobs.

Which of these perspectives best explains the differences in placement outcomes in the UPC clergywomen placement study? Were the differences in the women's experiences in seeking positions in the ministry due to disparities in their abilities and training or credentials, or were they the consequences of some clergy-women being more willing to conform to the rules of the game as the higher price of their tickets?

The questionnaire contains indicators of variables associated with the two models of occupational attainment. The socialization model concentrates on individual characteristics. Most relevant in this regard is a question dealing with the nature of the degree the woman received from the seminary, i.e., whether it was the Master of Arts, the Master of Religious Education, the Master of Divinity (or Bachelor of Divinity), or an advanced degree such as the Doctor of Ministry or Doctor of Theology. We also had some indicators of the socialization model, but it would have been helpful to have had indicators of additional factors such as the women's levels of academic performance, the quality of the schools they attended and their socio-economic status backgrounds. Unfortunately, these data are unavailable in the UPC sample. To the extent that these variables are central to the socialization model, they constitute noteworthy gaps in the analysis of the model's utility for predicting placement outcomes and corresponding limitations on the breadth of the conclusions that may be drawn from the study.

Indications of the working of the placement structures are available in questions dealing with the respondents' placement strategies. Items dealing with their involvement with the formal placement systems of the denomination include questions about contacting appropriate denominational placement offices, working with Boards and committees having placement responsibilities, and completing and submitting appropriate forms for use in the denominational placement files. The questionnaire also includes items determining whether the women used a variety of supplementary placement resources such as dossier workshops and conferences. Analyses of these items may indicate the extent to which placement structures serve as allocation mechanisms, i.e., if clergywomen utilize them, will they result in the women getting a job?

Finally, the questionnaire contains items indicating the extent to which the respondents tried to circumvent the formal placement system and utilize informal paths to a job. These questions deal with contacting friends in the ministry, seminary contacts and specifically other clergywomen. These questions are important in view of the fact that so many women view the formal system as either biased toward male candidates or as being mere formal ritual that yields few concrete results. The question is whether "doing an end run" around the official placement structures is fruitful in leading to jobs in the ministry for women, as well as the extent to which this informal route to a job is more or less efficient in comparison to utilizing the denominationally sanctioned structures.

Measures of Possible Explanatory Variables

Table 9.5 contains the clergywomen's responses to the questionnaire items associated with these concepts. The socialization model concentrates on the characteristics of the individual—socioeconomic status background, values, academic performance, credentials, etc. The data available for analysis contains but three items dealing with concepts of this nature, i.e., seminary degree ("credentials"), marital status and age. The table indicates that 84 percent of the women had earned the M.Div. or B.D. degree. This figure is notable, because it reflects a significant increase of female enrollments in the divinity programs, curricula completed primarily by men in the recent past when most women were enrolled in programs leading to the M.A. or M.R.E. degrees. This pattern is consistent with other evidence that the M.Div. degree is fast becoming a "union card" for women as well as for men. Only 5 percent of the clergywomen had completed the M.A. or M.R.E. About 10 percent had completed graduate seminary degrees.

The distribution of marital status shows nothing surprising. In general the clergywomen are conventional in this regard—85 percent either had never been married or were married, or they were widowed. The same applies to age distribution. Two-thirds of the women were between the ages of 21 and 30 when they graduated from seminary, ages that roughly parallel those of most male graduates. About one-fourth of them were "middle-aged" when they finished school.

Table 9.5 also contains items dealing with the structures women used while seeking placement in ministry. Many of these avenues to jobs are similar to those considered in the previous study done in ABC. The responses indicate that most of the clergywomen conformed to denominational policy in the process of trying to find a job. More than four-fifths of them prepared and

TABLE 9.5   INDICATORS OF POSSIBLE CORRELATES OF PLACEMENT AMONG
PRESBYTERIAN CLERGYWOMEN

INDIVIDUAL CHARACTERISTICS	Percent
Seminary degree:	
Master of Arts/Master of Religious Education	5
Master of Divinity/Bachelor of Divinity	84
Doctorate or a Master of Theology	10
Present marital status:	
single, never married	34
married: first time	50
divorced: remarried	5
divorced: not remarried	9
separated	1
widowed	2
Age when graduated from seminary:	
21–30	67
31–34	8
35–44	16
45–54	7
55 and over	1

THE FORMAL PLACEMENT SYSTEM	Percent
Used the Vocation Agency while seeking employment (or the Div. of Court Partnership, Ser's—PCUS)	70
Used the Ministerial Relations Committee while seeking employment	51
Prepared a personal information form (PIF)	81
Submitted PIF to Vocation Agency	84
Used a dossier-writing workshop while seeking employment	11
Used a career counselling center while seeking employment	13

INFORMAL STRUCTURES	
Contacted friends about seeking employment	65
Contacted seminary acquaintances about seeking employment	49
Consulted with other clergywomen while seeking a call	40

submitted appropriate forms to be listed in the denominational
personnel file (PIF's). More than two-thirds sought work through
the Vocation Agency, the denominational office most centrally

responsible for facilitating ministerial placement. About half of them utilized the services of Ministerial Relations Committees, the local structures designed to facilitate linkages between churches and clergy.

Considerably fewer clergywomen took advantage of some supplementary programs designed to facilitate placement. There are career counseling centers and dossier/resume-writing workshops, resources designed at least partly to assist persons who are having difficulties in finding placement and who are experiencing other problems in their careers. While participation in them is not institutionalized to the extent that involvement in the other formal structures is established, they have been especially promoted among the women in order to help them cope with problems in the placement experience.

Since many clergywomen look upon these formal structures as either "useless" at best, or as tools of "the enemy" (a sexist system) at worst, some individuals try other routes to a job. These alternate paths to employment typically are sets of informal contacts. Instead of filling out sets of personnel forms and submitting them to denominational officials in accordance with established practice, women who are suspicious of the formal system contact their personal friends, their seminary acquaintances and/or other clergywomen already in the field. The data indicate that significant numbers of these women took these routes. Nearly two-thirds of them sought work through friends, about half used seminary contacts and 40 percent went through other clergywomen. There is obviously some overlap between these categories, but the frequencies indicate that they are also somewhat distinct.

The question at this point is *which of these paths to a job actually led to positions in ministry*. Was it one's personal attributes that led to contacts, interviews, and job offers? Or did getting these results depend on finding ways to make a recalcitrant placement system respond, however begrudging that movement may be? Was the allocation of ministerial positions as "contingent" on playing by the rules in the Presbyterian system as it was in the American Baptist arena?

Placement Outcomes and Individual Attributes

The socialization model argues that individual attributes such as how smart you are and what you can do are the best predictors of occupational attainment. Does this apply to the placement outcomes of clergywomen? In the earlier study, indicators of individual backgrounds, performance and credentials for the most part were *not* predictive of finding a job. The results of comparing the measures of individual characteristics and placement outcomes in this study are contained in Table 9.6. They tend to support the findings in the other project.

In terms of credentials, *the degree one earns in seminary is but marginally associated with placement*. It makes no difference whether one has completed the MRE, MDIV, or a graduate degree when the question is the number of contacts one receives, whether churches come to listen to one preach, or the number of actual interviews one participates in. There is a weak association between holding the MDIV degree and receiving relatively many job offers, which suggests that the churches value that degree more than others at the point of finally extending a call.

The table also supports what some individuals have perceived informally concerning a "trade-off" between type of job and salary level. Having completed the MDIV degree is associated with acquiring a position usually occupied by a man—mainly as pastor or associate pastor. Holding a graduate degree is related to getting another kind of job, one in which females have been more welcome in the past—usually a low-to-middle level position in a denominational organization rather than a local church. However, the MDIV then becomes associated with lower salaries (in the pastorate), while the graduate degree leads to higher incomes linked to denominational jobs.

Age is a factor in some placement outcomes also. It seems to make little difference in the earliest stage of the process, i.e., initial contacts or inquiries from churches. However, age does become a barrier to placement in later segments. *The older the clergywoman is, the fewer interviews she participates in and the*

TABLE 9.6 CORRELATIONS BETWEEN PLACEMENT OUTCOMES AND INDIVIDUAL ATTRIBUTES OF PRESBYTERIAN CLERGYWOMEN

	MA/MRE degree	BD/MDIV degree	Graduate degree	Age	Married	Divorced
Number of contacts	—*	—	—	—	—	—
Number heard preach	—	—	—	—	—	—
Number of interviews	—	—	—	-.08	—	—
Number of calls	—	.09	—	-.10	—	—
Obtained "male" position	—	.14	-.11	—	—	—
Salary	—	-.14	.36	—	-.25	—

*indicates a statistically non-significant correlation. Coefficients in this category averaged ± .02. All other coefficients listed in this table are statistically significant at the .05 level or beyond.

fewer actual calls she receives. This pattern may be the opposite of some traditional experiences of male clergy. Churches usually prefer older and more experienced men if they can attract them to their communities. They do not want to tolerate the misadventures of novices just out of the seminary. However, the data in the table indicate the opposite is true for women—churches appear to prefer younger women over older ones, which implies that the secular cult of youth and attractiveness may play a part in the churches' decisions in such matters.

Marital status has traditionally been a criterion of recruitment in church circles. Local churches particularly are fond of arguing that they need a married man for a pastor. The "public" reason given for this preference is a need for a pastor's wife to take on numerous responsibilities in the church, as well as the idea that a married pastor will fit in with the social life of the church more smoothly than will an unmarried person. Privately many church members often also say that they simply want the pastor to be married so that he will be "settled down," meaning that he will be less likely than a single man to "fool around" and possibly bring scandal to the community. The other major factor in the pastor's marital status concerns divorce and separation. In many church circles, divorce is still one of the few unforgivable sins of the clergy. Divorced ministers are said to be harder to place in jobs than are either married or never-married persons.

Table 9.6 indicates that these arguments may not apply to clergywomen. *Whether the woman was married or not was unrelated to placement outcomes at every step of the process.* The only outcome related to marital status was salary, with married women earning less than did those who were unmarried. Finally, divorce does not appear to be related to any of the placement outcomes. The oft-repeated cliche that "a divorced woman just cannot get a church" is not supported in these data.

Placement Outcomes and Placement Strategies

In the ABC study, the major determinant of simply finding any job at all in the ministry was the clergywomen's placement strategy. Women who conformed to denominational policy and became relatively well integrated into networks of relationships with denominational leaders at the regional and local levels tended to be much more successful in finding placement than were those who did not. The act of circumnavigating these denominational structures and seeking a job via informal routes tended to be counter-productive. However, these patterns did not apply to the men, for whom it made no difference which strategy of job-search they used. For a man who got a position, the outcome was unrelated to what he did. Occupational status was allocated unconditionally to the men but only conditionally for the women. The question at hand is whether these same patterns apply in the case of Presbyterian clergywomen.

The results of comparing placement outcomes to placement strategies are contained in Table 9.7. The patterns of relationships are highly consistent with those observed in the earlier study. In general, *women who conformed to denominational policy regarding placement procedures were much more likely to succeed in the placement process than were those who did not.* Using the Vocation Agency, the denominational office most directly concerned with placement, is related to favorable placement outcomes more than any other factor. Working with local placement structures, i.e., the ministerial relations committees, is also positively related to success. The routines of filling out and submitting denominational placement forms are associated with getting a job. Those women who worked with "the computer" (the P.I.F.) were more likely to receive a call than were those who did not. *In general, placement of the clergywoman is contingent upon her using the denominational structures set in place for that purpose.*

The supplementary placement structures do not appear to be as effective, however. It appears to have made no difference for any placement outcome whether the women utilized the Career Counseling Center. While these resources may serve other purposes such as dealing with life changes or personal crises, they have little effect on the clergywomen's getting a job. Furthermore, participating in a dossier-writing workshop appears to be *negatively* related to placement outcomes, if at all. That is, clergywomen who attended these sessions had *fewer* contacts by churches, *fewer* delegations to hear them preach and *fewer* interviews. Participating in the workshops was unrelated to the number of job-offers received. This pattern is probably best interpreted not as indicating that going to the workshops hinders one's efforts to get a job, but rather as demonstrating that it was primarily

TABLE 9.7 CORRELATIONS BETWEEN PLACEMENT OUTCOMES AND PLACEMENT STRATEGIES OF PRESBYTERIAN CLERGYWOMEN

	Used Vocation Agency	Used ministerial relations committees	Prepared P.I.F.	Submitted P.I.F.	Used career counselling centers	Attended dossier-writing workshop	Contacted friends	Used seminary contacts	Contacted women clergy
Number of contacts	.44	.25	.27	.27	—*	−.14	.12	.18	.33
Number heard preach	.22	.13	.12	.10	—	−.06	—	—	.15
Number of interviews	.35	.12	.20	.18	—	−.09	—	.17	.25
Number of calls	.20	.19	.13	.13	—	—	.10	.10	.18
Obtained "male" position	.14	—	.08	.10	—	—	—	—	.11
Salary	—*	—	.24	—	—	−.08	—	—	—

*indicates a statistically non-significant correlation. Coefficients in this category averaged ±.03. All other coefficients in this table are statistically significant at the .05 level or beyond.

the clergywomen who were experiencing difficulty receiving contacts and arrangement interviews who took part in the resume-writing sessions. The absence of a relationship between number of calls and workshop participation implies that the personal contact in the interview situation overrides any skills developed in the workshops concerning presentation of self on paper. I would also interpret the negative relationship between attending dossier-writing workshops and salary in the same mode as with number of contacts, i.e., those who were dissatisfied with their salaries were more likely to take part in the workshops than were those whose salaries were more acceptable to them.

Using informal contacts during the job search was also related to placement outcomes, especially working through other female clergy already "on the job." This pattern is different from that observed earlier in ABC, for in that case the informal route was found to be negatively associated with placement. *Women in this study who worked through other clergywomen tended to have more contacts, to be listened to, to be interviewed, to receive a call and to obtain a "male" position*. Note, however, that the correlation between these contacts and placement outcomes are stronger in the *early* stages of placement than in the late phases. Informal contacts make more difference in the number of leads and interviews than do number of calls and type of position.

Using seminary contacts and friends as contacts weakly relates to some steps in the placement process, but these patterns are less consistent than those involving other clergywomen specifically. Although the relationships between using informal routes and placement outcomes are weaker and more erratic than those involving formal placement structures, the analysis indicates that *in some ways informal contacts can be productive.*

Multivariate Analysis

The final stage of the analysis involves subjecting each placement outcome to a multiple regression analysis with certain predictor variables. We have determined that a variety of factors influenced the results of placement efforts when considered singly. However, we also suspect that these variables were not acting independently of each other. All of these factors (and more) operate simultaneously. Accordingly, we need to ask which of these factors associated with various placement outcomes remain significant predictors when the influence of all of the others is taken into account. This can be determined through a multiple regression analysis (see Kerlinger, 1979: Ch. 11) such as was done in earlier chapters. The results can help identify those few factors that should receive the most careful attention when trying to answer the question of what a clergywoman can do to enhance her chances of succeeding in the ministerial market place.

Table 9.8 contains the results of the regression analysis. The procedure employed was to regress each placement outcome with its unique set of correlates derived from the preceding analyses. For example, "number of contacts" was regressed with indications of using the Vocation Agency, using the ministerial relations committees, completing and submitting the PIF forms; and with contacting friends, seminary acquaintances and other clergywomen. (Attending the dossier workshops and perceiving system barriers were not included in the regression, because they appeared not to be causally antecedent to number of contacts.)

In general the results indicate the primary importance of using the formal placement structures, as well as the utility of certain informal contacts, the impact of unique situational needs and educational experiences. The primacy of formal placement procedures shows up clearly in relation to number of contacts. Working through other clergywomen also leads to contacts, but the informal route appears to be less predictive than does the formal one. The same thing applies to having one's preaching heard, for using the Vocation Agency was the only significant predictor remaining in that equation. The primary influence of the formal system seems to diminish when one moves to the stage in the placement process of actual interviews. The largest beta coefficient is still associated with working through the Vocation Agency, but other factors become important. Informal contacts play a large role in obtaining interviews, with the seminary contacts possibly being in a strategic position to open those doors. Also, as appeared in the bivariate analysis, the number of situational needs or impediments play roles here as well, with number of interviews being negatively related to the number of pragmatic obstacles inherent in one's domestic situation.

An important shift takes place when we reach the stage of actually receiving a job offer. At this point, importance of the denominational offices recedes into the background, and the influence of local placement structures looms larger. The primary

TABLE 9.8 MULTIPLE REGRESSIONS (beta) OF PLACEMENT OUTCOMES WITH SELECTED CORRELATES, AMONG PRESBYTERIAN CLERGYWOMEN

	VOC agency	Min. rel'ns comm'y	Fill out PIF	Turn in PIF	Friends	Seminary contact	Women clergy	Needs score	Age	MDIV	Graduate degree	Married
Number of contacts	.28	.12	ns*	ns	ns	ns	.15	—#	—	—	—	—
Number heard preach	.19	ns	ns	ns	—	ns	—	—	—	—	—	—
Number of interviews	.21	ns	ns	ns	—	.11**	.16	-.14	ns	—	—	—
Number of calls	ns*	.16	ns	ns	ns	ns	ns	-.16	ns	ns	—	—
Obtained "male" position	ns	—	ns	ns	—	—	ns	—	—	.20	ns	ns
Salary	—#	—	ns	—	—	—	—	-.18	—	-.15**	ns	ns

*Indicates a statistically non-significant slope coefficient.
A line through a cell indicates a variable not entered in the regression.
**p < .10

denominational determinant of receiving calls to a job appears to be using the ministerial relations committees, local gatekeepers whose sponsorship evidently should not be underestimated when it comes to the final decision of whether or not a candidate receives an offer. It is important to note also that the use of informal contacts seems to be basically *irrelevant* to that issue.

When the question about placement outcome becomes qualitative rather than quantitative, i.e., the *kind* of position rather than the number of contacts, another shift takes place. The regression analysis indicates that the major determinant of whether the clergywoman is able to obtain a traditionally "male" position is simply the seminary program she completed. Those who earned the MDIV degree are more likely to enter that domain than are those who completed the MA, MRE, or graduate programs. Both the formal and informal placement strategies appear to make little difference for type of position. Somewhat the same pattern applies to differences in salary. In the final analysis it seems that one's bargaining position associated with one's flexibility and mobility is the main determinant of remuneration, coupled with the fact that lower salaries are associated with the "male" pastoral positions than with other (often denominational) posts.

Conclusions

Sociologists have long been imbued with the idea that "things are not as they seem." The structure of social life often appears to be one thing to the participants in social systems but something quite different to the detached observer. This dictum has led to important insights into hidden social patterns, latent functions and obscure infra-structures. Some clergywomen should pay attention to the admonition. *The workings of the placement process are not what they seem to be!*

Probable misperceptions of placement occur among some clergywomen in two ways. First, *the system is not necessarily the enemy.* It is also not unresponsive by nature to clergywomen's efforts to make it work. In the placement process, placement strategy appears to be the major determinant of female ministers' placement outcomes. Among strategic alternatives the formal structure is preeminent. In the early stages, i.e., seeking contacts and job interviews, using the formal denomination-wide system is the most efficient predictor of success. At later stages—waiting for the job offer—the institutionalized local structures (MRC's) are the most effective for bringing about the desired result. As far as ignoring the formal system and working through informal channels is concerned, doing this kind of "end-run" appears to help at the outset in terms of contacts and interviews, but at the critical stage of the job-offer the informal strategy fades to irrelevance. Being integrated into the formal system at that point is what counts the most.

As in the earlier study (Lehman, 1980), *occupational attainment at the point of final placement is largely contingent upon conformity with denominational norms.* In this context, the formal placement system emerges as a set of allocation structures. Final occupational attainment is allocated only conditionally—if the woman candidate conforms to system policy.

In the ABC study (Lehman, 1980), men were placed (or not) in a job in the ministry no matter what placement strategy they used. This pattern existed because their candidacy itself was not defined as "problematic." The women candidates' presenting themselves for jobs in ministry, on the other hand, was problematic from the outset. The women who succeeded did so mainly to the extent that they conformed to denominational policy by utilizing the formal structures. While we can make no statements about the males in this study, the patterns concerning the women are largely the same as those noted in ABC. The "price of their ticket" seems to be "being a good girl" and "doing as you are told."

Things may not be as they seem for clergywomen in another sense. Many of them conceptualize placement in ministry primarily as a matter of coping with obstacles. Our analysis raises serious questions about the adequacy of this characterization of what getting the job is about. *Having success at any stage of the placement process was basically unrelated to perceiving the presence of any type of obstacle. Desirable placement outcomes were also independent of any type of coping response.* This is not to say that the problems are not really there or that they do not need to be addressed by the person involved. Rather it is to say that their presence or absence is unrelated to actual results in the process of placement. In this sense, the perceived "barriers" may not be barriers at all. The participants in the placement process who define it as basically a matter of coping may be focusing their attention on the wrong things. Developing other perceptions of the system of placement, i.e., coming to perceive it as a *set of structures to be actively manipulated rather than passively coped with*, probably would serve their interests better.

Viewing the placement process as a matter of actively exploiting the formal placement system is likely to be productive for women in ministry for at least two reasons. *First, women seeking positions as ordained ministers need effective advocacy if they are to succeed at all.* They need such support even more if their candidacy is ever to be treated as matter-of-factually as men's. This requirement exists simply because women's entry into the ordained ministry is stigmatized from the outset. The position of "pastor" is highly sex-typed. It is "normal" for men to occupy the post. It is "not normal" for women to do so. Clergywomen are "a problem" for lay church members because they constitute a major departure from traditional patterns of church leadership, those members have no clear guidelines as to how to relate to women in ministry, and they are afraid that the controversy likely to be associated with the issue will disrupt the sense of community in their local congregation. Clergywomen constitute a "problem" for denominational leaders as well, for they tax administrators' ability to manipulate traditional structures to meet the needs of both clergy and congregation.

Effective advocacy is more likely to be forthcoming from persons working in conjunction with the formal placement structures than from other sources. Denominational functionaries associated with official personnel departments, regional and local offices, ministerial relations committees and theological seminaries work in the context of structures already established for exchanging information associated with recruitment and placement of clergy. They are the people most likely to be "in the action" as vacancies and candidates become paired off. The denominational executives are the ones with the greatest amount of information about churches seeking new leadership and about clergy seeking new opportunities. They are strategically located to either extend or withhold recommendations. They typically have direct input into the pool of information with which the congregation's search committee is likely to work. Their opinions and recommendations frequently carry the full weight of the denomination's authority, if not in a directive sense then in a symbolic mode.

Depending upon informal contacts to the exclusion of formal placement structures does not involve the same kind of advocacy either in type or amount. The amount of information held and transmitted by friends or other clergywomen is extremely limited in comparison to that of the formal placement system. Such persons are rarely integrated into the broad network of relationships within which vacancies and candidates are discussed. To depend on them exclusively is really to limit the range of one's opportunities. They can provide contacts, but not really *effective* advocacy.

Moreover, *to ignore the formal denominational placement system places the clergyperson in a situation of most likely alienating the network of decision makers most likely to be in positions to help*—the second reason. Since women in ministry are still novel at best and controversial at worst, their candidacy is problematic from the start. While most people working in formal placement agencies would probably prefer that their work were less complicated, they are also most likely willing to take on the challenge and try to serve the interests of women in ministry.

However, if the female candidate—like a member of any other minority group—decides to ignore these people, she complicates her own situation unnecessarily and to her own detriment. Not only does she forfeit what the system can provide, but also her candidacy takes on a "double stigma." She is now viewed as not "playing by the rules." Whether intentionally or not, she is asserting that she does not need denominational administrators and that she considers their potential contribution unnecessary if not undesirable. Already an object of suspicion, she now reinforces the conclusion that her candidacy should not be treated as a routine matter. She takes on the image of the "outsider" who should not be trusted without a great deal of additional evidence—a "poor risk" for being entrusted with the pastoral leadership of a church.

This point is not to argue that clergywomen should forego specific forms of assistance their sisters in ministry and other friends can provide. The evidence obtained in this study supports the perception that these informal relationships can be the source of contacts with churches and other organizations with vacancies. Some of those contacts may lead to interviews with search committees. In these ways the informal sources of information can be helpful. However, they are likely to be productive only in the early stages of placement—contacts and interviews. Beyond that point it is contact with the local ministerial relations committee—a part of the formal system—that remains predictive of obtaining a call or job offer. Furthermore, even in the early stages, involvement in the formal placement system (using the Vocation Agency) remains more predictive of positive outcomes than does informal contacts.

The obvious conclusion is to use *all* ethical resources available for identifying vacancies and getting one's credentials in the hands of those seeking to fill them, denominational and personal, formal and informal. But if there is reason to pick and choose between various routes to a job, the evidence available up to now suggests that it is a mistake to eliminate the formal placement systems. They may not always seem like one's best friend, but in the final analysis they could be *the only friends who count* in the struggle to find a job.

CHAPTER 10

Epilog

So where do we stand? After having asked and answered these questions about church members' receptivity to women as ordained clergy, what do we know now that we did not know at the outset? We think we have learned a great deal.

The study we reported in the previous chapters produced observations that can be of singular importance to persons making decisions concerning women in the ministry. Women themselves who are contemplating the pursuit of a religious vocation need to know these things—what do church members really think about the idea? What concerns are upper most in the members' minds as they try to come to grips with the concept of having a woman as pastor? What is the best way to go about seeking a position after I complete a seminary education? Likewise, denominational officials need to know what members actually think and feel about women in ministry. In the absence of such information, numerous policy decisions those officials make in dealing with the issue will be informed only by their culturally transmitted preconceptions, stereotypes and misplaced fears. The lay members of congregations confronting the prospect of calling a woman as pastor (or other staff) need to know what actually happens to most congregations when female pastoral leadership is set in place—not the ''horror stories'' that typically float around a community when the idea first comes up. In the case of each type of person involved in the drama, there is a danger that critical decisions will be made either in the absence of information (worse) in the presence of *incorrect* information which derives from irrational fears and which has the capacity to propagate itself like a cancer. People need to know what we have described—they have needed to know it for many years.

Some cynics may answer that we know little more now than we did when we began. One such argument is that this type of research can only deal with the "obvious"—that the information with which we have dealt is really common knowledge. This is possible, of course, but it is hardly likely. It is a familiar cliche, but true in this instance, that "hind sight is better than foresight." Looking back on it, it does seem obvious. As careful research unveils patterns of reality that make sense once they are understood, those perceptions usually take on the aura of familiarity and obviousness. This reaction is actually a hallmark of good research. It *does* make sense. However, this perception of self-evidence does not really falsify the assertion that the information was *not* generally known prior to the undertaking. Before the study was done, the patterns of reality were not "obvious" at all, although it is gratifying to researchers when the results of their work have that appearance after the fact. In short, what we have reviewed is genuinely new knowledge.

A second objection to claiming that this type of study is productive is the argument that survey research is superficial—that it doesn't go deeply enough into people's hidden motives but instead deals only with the surface of their lives. To some extent this assertion is correct. Survey research is not psychoanalysis, and it never can be. But it doesn't have to be! Survey research doesn't need to obtain deep psychological data to be successful. Witness, for example, the way in which modern survey techniques use a few simple questions to predict election outcomes successfully even in close races. Remember, also, the way in which those methods are used routinely to provide the basis for large corporations to invest millions of dollars in particular products and markets and come out making a profit. Survey research *is* useful. It produces information that has proved important in making informed decisions in many areas of life—politics, the economy, mental health and social welfare being a few of the more obvious examples. Here is one instance in which it can contribute to the making of informed decisions by people in religious institutions.

In this final chapter, we want to set forth a few basic conclusions that flow from the evidence we have studied. We also want to suggest what the future might plausibly hold for the entrance and acceptance of women in the ordained ministry. Before we do, however, we want to summarize some corroborating evidence obtained from a different source, i.e., from the clergy women themselves, those women who were serving as pastors of the churches we studied. Their voices should be heard too, for their perceptions flow from a different perspective on those events, one which is just as important as the frame of reference of the church members. They were the ministers involved in the interaction we described. Do they perceive the events in the same ways as the members of the congregations? Or do they view what happened differently? Would we reach the same conclusions about what is happening if we had data from one of these groups or the other?

Observations of the Clergywomen Themselves

After finishing the interviews with the members of churches where women had been serving as pastor, we contacted the clergywomen and collected data which was parallel to that obtained from the laypersons. The women stood in varying relationships to the congregations involved. All of the ministers-at-large had completed their stint as interim pastor. About one-half of the installed pastors had resigned their charges, and the others were continuing in their pastoral positions.

We wanted to obtain the perceptions of the clergywomen about what had happened in their churches during their stay as pastor (and what was still happening in the cases of those who were continuing as pastor). We got this information in two stages. First, we sent each clergywoman in the study a copy of the interview questionnaire used in the interviews of her (former) members. We asked each one to "project" herself into the mind of a "typical" member and to fill out the form as though she were that abstracted person. After each clergywoman returned the completed form, we reviewed it and called her to discuss it. We wanted to be sure that we understood what she was saying, that we weren't "putting words in her mouth," and that there was an opportunity for her to reflect on the situation and provide whatever additional information she thought was important for us to know.

The women ministers involved in the study were exceptionally cooperative. Their first question, of course, was "What did the members say?"—or—"When can I get a copy of the results?" (Many of them probably also wonder whether this is the last time someone is going to contact them to fill out a questionnaire or conduct an interview. They have been questionned intensely in recent years!) Nevertheless, they dealt patiently with our questions and provided some important new information. In discussing these details, we shall not try to distinguish between what was written and what was obtained by phone. We shall concentrate on the overall patterns in their impressions.

The first question dealt with the church's initial reaction to them. All of the clergywomen but one indicated that there were some "horror stories" about clergywomen before they came. In response to first learning about the possibility of having a woman as pastor, the usual range of dire consequences was predicted. Members thought others would stop coming to church, some fewer felt others would stop contributing financially, and some thought others would move away to other churches. Some members predicted major schisms in the congregation between the "pro-woman" people and those opposed. We have already noted some of these patterns in the data from the members themselves (above), but it is interesting to note the extent to which the information was shared openly with the women pastors. Nearly every clergywoman had her favorite story about the member (male or female) who was among the most opposed when she first arrived but who later proudly confessed to a conversion to the ranks of supporters of the new woman pastor—and how genuine that new support actually was.

Accordingly, nearly every pastor also indicated that none of the terrible predictions materialized. At first a few families stayed home from church, but most of them returned before long. Even fewer actually reduced their level of giving to the church. Actual defections from the church were extremely rare. Remarks by the laypersons corroborate these reports. Usually within a few weeks, the congregation was working with the clergywoman to pursue the range of goals and programs found in most UPC congregations, as it typically occurs under the leadership of a man. Even in one church where the congregation was described as feeling "blackmailed" into accepting a female minister-at-large, pastor/member relationships quickly settled into typical routines fairly soon after the clergywoman began functioning as interim pastor.

We were particularly interested in the clergywomen's descriptions of kind of change that took place while they were working in a church, and how much actual change occurred. As with the reports of the members, we have categorized changes in stereotyping, preferences for men or women in clergy roles and overall willingness to accept a clergywoman as pastor in the future.

About one-half of the ministers thought that there was less stereotyping of clergywomen after they had worked there than before they came. A few reports of "no change" involved the members' having *previously* encountered another woman minister in pastoral roles, which considerably diminished the amount of perceptual change associated with interacting with the present clergywoman. These members had already begun to change their minds. Other reports of little decline in stereotyping, however, indicated that in these cases the clergywoman simply felt that the members were about equally prejudiced after having worked with her as before. On the one hand, such a portrayal seems to be unduly self-effacing, because tables comparing the specific churches on these matters indicate no significant differences from one church to another. On the other hand, it is clear that not everyone did change his/her mind about women in ministry during the encounter. The discrepancies may be more apparent than real.

The interviews with the clergywomen also dealt with the perceived gender preferences of their members. The women reported more attitude change concerning sacramental and liturgical roles than on other dimensions. Seventy percent said that their members preferred men for these functions less after seeing them in the roles than before. This pattern is consistent with the data from the members which indicates more change on this dimension than on the others. It is probably the highly "public" nature of the sacramental functions that makes them the arenas where preferences are most likely to change and the points where change is most apt to be noticed.

Just the opposite is the case on the organizational dimension. About 60 percent of the women reported that after contact with them members still preferred men for leading the organizational components of church life. Leading the session, leading congregational meetings, developing a budget and church programs are still considered the appropriate provinces of men in those churches as perceived by the clergywomen. To some of the pastors the problem is still a matter of churches having difficulty with women taking roles involving direct organizational "authority." In our culture, authority-laden roles traditionally have been played mainly by men. Again, this perception is consistent with reports of the members themselves, for they indicate less change on the organizational dimension than on some others.

The women reported a similar situation regarding the pointed question of who their members preferred for the position of "pastor." Sixty-five percent of them said that their members still prefer a man in that position. This is also supported in their statement about members' preferences concerning the work of clergywomen "in general." Two-thirds of the women said that overall the church members still prefer a man as pastor or senior minister even after contact. Laypersons may become convinced that a woman is "capable" of being a pastor, but often they still "prefer" a man. Sacred culture is slow to change.

The pastors' comments suggest a few unresolved issues. One problem in the dynamics of members' reactions to clergywomen serving as their pastor seems to be a matter of "generalization." Several of the pastors and ministers-at-large perceived that the members of the churches they served found it acceptable to work with "me" but not with "a woman." Members warmed up to the specific clergywomen they encountered, but they often failed to view them also as representative of a class of people known as "women ministers." "Our Barbara is wonderful, but it would be hard for any other woman to measure up to her!" was a frequent comment by members we interviewed. The changed attitudes were person-specific. They didn't apply to clergywomen "in general." Approximately one-half of the clergywomen themselves reported that they thought the members related to the experience in this way. Again, however, the reports of the members do not entirely corroborate these impressions. There clearly was *some* attitude change toward clergywomen as a class of objects rather than toward a specific individual. It is unrealistic to expect *everyone* to change! Changes in attitudes toward clergywomen in general are also relatively equally distributed among the churches. Perhaps we have a little selective perception going on here.

A few of the women also said that they probably were "adopted" by the churches where they served—adopted not only in the sense of being accepted as "one of us" but also in the sense of being "a child." "Our Barbara" was adopted as a "daughter of the church"—as a "daughter" in a cultural sense, i.e., as a dependent person rather than as an autonomous leader, as a child to be protected and nurtured rather than as a spiritual guide to provide wisdom for life's complexities and frustrations! In instances where this is the case, it is but another manifestation of the classical "insulting compliment." It says, "We will accept you as a nice novel individual among us, but we will not take you seriously as our minister." It is a special form of tokenism. To the extent that this is the case, contact with the clergywoman in the pastoral role has not worked in the way some people might have hoped. However, with so many cultural forces working against the program, it would be naive to expect to encounter none of these ways of derailing its effects.

It is my suspicion that these highly tokenistic descriptions of members' reactions involve some truth. No doubt they reflect specific incidents in which the clergywomen experienced being "put in their place." At times such actions probably were deliberate. However, most of the time such events stem from subtle and tenacious assumptions about sex roles that pop up in the actions of even well intentioned individuals—a slip of the tongue or a faux pas that even the actor doesn't recognize. They reflect ways in which the subtle, traditional sex-role distinctions are hard to "get hold of" and to change. It is the effect of a culture in its profoundly basic power to structure reality. Nevertheless, intentional or not, such events reflect ways in which contact designed to change people's attitudes has not worked as thoroughly as was envisioned.

However, others among the women pastors explicitly denied such experiences. These women emphasized how *well* they had been accepted as leaders in all forms of church life—in public and in private, in the warmth of worship and in the cold politics of debate, in the humility of personal counselling sessions and in the pride taken in congregational successes. There were no put-downs or insults, either intended or accidental. These other clergywomen reported glowing comparisons which their members made between them and their male predecessors. Some men who had served as pastor in the immediate past were described as a series of "clerical disasters" in the life of the church. There had been moral problems, professional incompetence, resignation and capitulation in the face of the seemingly insurmountable challenges inherent in the pastoral role. These clergywomen had shown them what women in ministry could do, and the people responded with expressions of gratitude and praise.

My suspicion is that it would be a mistake to generalize from either of these extremes in assessing the impact of the encounter with a woman as pastor. Church members in general and in any particular congregation are probably more heterogeneous in attitude and action than either type of report alone would imply. The same goes for clergywomen. On the one hand, sex roles are basic to the fabric of our society and to most individuals' concepts of what is natural and/or proper in the structures of social situations. Notions about what is appropriately male and female are both widespread and deep-seated. When such fundamental concepts of reality are challenged, many people react with confusion, anxiety, anger and obstinacy. A clergywoman who is the agent of such a challenge is likely to sense these reactions for two obvious reasons, i.e., she is going to be uniquely sensitive to any cues about reactions to her, not because she is a woman but because she has been trained to be sensitive to others and objectively needs such feedback in order to decide how to proceed with her work; secondly, she is the specific agent of the challenge in the congregation, and it would be naive to expect negative reactions to focus anywhere other than on herself. Add to this the middle class conventionality that typifies most Protestant congregations, and powerful forces (initially) present the woman minister with emotionally-charged, negative reactions.

On the other hand, there are good reasons to expect some clergywomen to report basically positive experiences as well. Like the rest of us, women in ministry are not monolithic, and the situations into which they are projected differ widely too. On the note of idiosyncrasy, it is probably no accident that all of the interim pastors reported that their congregations viewed them not as typical of other women in ministry but as "exceptions." This pattern supports the data from their churches. As a group the women interim pastors were both highly competent and very self-confident. They were accustomed to excelling. No doubt only the best candidates were selected as clergywomen to participate in the minister-at-large program. It is clearly in the interest of the sponsoring agency to have its best examples "out there" representing women in ministry can change people's minds about clergywomen. The ministers-at-large were a competent lot.

However, it is important to remember that the churches served by ministers-at-large manifested no more changes in levels of receptivity than did the congregations served by women who had been installed as pastor. Not only were these pastors also highly competent as a group, but their members' responses to them in terms of attitude change were just as positive. It is also significant in this regard that the members' perceptions of the relative effectiveness of the woman who was serving their church was *not* related to the extent to which they changed their mind about women in ministry. The apparent basis for attitude change was less a matter of calculated evaluation and more an effect of having to bring their attitudes in line with their church commitments. Accordingly, it is probably not necessary to think in terms of using only "superwomen" in a minister-at-large program. The useful range of levels of ability may be rather broad.

It is also important to bear in mind that not only do clergywomen differ among themselves but also local congregations are heterogeneous. This point especially applies to what they have experienced in terms of pastoral leadership in the recent past. The anecdotal reports of the members (at the end of the interviews) included references to unfortunate experiences with a few ministers who had served their congregations before the clergywoman came on the scene. These stories corroborate the reports of the women pastors. Evidently some of the women were able to bring stability into a number of church communities where recent events had engendered a great deal of disappointment, conflict and stigma. The women were able to make the people feel good about themselves again and to rally their confidence and support. With no intention of denigrating these particular clergywomen on their work, it is likely that the congregations in questions would have experienced the resurgence of vitality and self-confidence in response to the leadership of any competent minister, male or female. It is simply fortunate for clergywomen in general that the particular women pastors happened upon the scene at the right moment. They were able to demonstrate that women can provide quality pastoral leadership right at the time when the members were uniquely open and receptive to it.

In general, then, there is evidence that the extremely negative and extremely positive reports of the clergywomen should be tempered a bit. On balance it seems that the members responded positively to them. Many members changed their minds about women in ministry. However, we have not reached the promised land. The amount of change was moderate. Still we should not despair of ever reaching that land, for the changes that did take place were consistent across nearly every dimension of receptivity, and they were real. Contact with women in the role of pastor does change most members' minds, but it doesn't bring about a revolution.

On this note, several of the clergywomen volunteered their impressions concerning whether or not the contact hypothesis is applicable to changing receptivity to women in ministry. As one would expect, some of these perceptions were positive, and others were negative. Among the interim pastors, the one who was most emphatic about the program having worked had some very powerful evidence in support of her argument. One church where she had served as interim pastor had elected to install another clergywoman as pastor when she left. The members had changed their minds enough to cross the threshold of making an open-ended commitment to a woman pastor. This outcome is the acid test.

Most of the other ministers-at-large, along with respondents from their churches, reported that many members wanted the woman interims to remain as pastor. The ministers-at-large were prevented by contract from accepting such overtures, and there is no evidence to suggest that they encouraged such speculation. Yet the fact that these other minister-at-large churches did not actually call a clergywoman as pastor after the contact experience seems to reinforce the perception that some members do not generalize very much from the particular woman interim pastor to clergywomen in general. In the interest of enhancing the pastoral opportunities of women in ministry, these patterns may be a basis for reconsidering the prohibitions against their being considered candidates for pastor of the churches they serve as interim minister.

One-half of the clergywomen in the study who had been installed as pastors also argued that the contact hypothesis was applicable to women in ministry. These five women reported that their congregations previously had been served by women who were either seminary students working in an internship situation or seminary graduates who were there as interim ministers. Both these women pastors and many members of their churches reported that these previous contacts with women in the role of pastor (or student minister) had "broken the ice" for the clergywoman who eventually was installed. This pattern provides additional evidence that contact does "work." It supports the arguments that some "generalization" does take place. However, it must be viewed with caution, because we did not survey those other churches where women seminarians served or where women had another form of temporary assignment but where no woman was called subsequently. The evidence is consistent with patterns we have observed in this study, but it is not conclusive.

The women who indicated that in their opinion the clergywoman/congregation contact had *not* worked were in the minority. The woman interim who was the most adamant in this evaluation seemed to be implying two quite different points. First, the members who had experienced her leadership as interim pastor responded very positively to her. They were both effusive and public in heaping praise upon her. But they did not seem to generalize. They saw her as an exceptional woman and responded to her appropriately, but there was little evidence that they would ever call another woman as their pastor. Second, even though her success was well known in the area through media accounts and word-of-mouth exchanges, no other church had given any evidence of seriously considering her when there was a vacancy on their staff. The door had not really been opened for *her* in any meaningful way. To the extent that such a pattern has the potential for being widespread, perhaps it would be worthwhile considering creating more efficient structures to facilitate movement from the status of interim pastor to the status of installed pastor in another situation. Churches willing to consider such persons would then be dealing with known entities rather than unknowns, and their level of risk would probably be lower than in many routine installations of new pastors.

We asked the clergywomen about some specific issues during the interview. Perhaps the most noteworthy of the things discussed was the language issue. As noted elsewhere in this report, the problem of sexist language is an important theme in the feminist critique of traditional church life and thought. Evidence of the challenge is clear. The religious press has produced a number of important works on the subject, and it is a pervasive issue in theological seminary circles. The intensity with which some feminists within the denomination raise the issue of linguistic changes at least equals that experienced in secular circles. One's position on the issue is often regarded as a "litmus test" of one's orientation to the entire range of matters which the feminist movement is calling into question.

Every clergywoman included in the study indicated that the problem of sexist language was (or would be) a sensitive subject in the churches they served. Two of them, one an interim pastor and the other an installed pastor, also stated that they think the issue is being overemphasized in the movement and that it has become too much an end in itself and trivialized. All of the others argued that they consider the issue important but that there are other *more* important goals to pursue in the role of pastor. The two persons who basically rejected the sexist language issue as a problem to be attacked asserted that they spent no time dealing with it, and they were critical of those who "wasted" their time in such pursuits. The matter was considered entirely too "offensive" to take up.

All of the remaining clergywoman in the study considered the problem of sexist language to be sufficiently important to deal with. They were also unanimous in their preferences for strategies with which to approach it. They all counseled to "go slow." Seven out of these thirteen asserted that they had incorporated inclusive language in their liturgies, but they tried to do so in a "matter-of-fact" way. They also tried not to present the language issue as "a problem" to be confronted by the congregation. They felt that to do so would be too divisive, would serve to construct unnecessary barriers between themselves and the congregation, and would diminish their effectiveness in dealing with other problems in the life of the church. They felt that such prices were too high and that a "gradual" approach was to be preferred.

Several of the clergywomen reported feeling uncomfortable in the apparent cross-pressures involved in this situation. On the one hand, they had encountered a heavy emphasis on changing sexist language while students in seminary. A few had been participants in the campus efforts to encourage the seminary to use sexually inclusive symbols. The tendency was to depart from seminary upon graduation with the goal of eliminating sexist language from the life of the church. On the other hand, they sensed the extent to which the issue of inclusive language was in some ways a "non-issue" in most local churches prior to their arrival, and they anticipated considerable resistance if they decided to make it a matter of programmatic controversy in their churches. Instead they chose to introduce inclusive language into church life in as inoffensive a way as possible. However, remembering the emphasis placed on linguistic problems in seminary circles, *they (initially) thought that they were the only ones "giving in" to gradualism, and they felt guilty about it.* They felt as though they had betrayed their sisters! A few of them reported that they had tried hitting the issue hard once or twice in their first jobs, but the reaction was so unpleasant that they abandoned further efforts at direct confrontation over the matter, and they did not approach it directly in subsequent positions.

Most of the clergywomen indicated their approach to inclusive language seemed to "be working." By making subtle linguistic modifications now and then, they were able to lead the members into the use of inclusive forms often without their being aware of the changes. In one congregation the clergywoman experimented one Sunday by reverting deliberately and abruptly to the former, traditional sexist language after a long period of gradual change. Some members of the congregation (both male and female) became angry at the reversal! Perhaps to many members it is "sudden change" that is the issue as much as the content of the symbols themselves!

Finally, we asked the clergywomen if there had been any particular event (or kind of event) that symbolized their being accepted as pastor of the church. Was there any "big plus" in what had happened to them in their churches that said to them, "I've made it! They really are relating to me as their minister!"? The answers were quite diverse, of course, but a few patterns emerged in their responses. First, only four could think of *nothing* so symbolic or noteworthy. Most of the women did see certain kinds of events as significant. Second, the interim ministers were unanimous in mentioning actions by the church associated with their departure. There were parties and dinners and gifts. Often the organizers of these activities and some of the "biggest givers" were members who had been strongly opposed to the clergywoman at the outset of her ministry there. These ritual recognitions also involved litanies of regret at her leaving and included statements indicating a desire that she stay on as the installed pastor of the church.

Third, one kind of event was mentioned more than any other as the opportunity that seemed to "open the people up" to being ministered to by a woman. That event was the death of a member (or relative) and the necessity for dealing with the bereavement and the funeral ceremonies. As many other ministers have experienced for years (centuries?), simply "being there" and showing the love associated with the Christian life opens the doors of people's hearts to the minister's presence, compassion and skill. Those pastors who tread softly on the souls laid bare before them in bereavement situations usually are rewarded with a level of reciprocated love and support that defies rational explanation. No other single type of event was mentioned more often as the thing that cemented the clergywoman's relationship with the congregation as their pastor.

In general, the reports of the clergywomen support the patterns observed in the responses of the members. Did contact with the clergywoman in the role of pastor have any influence on members' receptivity to women in ministry? The ministers themselves tend to say "yes." The members' responses were both positive and negative, but the positive reactions clearly prevailed. After members' had interacted with tthe woman pastor, levels of resistance seemed to be lower than they were before she came. The amount of change was not great, but it was more than could be accounted for by chance alone, and it was consistent across all dimensions. Whether it was "enough" remains a matter of the reader's values and aspirations.

Some Conclusions

We come now to the point where we must draw the results of the study together and indicate what generalizations can be made from it, however tentative those statements may be. Several points appear to have sufficient empirical support to be given the status of "conclusions." A few of them will be a bit repetitious of materials we have already reviewed in the previous chapters, but they are sufficiently basic to warrant stating them again.

1. *The current feminist movement is challenging the churches to practice what they preach.*

Nearly a quarter century has passed since most mainline denominations in the United States issued pronouncements endorsing the ordination of women as clergy. During that time thousands of women, mostly young adults but also significant numbers of middle-aged and older persons, have responded to the open door and have asserted that they were pursuing a call to ministry. Over the decade of the 1970's and beyond, the enrollments of women in theological seminaries increased virtually at a geometric rate. By the early 1980's, women actually constituted a majority of the student body in some leading theological seminaries, and they were found in most other such schools in large numbers. Many of these women were enrolled in educational programs normally leading to a pastorate with local congregations. The range of their aspirations and commitments closely paralleled that of male seminarians.

The women are in the system. They are knocking on the door of the churches and asking to be accepted as clergy in all of the ways traditionally reserved for men. The ball is currently in the congregations' court. As church members encounter this situation, they view themselves as evaluating the peformance of the women in order to decide whether to really accept them as ordained ministers. In fact it is the churches who are on trial. The women ministers are saying, in effect, "You profess to be the guardians of the values of universalistic justice and equality before God. We are also equal. Our call is equal to that of men. Let us work out our Christian vocation!"

2. *Church members are not monolithic in their response to clergywomen.*

We started out asking whether the church members, especially the laity, were open or closed to the concept of women as pastors and other forms of minister. As usually happens, the research has indicated that the question, articulated in that form, cannot be answered. The evidence suggests that the world of church members is much more complicated than the question assumes. It is not a situation of "either/or" but rather of "both/and." Some members are receptive to women in ministry, and others are opposed. Some are willing to give it a try, while others are not.

Furthermore, the members differ widely in their acceptance of clergywomen depending on what facet of "acceptance" is at issue. Is it stereotyping? Is it preferences? Is it a matter of what women clergy *can do* or a problem of whether they *ought* to do any of it? We get different answers depending on which dimension of receptivity we deal with. The response is as complicated as the women to whom it is made.

3. Church members are not always consistent in their response to clergywomen.

There are many ways in which church members indicate inconsistency in their reactions to women as ordained clergy. On the one hand, they may argue that women are capable of performing the ministerial roles they personally consider most desirable, and on the other hand they assert that they prefer a man for their pastor. Similarly, numerous members said that they had no preference for men (or women) concerning specific functions clergy perform—leading worship, preaching, administering sacraments, counselling—virtually every task for which clergy are traditionally responsible. At the same time they indicated that they prefer a man as the individual with the title of "pastor" of their congregation. This pattern probably reflects the influence of culture's power to control not only overt actions but also deep seated feelings. People do not readily turn away from traditions and customs they hold dear. They are uncomfortable with such change. We have seen this hesitancy historically in the nation's reluctant responses to other innovations, i.e., to labor unions, the social security system, civil rights and the Susan B. Anthony silver dollar. Here we see the same hesitancy to change in relation to two powerful sources of meaning—two basic symbols that are conjoined in one movement—the distinctions between the sexes and religious tradition. It is small wonder that people react to efforts to alter these areas of life with some irrationalities in their actions.

4. Nevertheless, the predominant response of church members to women in ministry is clearly positive.

Even though there are wide disagreements among individuals concerning what to do about the "clergywoman problem," the evidence is clear that most of them are willing to make some changes in the area. As individuals speak for themselves, they typically manifest high levels of receptivity to women as clergy. About 75 to 80 percent of lay members view women as temperamentally fit for the pastorate, as stable and reliable workers and as potentially strong church leaders. They hold few stereotypes of women as clergy. Very few members think women cannot do the job at all. Similarly, they tend *not* to prefer men performing specific clergy functions in the liturgical and organizational life of the church. Few lay members are willing to endorse discrimination against women in the congregation's hiring practices in the absence of congregational consensus. The clergymen tend to be even more positive in their acceptance of women as clergy. These patterns bode well for the prospects of clergywomen being integrated into the profession on an institutionalized basis and eventually no longer as a novelty. Individual church members are willing to change.

5. *However, the resistant minority has a powerful voice in the current debates, and they influence congregational decisions far beyond the strength of their numbers.*

Congregational solidarity is an important value—indeed, a central one in some circles—which plays a significant role in congregational decision making. Most members place high importance on maintaining harmonious relations within the congregation. Similarly, most denominational officials give considerable weight to the maintenance of concord within and between local churches. The church is supposed to be the community of love, and it is unusually painful when it becomes an arena of rancor.

This traditional notion of the kinds of social relations that are supposed to prevail in the congregation is especially important in view of the fact that the vast majority of church members expect a woman's candidacy for a ministerial position to generate conflict in the community. Most members think that if a woman were called to serve the church, particularly as pastor, significant numbers of members would stay home in protest, would withhold or cut back their financial contributions to the church or would leave altogether to join another congregation. This perception of the negative consequences of recruiting a woman for pastoral position prevails in most congregations. Almost everyone expects the worst to happen.

The consequences of this perception constitute another illustration of the importance of the mere "definition of the situation," a dictum which says that situations which are defined as real are real in their consequences. Applied to this case, it means that if members perceive that others will leave the church or otherwise reduce the level of their commitment to the congregation in response to the introduction of a clergywoman, they will act to prevent those consequences from happening. It matters little whether the anticipated reaction of others is correct or not. It is defined as correct by the members who, in turn, act as if it were correct. The consequence is that individuals who would act one way if they followed their own orientations to clergywomen ultimately act the opposite way in order to avoid intra-church conflict. Wanting to prevent other members' withdrawal from church life in protest over a woman minister, they decide to placate the negative minority by rejecting the clergywoman themselves. It is not their own attitudes toward women clergy that make them act this way, but rather it is their love of their congregation and their perceptions of the attitudes of others that lead them to resist. Even though the majority of members are clearly in favor of having a woman as pastor, the minority who oppose female leadership ultimately prevail in the name of church viability. It is quite clear that if a member has a high level of investment of self in the congregation *and* perceives that a clergywoman would generate conflict there, that person is likely to prefer having male pastoral church leadership. It makes little difference that members do *not in fact* withdraw from church participation after a woman comes on the scene. The fear and perception of possible schism is sufficient to affect behavior. Concern for church viability is a powerful predictor of receptivity to women in ministry.

This pattern is suggested in yet another pattern in the data. *The more the personal investment and involvement in the local congregation, the more resistant members are likely to be toward women in ministry.* Local lay members were less receptive on the average than pastors, and the pastors in turn were less receptive than special clergy. For local lay members, the *local* congregation is what "church" is mostly about. It is *this* church in *this* community. *This* is *my* church, regardless of the existence of a religious community (or church) beyond the local level. *This* church is where my family, neighbors and other friends seek guidance and opportunity for living out their religious commitments. If something happens to fracture that community, I am likely to be hurt personally. I want to avoid that if at all possible.

The same isn't true nearly to the same degree for the pastors. Typically, indeed almost always, they are not natives of the local community in which they are working as pastor. They were called there, they will spend several years laboring in that particular field, and then they will depart for other endeavors. They do have some vested interest in the local congregations' health and happiness. If nothing else, discord in the congregation they are serving reflects badly on their pastoral leadership. They are not supposed to let such things happen. Nevertheless, if things don't work out, they can usually leave that congregation fairly easily and work with another one. The level of their personal investment is not nearly as high as is that of the local lay members. The pastor can "take it or leave it" more easily than can the local layperson.

At the opposite extreme from lay members are the special clergy. As denominational officials, college or seminary faculty, or workers in other institutional settings, they can afford to be even more cavalier about the consequences of introducing controversy into the life of local congregations. Occupationally they typically see themselves as concerned with "bigger" issues than local church life. They experience the fallout of congregational conflict only indirectly. In this frame of reference, therefore, it is not surprising to see the patterns of receptivity and resistance to women in ministry ordered as they are among these three categories of members. Lay members are least receptive, pastors more receptive, and special clergy the most receptive. The extent of their respective direct concern over local church solidarity would lead one to expect these differences. The more distant they are in the church structure from the local church scene, the more likely they are to be in favor of introducing women in ministry. In terms of promoting controversial issues, this distance is functional. If the cause is defined as just and proper, then one should press for its acceptance. The point here is simply that we should not be surprised to see local lay members more resistant to these causes than are remote church officials.

6. *Some of the differences in receptivity to clergywomen are predictable in view of other characteristics of the members.*

People's attitudes don't "just happen." They develop out of day-to-day experiences in the real world, and knowable differences in those experiences can be used to predict which people have which types of attitudes. It is considered common knowledge, for example, that regional differences are predictive of differences in race prejudice. We likewise know that cultural differences lie behind our attitudes toward various kinds of food. The same principle applies to people's attitudes toward women in ministry.

The research indicates that there are at least three kinds of reasons why members differ in their receptivity toward female clergy, i.e., their orientations toward sex roles in general, the level of their traditional religious commitments, and the type of congregation of which they are members. As one would expect, members with traditional attitudes towards sex roles in general also tend to have traditional attitudes toward women in ministry. The same factors that predict different levels of "sexism" in general also predict variations in acceptance of clergywomen. Males, older persons and those with lower levels of formal education tend to be more resistant to women in ministry than do females, younger persons and the more educated. Of these factors, sex is the strongest predictor. Men have significantly lower levels of receptivity than women in terms of their tendency to stereotype clergywomen, to prefer male pastoral leadership and to be willing to discriminate against female candidates for local church positions. Unfortunately, sometimes the "MCP" image is not without some basis in fact.

Traditional religiosity is also related to differences in attitudes. Members who hold traditional religious ideology and participate in traditional ritual behavior to a high degree are those with few inclinations to accept clergywomen. Those with nontraditional ideologies and few traditional ritual involvements are people with greater tendencies to accept women in ministry. "Traditionalism" tends to be a generalized trait rather than a specific one.

Finally, the type of church that members belonged to is predictive of their attitudes toward clergywomen, although the relationships are not strong. The general pattern is for members of large churches with multiple staff, stable budgets and one denominational affiliation to be relatively *resistant* to women in ministry, while small churches with solo pastorates, problem budgets and dual denominational alignments tend to be more *accepting* of them.

7. *Fears of congregational conflict notwithstanding, contact with women in the role of pastor tends to be a positive experience for church members. The experience transforms resistance into acceptance.*

The contact hypothesis is applicable to the situation of church members interacting with a woman in the role of pastor. Members of churches where women have served as either interim pastor or installed pastor are more receptive of women in ministry than are those in congregations who have not had that experience. Where clergywomen have taken the role of pastor, members of the congregation tend to stereotype them less, tend to have fewer preferences for men in pastoral roles, and tend to be less willing to discriminate against women appylying for positions in their church. Contact works.

Furthermore, none of the "horror stories" about members withdrawing from church participation in droves come true when a clergywoman arrives on the scene. If anything, the opposite happens. The congregation tends to stabilize as it works through the realities of the new situation. In a few cases, the church grows, but there is no evidence that it develops any more under the leadership of a woman than a man. There simply appears to be no difference directly attributable to the sex of the pastor.

Other changes also take place in members' orientations to women in ministry as a result of contact with a woman in the role of pastor. For one thing, the influence of some other factors previously related to differences in attitudes pales into insignificance. In the face of the direct experience with the woman as pastor, the former attitudinal differences between men and women, young and old, etc., tend to diminish considerably. The direct experience tends to homogenize those attitudes and to unify the congregation ideologically. Any remaining differences in attitudes toward clergywomen after direct contact tend not to be predicted by those same factors but instead tend to become more idiosyncratic. The contact experience tends to override the influence of other experiences in its power to shape orientations toward female church leadership.

Secondly, the patterns of members' preference for men in clergy roles change significantly. Prior to direct contact with a woman as pastor, members tend to like or dislike the idea of female church leadership mostly on organizational grounds. That is, whether or not members favor a woman in ministry tends to be determined mostly in terms of how well she is likely to do at running the church as an organization. Preferences for men or women as pastor are related more to this aspect of church life than to its liturgical and sacramental activities prior to contact. After members experience a woman as pastor, however, these patterns change. The clarity of these organizational concerns tends to break up. The organizational leadership criterion is no longer the one mostly applied to preferences for men or women in the position of pastor. After contact, preferences for men or women as pastor become grouped together as liturgical or sacramental concerns. Furthermore, the liturgical arena remains the only clear one in which women pastors are be accepted or rejected after contact. The others, such as the organizational one, become less clear after contact. This outcome suggests a decline in the extent to which sexism is institutionalized in the congregation after a woman has been experienced in the role of pastor. Aside from liturgical concerns, other factors become unrelated to each other, suggesting that they become less matters of congregational concensus and more idiosyncratic preferences.

Finally, the factor most consistently predictive of differences in receptivity to women in ministry—having traditional ritual involvements in the church—seems to be the very thing that helps members change their minds about female pastoral leadership. Prior to contact, members who are relatively high in ritual church participation tend also to be *low* in receptivity toward clergy-women. Traditional involvements are associated with traditional attitudes. However, this very form of organizational commitment to the local church plays an important role in producing changes in attitudes toward the very non-traditional pastor—the clergy-woman. In effect, the high level of ritual commitment keeps the member "locked in" to the interactional life of the congregation. It keeps him/her coming to church to participate in worship and related activities. This also forces the individual involved to enter situations in which he/she must then interact with the woman in her role as pastor, an act which by definition is counter-attitudinal where the orientation is conservative. It also forces such members to interact with other members who do not share the negative attitudes toward women in ministry. This situation typically arouses "cognitive dissonance" in those members. Since it is relatively difficult psychologically to alter the overt behavior, i.e., to stop coming to church, given the personal commitments to the church, the dissonance is reduced by changing attitudes toward women as pastor. By maintaining a high level of ritual commitment once the clergywoman arrives on the scene, the members thrust themselves into dissonance-arousing situations and in effect force attitude change upon themselves.

8. The denominational placement system may be the "best friend" of clergywomen seeking positions in ministry.

Women seeking to break into the traditionally male ranks of ordained clergy have several avenues before them for obtaining ministerial positions. They can choose to work through the denominational placement structures set in place for that purpose, or they can elect to take other paths to a job. In some circles of clergywomen, the formal placement systems are viewed with suspicion at best and considered "the enemy" at worst. These women expect those structures to be fundamentally unresponsive to women's placement needs, largely because they define them as but little more than one portion of a basically sexist church structure. Operating with this set of assumptions, women sometimes select routes to ministerial positions other than those of the placement structures. Occasionally these moves are successful, but more often than not the women who take such routes experience less success in finding a job than they would have if they had gone through routine channels.

The reasons for these unsatisfactory outcomes are basically two in number. First, clergywomen who try to circumnavigate the denominational placement system stand in danger of alienating the placement personnel who work within it. The consequence of this is that women then get punished for *not* using it. Women's candidacy for pastoral positions is a matter of controversy simply because it defies tradition. They enter the arena to compete for jobs already stigmatized by the simple fact of their sex. When they refuse to follow normal placement procedure, they take on a "double stigma," for now in effect they have announced that they refuse to "play by the rules" and that they intend to obtain a position in ministry by deviant means. Since denominational officials are accustomed to working within those rules, their typical reaction is to reciprocate the contempt and to view the woman as a potential enemy. Just as the women look upon the system with suspicion, the persons working within the system view them as equally suspicious and not to be trusted with a position in ministry.

The second reason why trying to do an "end run" around the formal placement system can be counterproductive for women (or anyone else, for that matter) is that the system may in fact be the "best friend they have." It is often fruitful to contact personal friends to find out about job openings. One can make an initial contact with a potential employer through such informal contacts. Unfortunately, however, the initial contact is usually as far as those relationships can take one. In contrast to this limitation, the formal placement system is structured in such a way as to take one from initial contacts through to interviews with search committees, and it can provide strategic advocacy among the persons who will ultimately make decisions on whom to hire. Each step of the recruitment/placement process is linked to each other step within the formal placement process, so that one is more likely to get one's name before the appropriate people at each step of the way by following that route. In the final analysis, there is no guarantee that anyone—man or woman—will be placed in a ministerial position as a direct result of using the sanctioned procedures established by the denomination. However, *not* using that system is virtually guaranteed to set unnecessary obstacles in way of job placement. So the admonition to women seeking placement would be that if they want to *eliminate* any paths to placement in ministry, they should *not* eliminate the formal system. In the final analysis, it may not seem like their very best friend, but *it could be the only friend that "counts."*

What of the Future?

We venture to make a few predictions about women in ministry. They apply primarily to the denomination we examined in this study, but I suggest that they are largely applicable to other Protestant bodies as well. Differences in theology and church polity are frequently the focus of attention when comparing various denominations, and those differences are real. However, it is yet another matter to assert that denominational uniqueness in theology and polity are always the primary forces shaping people's decisions to enter the ministry and to endorse another's ministry. There is some evidence that at times other factors play the key roles in those matters. In short, I'd risk a guess that in the case of the emergence of women in ministry, there is more in common among Protestant bodies than there is that which distinguishes them. I would also risk the assertion that most of the predictions below are applicable to all "mainline" Protestant bodies to some degree.

1. *The pressure by women to obtain complete acceptance as or-*
   dained religous leaders will remain in effect in the foreseeable
   future.

The feminist movement *has* come to the churches, and it is not
likely to go away. The surge of pressure that is gradually revolutionizing the status of gender in American life, built as it is on
arguments of equality, justice, universalism and dignity, is now
also focused on religious institutions. The linkage between these
values and those which Judaeo-Christian religious organizations
supposedly espouse is too blatant to ignore. More and more conventional women are taking note of these facts and are taking the
very *un*conventional step of declaring themselves called to forms
of ministry previously reserved for men. They are heading for
theological seminaries in unprecedented numbers. They are graduating and expecting to find placement in some form of ministry,
often one which involves ordination. The "masculine mystique"
(if there is such a thing) which pervaided clerical roles and functions in the past is being stripped away. Today the ordained
ministry has been legitimated as an option for dedicated Christian
women, and they will continue to elect to move in that direction.
The women are in the system to stay.

2. *The level of frustration of women seeking to move into the*
   ministry is more likely to increase than decrease.

Enrollments of women in theological seminaries has been increasing at a rate analogous to a geometric progression. While this
trend cannot continue indefinitely (since extending it to infinity is
mathematically impossible in a finite world), it has not begun to
abate as yet. However, the rate at which local congregations are
opening their pulpits to women and installing them as pastors is
analogous to an arithmetic progression. A few churches accept
ordained female leadership each year, but not nearly as many as
the number of women graduating from seminaries. One conclusion is inescapable. The number of women ministerial candidates
is increasing at a rate much greater than the number of churches
willing to accept them as ministers to their congregations. At present the ratio of female candidates to receptive churches is increasing rather than decreasing. Unless the officials of denominations
which have endorsed the status of women as ordained clergy
adopt a much more vigorous and imaginative set of programs to

facilitate the movement of women into ministries, the number of women whose aspirations are being frustrated will increase, the volume and frequency of their calls for justice will also increase, and their talents will stand to go to waste.

3. *If women are allowed to function as ordained clergy in local congregations, they will succeed as fully as men.*

Even in the absence of any direct contact with women as ordained clergy, lay church members indicate overwhelmingly that they think women can succeed in that role as well as men. Eighty percent and more of the members surveyed held healthy and realistic images of clergywomen. They entertained few stereotypes of them, and they even asserted that women could perform the specific church functions they personally considered most vital to themselves as well as men. Whatever hesitancy they felt about asking women to assume clergy roles in their own congregation was in large measure a function of how they thought others felt about the idea. They feared possible controversy and schism.

These qualms notwithstanding, the evidence is clear that congregations continue to function normally after the introduction of female pastoral leadership. The rolls remain stable, the people meet their church budget and other routines of church life go on as usual. New members arrive, and old members sometimes move away, but these changes in the congregations served by women are normal alterations in the lives of the members rather than reactions to the clergywoman herself. They are due to changing jobs, job transfers, getting married or being retired— things that happen to congregations regardless of the identity of the person serving them as pastor. Churches' growth and decline is based more on trends in their surrounding communities than on the gender of their pastors. It seems that clergywomen succeed and fail no more than men. So the majority of members are correct in their opinions that clergywomen "can cut it." They can.

Furthermore, the study indicates clearly that whatever reservations might have existed among lay members before working with a woman as pastor diminish significantly as a result of the experience. The positive majority tends to expand its dominance over the ethos in the congregation. Stereotypes lose adherents and preferences for men in specific roles decline in number and intensity. Given the chance, clergywomen win opponents over. If they are given the opportunity to take the mantle of leadership, having demonstrated repeatedly that they will wear it well, clergy-women repay the investment churches make in them many times over.

4. *History will judge the churches at least partly on the basis of their response to the women-in-ministry movement.*

Church history has already presented us with a highly varied report card on the way the bearers of the faith deal with the ethical dimensions of issues they face. There has been some good news and some bad. In just the last century, church members have earned high grades in the way they have upheld high moral standards in some situations where those values were being challenged—Quakers campaigning in opposition to human slavery, German churches in opposition to Nazi totalitarianism and pogroms, world-wide organized efforts in behalf of refugees, global famine relief efforts, constructing and supporting medical facilities for the indigent, and many more. Time and again the churches have been able to see through superficial rhetoric to the normative core of issues that simply could not be ignored. Most observers would argue that in those moments the faithful came down on the right side of the conflict and practiced what they preached.

Unfortunately, however, there have been other times when they appear to have missed the mark altogether. In the distant past, the inhumanities of the Inquisition were justified on religious grounds, as was the bloody Lutheran campaign against the Anabaptists. The arrogant colonization of preliterate peoples was legitimated in terms of their need for eternal salvation. Today some large Christian bodies glorify nuclear weapons as God's tools against the evils of the other side. The Sunday morning worship hour is still the most segregated hour of the week. Time and again, the hind sight of history has raised serious questions about the basic ethics involved in numerous social and political policies which the churches have either pursued themselves or have endorsed in the actions of others. Repeatedly representatives of other institutions, most notably the law, the press and literature, have ended up beating the churches at their own game—representing and safeguarding basic human values. On one issue after another, the churches have been "caught with their platitudes down."

Will the churches' reactions to the current feminist movement become something of which they will eventually be proud or ashamed? The way in which they respond to women wishing to participate in the full range of ministries of the Church will be a major determinant of how future ethical historians evaluate the churches' coming to grips with the human movements of the twentieth century. The inconsistencies between claiming to be the defenders of the highest moral values on the one hand and barring any group of people from full participation in the church's ministries on the other are too apparent to gloss over. Just as the clergywomen have perceived such contradictions, other observers have taken note of the hypocrisies involved in conservative church positions. Indeed, secular policy makers are already outdistancing religious communities in the area of women's rights. Legislation proscribing sex discrimination is already codified at both national and state levels. In some ways secular leaders are already ahead of the churches in implementing the values of equality and justice in situations where sex roles are in question.

The churches cannot afford the embarassment which could derive from maintaining a conservative stance toward women in ministry. There is little question that women are capable of doing the job. It is a matter of whether or not they will be allowed to do it. If the churches boldly endorse women's broadening sense of call to ministry, history is likely to give them high marks. If they refuse to recognize the legitimacy of women's call to serve in places heretofore reserved for men, they will surely find the judgment of history against them.

Bibliography

Allport, Gordon W.
  1958 *The Nature of Prejudice.* Garden City, New York: Doubleday and Co.

Amir, Yehuda.
  1969 "Contact Hypothesis in Ethnic Relations." *Psychological Bulletin* 71:5 (May): 319–342.

Babbie, Earl R.
  1979 *The Practice of Social Research.* 2d rev. ed. Belmont, California: Wadsworth Publishing Co.

Basow, Susan A.
  1980 *Sex-Role Stereotypes: Traditions and Alternatives.* Monterey, California: Brooks/Cole Publishing Co.

Beck, Marc.
  1978 "Pluralist Theory and Church Policy Positions on Racial and Sexual Equality." *Sociological Analysis,* 39:4 (Winter): 338–350.

Blizzard, Samuel W.
  1958 "The Protestant Parish Minister's Integrating Roles." *Religious Education,* 53 (July): 374–380.

Bock, E. Wilber.
  1967 "The Female Clergy: A Case of Professional Marginality." *American Journal of Sociology,* 27 (5): 531–539.

Bogardus, Emory S.
  1951 "Measuring Changes in Ethnic Relations." *American Sociological Review,* 15: 48–51.

Bureau of the Census.
  1979 *Statistical Abstracts: 1979.* Washington, D.C.

Carroll, Jackson W., and Robert L. Wilson.
  1978 *The Clergy Job Market: Over-Supply and/or Opportunity.* Hartford: Hartford Seminary Foundation.

Carroll, Jackson W., Barbara Hargrove and Adair Lummis.
1983 *Women of the Cloth*. New York: Harper and Row.

Chalfant, H. Paul, Robert Beckley and C. Eddie Palmer.
1981 *Religion in Contemporary Society*. Sherman Oaks, California: Alfred Publishing Co.

Charlton, Joy.
1978 "Women Entering the Ordained Ministry: Contradictions and Dilemmas of Status." Paper presented at the Annual Meeting of the Society for the Scientific Study of Religion, Hartford, Connecticut, October 26–29.

Colman, Penelope Morgan and Ann Dubois Conrad.
1978 *Resource Book for Placement, Acceptance and Support of Clergywomen*. Office for Women in Ministry, The Vocation Agency, United Presbyterian Church, USA, 406 Interchurch Center, 475 Riverside Drive, New York, New York: 10115.

Colwill, Nina L.
1982 *The New Partnership: Women and Men in Organizations*. Palo Alto, California: Mayfield Publishing Co.

Commission on Women in Ministry.
1976 *A Resource Guide for Women in Seminary*. New York: National Council of Churches.

Cook, Stuart W.
1969 "Motives in a Conceptual Analysis of Attitude-Related Behavior." In *Nebraska Symposium on Motivation*, edited by W. J. Arnold and D. Levine. 17: 179–235.

Cooley, Charles H.
1962 *Social Organization*. New York: Schocken.

Daly, Mary
1975 *The Church and the Second Sex*. New York: Harper and Row.

Dempewolff, J. A.
1974 "Some Correlates of Feminism." *Psychological Reports*, 34: 671–676.

Department of Labor, U.S. Bureau of Labor Statistics
1980 *Perspectives on Working Women: A Databook*. Washington, D.C.: U.S. Government Printing Office.

Deutsch, Morton and M. E. Collins
1951 *Interracial Housing: A Psychological Evaluation of a Social Experiment*. Minneapolis: University of Minnesota Press.

Deutscher, Irwin
1973 *What We Say/What We Do*. Glenview, Illinois: Scott-Foresman.

Dillman, Don A.
1978 *Mail and Telephone Surveys: The Total Design Method*. New York: Wiley.

Driedger, Leo
1974 "Doctrinal Belief: A Major Factor in the Differential Perception of Social Issues." *The Sociological Quarterly*, 15 (Winter): 66–80.

Epstein, Cynthia Fuchs
1970 *Woman's Place*. Berkeley: University of California Press.

Etzioni, Amitai
1964 *Modern Organizations*. Englewood Cliffs, New Jersey: Prentice-Hall.

Feagin, Joe R. and Clarice Booker Feagin
1978 *Discrimination, American Style: Institutional Racism and Sexism*. Englewood Cliffs, New Jersey: Prentice-Hall.

Festinger, Leon A.
1957 *A Theory of Cognitive Dissonance*. New York: Harper and Row.

Freeman, Jo
1975 *The Politics of Women's Liberation*. New York: Longman, Inc.

Friedan, Betty
1963 *The Feminine Mystique*. New York: Dell Books.

Gorsuch, Richard L. and Daniel Aleshire
1974 "Christian Faith and Ethnic Prejudice: A Review and Interpretation of Research." *Journal for the Scientific Study of Religion*, 13 (September): 281–307.

Hacker, Helen M.
1951 "Women as a Minority Group." *Social Forces* 30 (October): 60–69.

Hale, Harry, Morton King and Doris Jones
1980 *New Witnesses: United Methodist Clergywomen*. Nashville: Board of Higher Education and Ministry.

Hall, Richard H.
1982 *Organizations: Structure and Process*. 3d rev. ed. Englewood Cliffs, New Jersey: Prentice-Hall, Inc.

Harrison, Paul M.
1959 *Authority and Power in the Free Church Tradition*. Princeton: Princeton University Press.

Henley, Nancy M. and Fred Pincus
1978 "Interrelationship of Sexist, Racist, and Antihomosexual Attitudes." *Psychological Reports* 42 (February): 83–90.

Hennig, Margaret and Anne Jardim
1977 *The Managerial Woman*. New York: Doubleday.

Hertzler, Joyce O.
1965 *A Sociology of Language*. New York: Random House.

Hoge, Dean R. and David A. Roozen, eds.
1979 *Understanding Church Growth and Decline, 1950–1978*. New York: Pilgrim Press.

Holsti, Ole
  1969 *Content Analysis for the Social Sciences and Humanities*. Reading, Massachusetts: Addison-Wesley.

Horowitz, Eugene L.
  1965 "Development of Attitudes Toward Negroes." In *Basic Studies in Social Psychology*, edited by Proshansky and Seidenberg. New York: Holt, Rinehart and Winston.

Jacquet, Constant H. Jr.
  1973 *The Status of Women in Various Constituent Bodies of the National Council of Churches—Results of an Inquiry*. National Council of Churches, 475 Riverside Drive, New York, New York 10027.

Jacquet, Constant H. Jr.
  1978 *Women Ministers in 1977: A Report*. National Council of Churches. 475 Riverside Drive, New York, New York 10027.

Jones, Arthur R., Jr. and Lee Taylor
  1971 "Differential Recruitment of Female Professionals: A Case Study of Clergywomen." In *The Professional Woman*, edited by Athena Theodore. Cambridge, Mass.: Schenkman.

Kanter, Rosabeth Moss
  1975 "Women and the Structure of Organizations: Explorations in Theory and Behavior." In *Another Voice*, edited by M. Millman and R. M. Kanter. Garden City, New York: Doubleday.

_____.
  1977 *Men and Women of the Corporation*. New York: Basic Books.

Katz, Daniel and Robert L. Kahn
  1970 *The Social Psychology of Organizations*. New Delhi: Wiley Eastern Private, Ltd.

Katz, Elihu
  1957 "The Two-Step Flow of Communication: An Up-to-Date Report on an Hypothesis." *Public Opinion Quarterly* (21): 61–78.

Kerckhoff, Alan
  1976 "The Status Attainment Process: Socialization or Allocation?" *Social Forces* 55 (2): 368–381.

Kerlinger, Fred N.
  1979 *Behavioral Research: A Conceptual Approach*. New York: Holt, Rinehart and Winston.

Lehman, Edward C., Jr.
  1979 *Project SWIM: A Study of Women in Ministry*. A research report to the Ministers Council, American Baptist Churches, Valley Forge, Pa.

_____.
  1980 "Placement of Men and Women in the Ministry." *Review of Religious Research*, 22 (September): 18–40.

————.
1981a "Patterns of Lay Resistance to Women in Ministry." *Sociological Analysis*, 41 (January): 317–338.

————.
1981b "Organizational Resistance to Women in Ministry." *Sociological Analysis*, 41 (Spring): 101–118.

————.
1982 "Changing Receptivity to Clergywomen: An Application of the Contact Hypothesis." Paper presented at the annual meeting of the Association for the Sociology of Religion, Providence, Rhode Island, October.

Liska, Allen E.
1974 "Emergent Issues in the Attitude-Behavior Consistency Controversy." *American Sociological Review*, 39 (April): 261–272.

Liska, Allen E.
1975 *The Consistency Controversy: Readings on the Impact of Attitude on Behavior*. New York: John Wiley and Sons.

McClendon, McKee Jr.
1976 "The Occupational Status Attainment Process of Males and Females." *American Sociological Review*, 41 (February): 52–64.

Newcomb, Theodore M., Ralph H. Turner and Philip E. Converse
1965 *Social Psychology: The Study of Human Interaction*. New York: Holt, Rinehart and Winston.

Office of the General Assembly
1967 *The Constitution of the United Presbyterian Church in the United States of America: Part II–Book of Order*. New York: United Presbyterian Church.

Otto, Luther B. and Archibald O. Haller
1979 "Evidence for a Social Psychological View of the Status Attainment Process: Four Studies Compared." *Social Forces*, 57 (March): 887–914.

Peek, Charles W. and Sharon Brown
1980 "Sex Prejudice Among White Protestants: Like or Unlike Ethnic Prejudice?" *Social Forces*, 59: 169–185.

Petty, Richard and John T. Cacioppo
1981 *Attitudes and Persuasion: Classic and Contemporary Approaches*. Dubuque, Iowa: William C. Brown.

Ruether, Rosemary R.
1974 *Religion and Sexism: Images of Women in the Jewish and Christian Tradition*. New York: Simon and Schuster.

Russell, Letty M., ed.
1976 *The Liberating Word: A Guide to Non-Sexist Interpretation of the Bible*. Philadelphia: Westminster.

Schofield, Janet Ward
    1978 "Conceptual Problems in Desegregation Research." Paper presented at the annual meeting of the American Psychological Association, Toronto, Canada, August.

Sewell, W. H. and R. M. Hauser
    1975 *Education, Occupation, and Earnings: Achievement in the Early Career.* New York: Academic Press.

Smith, Donald P.
    1973 *Clergy in the Cross Fire: Coping With Role Conflicts in the Ministry.* Philadelphia: Westminster Press.

Stark, Rodney and Charles Y. Glock
    1970 *American Piety: The Nature of Religious Commitment*, vol. 1. Berkeley, California: University of California Press.

Stark, Rodney, and Charles Y. Glock
    1971 *Wayward Shepherd: Prejudice and the Protestant Clergy.* New York: Harper and Row.

Stendahl, Krister
    1966 *The Bible and the Role of Women.* Philadelphia: Fortress Press.

Steward, Margaret S., David S. Steward and Judith Dary
    1979 "Women Who Choose a Man's Career: A Study of Women in Ministry." Mimeographed.

Stromberg, A. H. and Shirley Harkess, ed.
    1978 *Women Working: Theories and Facts in Perspective.* Palo Alto, California: Mayfield Publishing Co.

Tavris, Carol and Carole Offir
    1977 *The Longest War: Sex Differences in Perspective.* New York: Harcourt, Brace, Jovanovich.

Taylor, Marvin J.
    1982 *Fact Book on Theological Education.* Vandalia, Ohio: American Association of Theological Schools.

Tedin, Kent L.
    1978 "Religious Preference and Pro-Anti Activism on the Equal Rights Amendment Issue." *Pacific Sociological Review*, 21 (January): 55–56.

Turner, Ralph H.
    1957 "Role Taking, Role Standpoint, and Reference Group Behavior." In *Sociological Theory: A Book of Readings*, edited by Lewis A. Coser and Bernard Rosenberg. New York: Macmillan.

Warren, Roland I.
1972 *The Community in America*. 2d rev. ed. Chicago: Rand McNally and Co.

Weidman, Judith L. (ed.)
1981 *Women Ministers: How Women Are Redefining Traditional Roles*. New York: Harper and Row.

Westhues, Kenneth
1976 "The Church in Opposition." *Sociological Analysis*, 37:4, (Winter): 299–314.

Wolf, Wendy C. and Neil D. Fligstein
1979 "Sex and Authority in the Workplace: The Causes of Sexual Inequality." *American Sociological Review*, 44 (April): 235–252.

Wolf, Wendy C. and Rachel Rosenfeld
1978 "Sex Structure of Occupations and Job Mobility." *Social Forces*, 56: 823–844.

Wood, James R.
1970 "Authority and Controversial Policy: The Churches and Civil Rights." *American Sociological Review* 35: 1057–1069.

————.

1981 *Leadership in Voluntary Organizations: The Controversy Over Social Action in Protestant Chruches*. New Brunswick, New Jersey: Rutgers University Press.

Zimbardo, Phillip G.
1969 "Comments." In *Nebraska Symposium on Motivation*, W. J. Arnold and D. Levine, eds., vol. 17: 232–235.

List of Tables